REA

'MAIN LIBRA

D0927956

Copyright © Angela Patmore 1979, 1986

All rights reserved

First published in 1979 by Stanley Paul & Co. Ltd,
an imprint of Century Hutchinson Ltd,
Brookmount House, 62–65 Chandos Place, Covent Garden,
London WC2N 4NW

Revised edition 1986
Century Hutchinson Australia Pty Ltd
PO Box 496, 16–22 Church Street, Hawthorn, Victoria 3122, Australia

Century Hutchinson New Zealand Limited
PO Box 40-086, Glenfield, Auckland 10, New Zealand

Century Hutchinson South Africa (Pty) Ltd
PO Box 337, Bergvlei 2012, South Africa

Set in Times by Book Ens, Saffron Walden, Essex

Printed and bound in Great Britain by Anchor Brendon Ltd
Tiptree, Essex

British Library Cataloguing in Publication Data

Patmore, Angela

ISBN 0 09 166070 X

2316365

Contents

Introduction

Introduction

Sport is a word applied to many different things: I have applied it to only one. This book is not about hunting, fishing or mountaineering, or the 'friendly' sport played in clubs and parks, nor is it about jogging, keep-fit, or physical recreation with bats and balls. However valuable these activities may be, they seem to me inherently different from sport as I have described it. Games people play in small groups for their own amusement are essentially still games, though they may indeed make use of sports equipment, and be very good for our health and even our spiritual awareness: games often appear to have mystical meaning, and may be played for this reason alone.

The sport referred to in this book is organized, high-level, competitive, spectator sport, which is often, though not always, international and in which the players are often, though not always, paid. I have tried to avoid the subject of payment; wherever 'professional sport' is mentioned, it is intended to refer to spectator sport. I believe any sportsman sufficiently competent and dedicated to be performing his skills in front of large numbers of spectators should be called professional, and richly deserves to be paid for what he does.

Spectator sport percolates down through many amateur and junior systems to the school curriculum. When sport is organized as part of a child's education for reasons other than tiring him out or passing the time of day, we may assume that this is in order to discover children with potential, who may be encouraged to develop their skills at a higher level. Different nations have evolved more or less democratic ways of selecting their future sports performers at an early age. I am not qualified to discuss the relative morality of their methods: what seems to me significant is that an obsession with sports contests should have so pervaded many different cultures through all of history to have made selection necessary.

One fascination unites all the people of the world who have ever gone through a turnstile or looked through a gap in the stadium fence at sportsmen 'playing'. This is the question, 'What will they do now?' Sport is not like a novel or a play, with the ending already decided. It is alive and dynamic. Anything can happen really, anything at all. Human beings under pressure are wonderfully unpredictable; their nature is a puzzle to us all, and psychology has only scratched the surface. When human beings are placed in an arena, and their hopes and fears exposed in front of thousands of observers, they are likely to do extraordinary things. This is especially true if someone has told them, 'Don't let us down, now,' or 'This is for the whole ball of wax.'

Spectators are greatly interested in what sportsmen do under these circumstances. Like sport's many self-ordained experts, spectators can be very harsh when the sportmen's actions do not meet with their requirements. This book is not about the spectators or the *cognoscenti*: it is about the people under their scrutiny whom we call sportsmen.

Sports*men*. There are not many female athletes in this book because, firstly, as a woman I have naturally preferred to watch men's sports and, secondly, the subject matter touches frequently on emotional ordeals brought about by competitive pressure, which have caused many athletes to falter or break down. In the reader's mind there are likely to be associations between women and emotional frailty which I wish to avoid as they may muddle our findings.

The sports examined are not selected at random either. I have deliberately chosen sports which for one reason or another push the players towards the frontiers of speed, pain, fear, release and violence. Readers who imagine they know nothing about one or two of the sports discussed might bear this in mind. I have tried not to dwell on technicalities: my concern is with the experiences of the players, and the strange pressures confronting them.

At first sight this book may appear to denigrate spectator sport by suggesting how very cruel it may sometimes be, and how close to the wire it has brought gifted people. To this criticism I can only answer that I have watched sport avidly all my life, both as a hobby and a job, and I believe sport is valuable and important, perhaps more so than we realize. And even more valuable and important are the human beings who play it. Much has been written about their prize money and their joy. Little has been written about their fear and sadness.

I should like to thank all the people who have helped with my research: Chris Plumridge for his golfing acumen, Dudley Doust for his polymathy; Philip Hale and John Plummer for checking my Formula One material; Dr David Ryde the hypnotist; Dr David Cowan at the Drug Control Centre; Silva Mind Control's Philip Miele for information on the White Sox project; sports psychologists Dr Richard Suinn and Prof. H.T.A. Whiting; tennis's Jimmy Jones; coaches Denis Watts and Harry Wilson; and sports medicine's Dr William Armour. Thanks to Bernie Ecclestone, President of FOCA for his time, to old colleagues on Mark McCormack's *Tennis World* and *Golf International* for keeping me busy, to Delena Carey for typing the manuscripts, and above all to the sportsmen themselves – Ilie Nastase, Bob Willis, John Watson, Guillermo Vilas, Vitas Gerulaitis, Tom Watson, Dale Hayes, Mike Brearley, Björn Borg, Roger Osborne, Willie Johnston, Nick Faldo, J.P.R. Williams and John McEnroe – who very kindly talked to me about their experiences. Without their insights this book could never have been written.

Although this book was originally published in 1979, updated research serves to highlight the accuracy of the original findings.

1

The Experiments

Every age has its monsters; the twentieth century is no exception. Most of ours would appear to be of the genus *stress*. Stress has evolved with man from the dawn of his civilization, and shows no signs of ever becoming extinct. It thrives in an urban habitat, likes overcrowding and breeds on industrial technology. Man has therefore set to studying stress in great detail, aware that his survival may depend on his ability to deal with it, live with it, or get out of the way of it, should it come charging up the garden path. Stress may well be his number-one enemy. He has seen that it causes fatal illness on a large scale and war (in some cases) on a monumental one. It has also consigned rather large numbers of people to mental institutions, psychiatrists' couches, prisons and hospitals. We do not know if it causes cancer, but we have our suspicions.

What sort of monster is stress? What are its eating habits, and how can civilization be defended against it, if at all? Man has devised a number of ways of studying the problem, of painting the dinosaur on the wall. One ancient, massive and very efficient institution which is devoted exclusively to the production and exposition of stress we call 'sport'. We do not know how the term originated. Two of its obsolete definitions are, 'to force open', and 'to use, exhibit or set up, publicly or ostentatiously'. Perhaps it is an acronym: Seeing Pressure Overcome Resolves Tension. Our ancestors were a witty lot. Sport as we now know it seems to have been hit upon originally by the Athenians and Spartans, and taken up by the Romans, for the edification of their assembled masses, in the Circus Maximus in Corinth and the Colosseum in Rome.

In its ancient and classical form, the sport experiment frequently involved unwilling subjects: Christians, gladiators, and animals of varying degrees of ferocity. These were pitted against each other under controlled conditions in front of the largest possible numbers of observers. The experiments were considered very important; the arenas built to house them are among the most magnificent architectural achievements of man. The Colosseum itself accommodated 87,000 spectators when it was finished by Titus, in AD 80. The events were – and are – colossal.

The more modern sport experiments are conducted on a voluntary basis, although social sanctions naturally exist to prevent the subjects from actually running away. Schoolchildren are inducted into the sports system, in some countries from a very early age, so as to select and encourage the very best for future experimentation. Many of them, it must be said, enjoy the training immensely. They think it is all to do with cavorting about, and innocently conduct their own extramural sports contests, improvising where necessary with equipment and rules. Many of their heroes, for reasons which will later become apparent, are sports subjects they wish to emulate. Somewhere in the Greenwich Park area, there is a small boy who plays cricket and thinks he is Mike Brearley. Mike Brearley thought he was Jack Robertson; Robertson thought *he* was Wally Hammond; and Hammond probably thought he was somebody else. Most children love competitive sport, and this is very much in the interests of the multi-million-dollar conglomerates which produce and advertise sports 'goods' (as they are invariably called), because here is a further avenue to profit. Besides, children, and many adults, are apt to confuse competitive sport with play (as I have suggested in the Introduction), a confusion perpetuated by the large numbers of parties who stand to benefit from it. In fact, competitive sport is *not* play, as every professional sportsman quickly discovers. This kind of sport differs from play in that it is organized, and it is organized for the very good reason that large numbers of people may watch it.

For the benefit of any reader bewildered by this distinction, a brief definition of the sport experiment will avoid misunderstandings: by artificial means, by the use of symbols, tools, props, boundaries and time limits, conditions shall be imposed on subject or subjects which will excite the maximum degree of stress, both in the area provided and at the time designated. Death, where it is not presented as a possible stimulus, shall be represented or symbolized. Under these conditions, ability to withstand stress in the subject or subjects shall be measured, and be seen to be measured, in the performance of a chosen visible skill, in the area provided and at the time designated. 'Skill' shall signify any visible action or design which requires proficiency of execution and which shall be directed towards an agreed and visible goal. Success or failure shall be adjudged according to the subject's or subjects' ability to perform and direct the agreed skill towards the agreed goal, in the area provided and at the time designated. The exhibition of energies so generated shall be signified collectively by the term 'sport'.

To define sport in this manner is not to decry its value. Sport stands on the frontier of man's knowledge of himself. What he may learn by watching sport is not easily disseminated in any other way. Besides, there is no point in advocating that the experiment be changed: it has outlived many campaigns against it, and is likely to go on doing so. I am not opposed to sport, but I am opposed to the dishonesty and hugger-mugger in which it has now been shrouded, for these have prevented us from fully appreciating what sport is and what sport does to the human beings who take part in it. It is for the sake of these human beings, whose performances we are so apt to criticize when they do not conform to our expectations, that this book is written. To understand sport is to forgive them all.

Since most modern sport experiments are conducted on a voluntary basis, the sort of terminology used above may be construed as offensive, not least to the subjects taking part. Rather than run the risk of a sharp decline in the number of volunteers, most Western societies conducting sport experiments have thought fit to couch the requirements in more inviting terms. First, subjects are referred to, not as subjects, but as 'participants', 'athletes' (favoured in the US), 'competitors', or, more popularly, 'players'. This doesn't in any way alter the meaning, but avoids offending the taste. Second, there are huge rewards to be had, financial or otherwise. This is both a sop to the social conscience, and a means of ensuring the sportman's utmost motivation for the task at hand – an important consideration if the experiments are to be valid. The more successful subjects, or rather sportsmen, who seem capable of demonstrating their skills under large amounts of stress – which they generally call 'pressure' – and who can apparently perform in spite of innumerable obstacles and opponents put in their way, are groomed for stardom.

They are rewarded and reinforced according to the prevailing social norms, and qualify for inclusion in bigger and better experiments, which are conducted internationally, and under the auspices of national and international organizations. The bigger and better experiments are often referred to collectively as 'professional sport' (particularly if the athletes are paid), and are communicated through the media to millions of interested observers around the world.

The advent of television and the television satellite have ensured that the behaviour of subjects taking part in the stress events can be minutely examined, tabulated, classified, criticized and recorded for posterity. As journalist Hugh McIlvanney commented on the interminable 1978 World Cup coverage, [1]* 'the cameras spend so many hours examining so many aspects of the occasion that we almost feel deprived when we are not given a look at the centre forward's piles'. One recent experiment in the United States, called Super Bowl XX, was observed by over 100 million people, including 76,791 in an indoor stadium which cost £139 million to build (the Louisiana Superdome). Super Bowl XIX had 115,936 viewing 'live' and 100 million on TV. Some 200 million worldwide watched a tennis match between Billie Jean King and Bobby Riggs, 30,472 of them at the ring side. More than one thousand million viewers tuned into the World Cup final in 1986. The BBC–ITV negotiations over the rights to cover British soccer touched on a figure of £19 million for three seasons. Mere peanuts, compared with the expenditure of American TV on *its* football coverage. That deal shifted £328 million ($656 million), the largest sum in television history.

The need for televised sports coverage became apparent long before it was technically possible. The first flickering commercial motion picture was made by Woodville Latham and his two sons in 1895. It lasted four minutes and showed highlights of the prize fight between Young Griffo and Battling Barnett. In 1926 Jack Dempsey fought Gene Tunney in Philadelphia before an audience of 130,000. In 1927 the same fighters met in Chicago's Soldier Field. There were 145,000 spectators, brought there in twenty-four special trains: many of them were seated too far away from the ring to see who actually won. During the thirteen-second fiasco of a count, which the referee delayed until Dempsey had gone to a neutral

*Superior figures refer to the notes on pages 249–66.

corner, five radio listeners suffered fatal heart attacks. Television, when it came along, brought the sport experiment into the living room and covered itself with glory as 'the magic eye'. Hologram sports coverage cannot be far away, for the public greed for intimacy with the events is insatiable.

The nomenclature of sport experiments is interesting. Some are called 'trials' (as in horse trials) or 'tests' (both synonyms for experiments). 'Contest' indicates that subjects are being *tested with others*, and this has been of considerable importance in the design of all sport experiments, including those which we call 'tournaments', 'matches' and 'championships'. The simplest way to apply pressure to a subject on a sports field or in an arena is to provide him with opposition, or 'con-testants' who will try to prevent him from doing what he came to do. This is the impetus behind competition of all kinds. It is a dynamic method of applying pressure to all concerned, for each is striving to succeed in his performance while every effort is being made by others to disrupt it.

The ideal experimental model brings into contest *subjects of more or less equal ability*. The terms 'competition' and 'match' refer to such an ideal model, and sport contrives to guarantee some version of what Muhammad Ali's fight doctor Ferdie Pacheco calls 'a genuine championship fight between two equal men',[2] by its elimination, handicapping and 'knock-out' systems, and its methods of selection and qualification. When contests take place between subjects *not* of equal ability, the experiment is more or less devoid of interest: it is likely to reveal nothing new about the subjects taking part. It is often referred to as a non-contest or mis-match, and sport is organized so as to avoid this wherever possible.

But why should contests be so arranged as to pit subjects of equal ability against each other? Because in this case, and only in this case, is it possible to observe the *edge* which brings victory to one side and defeat to the other. The technical skills of the contestants, if the experiment has been set up correctly, cancel each other out. The sport experiment is not concerned with the particular technical skills the subject has brought with him to the contest. His skill is not really at issue – although he fervently believes it is – since his fellow-contestants also have it; they have been screened and selected very carefully indeed to ensure that their skill bears comparison with his. The deciding factor is not his skill, *but his ability to perform it under stress*. This is the sport experiment and it is very important that we should understand its contrivances. To see that sport pits equals against each other is to realize how important a factor pressure is going to be.

Under the exacting conditions of such events, which contrive to subject the participants to as much pressure as they can possibly withstand, it is hardly surprising that there are many casualties. Serious injuries of various kinds – physical, psychosomatic and emotional – are sustained by the subjects, who nevertheless usually continue to participate as long as they are eligible. Their motives vary. Some simply enjoy the fame and financial reward. Others relish the self-esteem that undoubtedly accrues to successful performers, who are able to compare themselves with others professing similar skills. Some enjoy particularly the strong sense of allegiance and camaraderie between teamed participants, for such intense communion is at a premium in a sophisticated society. Still others are deeply fascinated by the effects of the experiments on themselves, and by their reactions and abilities under pressure. Sport *may* provide sportsmen with insights that help them make sense of their lives. Most important of all, each performer values and enjoys his particular skill, which he has nurtured by long hours of rigorous training and self-sacrifice, to the extent that this skill may even become synonymous with himself, or symbolic of his individual worth. To be able to demonstrate this skill, to himself and to others, and under live experimental conditions, is an experience so important and exhilarating that he is willing to devote the best years of his life to its pursuit.

It is easily seen from a consideration of all the factors involved, that the predicament of the player or subject is both inherently tragic, and inherently heroic. In many Western societies his status is that of a folk-hero or god. Indeed, the Olympic Games were originated by the Greeks, not as an international charade of medal-winning and anabolic steroid regimens, but as the Games of the Gods, in honour of Zeus. They were a celebration of man's ability (then as now) to perform his skills in the face of fate which mocked him, and annihilation which threatened on every side. In so doing he achieved brief immortality, and poets glorified him in odes. Time was measured in olympiads, the four-year intervals between the Games, the first traditionally beginning in 776 BC. An Olympian was a god-like person, a competitor in the Games, or one of the greater Greek gods who were thought to dwell on Mount Olympus in Thessaly.

The notion that sport is 'only a game' is of comparatively recent origin. Leni Riefenstahl's epic film of the 1936 Berlin Olympics, and the vast neo-classical remains of the echoing Sportpalast and Hochenheim in Germany, are monuments of a far different belief, not all to do with Nazism (the Nazi salute was in fact very close to the old Olympic salute).[3] The American sportsman, regardless of his sport, is called 'athlete', from the Greek *athletes*, and *athlon* meaning prize. It is a reminder, in spite of all modern disillusionment, of ancient esteem.

Every career has an ignition point somewhere and in my case it was not watching a giant batting but merely watching a giant walking out to bat. The giant was Hammond.[4]

I wanted to be part of Cwmgors rugby so much. I wanted to be grown up. One Saturday, we young boys followed the Cwmgors team back from the field to the Welfare Hall where they had a shower. We hung around the changing-room, scraping mud off boots, handing in jerseys, anything to get in on the act. . . .[5]

If the golfer's object was merely to sink the ball in the hole, he could walk around the course with a bag of golf balls and drop each one in.[6]

I knew intellectually that being good at tennis wasn't a valid test of manhood – or of anything else of importance – but I was still tight before a match.[7]

May the best man win.

Defeat, particularly dramatic defeat, confirms our worst image of ourselves. We are not effective, after all, not truly competent, not manly in crisis.[8]

That sport is in some way symbolic has long been accepted. It is obvious to the most sceptical observer that a cricketer with a stick in his hands is not guarding three other sticks in the ground because he wishes to make a fence, and that the track athlete does not build up momentum for 1500 metres simply in order to break a piece of tape without the use of scissors. What is *not* generally agreed is how and why symbolism enters into sport, or what the symbols stand for. My own suggestion – that the symbols are a means to an end, which has to do with producing and overcoming stress – has been indicated already. At the end of the day, precisely *what* the symbols mean seems less important than that they do *have* meaning and significance, and that this is understood both by the subjects taking part in the experiment and by the spectators.

In fairness to the reader's roving imagination, though, something should now be said about the symbols themselves.

Gerald Ford, one of several presidents of the United States to take an avid interest in sport, used to play gridiron football in college. During his Vice-Presidency, and before he had begun falling down stairs on top of foreign ambassadors, Mr Ford made known his views on the importance of sport in society. 'The reason I make reference to those winning seasons at Michigan is that we have been asked to swallow a lot of home-cooked psychology in recent years that winning isn't all that important any more, whether on the athletic field or in any other field, national or international. I don't buy that for a minute. It isn't enough just to compete. Winning is very important. Broadly speaking, outside of a national character and an educated society, there are few things more important to a country's growth and well-being than competitive athletics.'[9]

The essential presence of a winning symbol is the single most important factor in any sport experiment, and not only for the motivation of the participants. The experiments are designed to pit man against stress, under controlled conditions so that the outcome may be observed. There must always be a winner, or winners, to symbolize that stress has been overcome. Without such a symbol, the spectacle would mean that stress had vanquished all the subjects. And since, at the highest competitive levels, these subjects also 'champion' the observers, the implications would be grave indeed. Winning is, of all sport's symbols, decisive in resolving tension and settling the odds. If the experiments are to prove anything, they must produce results, and results have to do with winning (and, although incidentally, losing).

Winning signals the end of the experiment. The purpose of all crafty restrictions on time and place in sport is to ensure that there is a winner or winners, and comprehensible measures of success and failure. Indeed, the restrictions on time and place force the pace towards such an outcome, and brook no uncertainty. In sport experiments where victory is not physically demonstrated (as in gladiatorial combat, or by a knock-out in boxing), it is shown symbolically by various contrivances. Those social commentators objecting to such contrivances – and there are many of them – argue that the competitive urge in man is 'wrong' and 'dangerous': sport should be purged of all these symbols of winning and losing. (They do not deny, of course, that they themselves wish to win this argument on competitive sport, and engage with vigour on behalf of their claims.)

There have been various attempts at purging sport of its outcomes, its pay-offs, scores, results, winners and losers. Thomas Tutko, an American sports psychologist, has suggested rules for what he calls Cooperation Golf and Cooperation Tennis, in which the object is not to win, but to exhibit shots for shots' sake.[10] A similar essay was made by Reginald Perrin's seminar groups with the sweet science of boxing in which the contestants attempted to punch *themselves* and were told by their seconds, 'Now go in and finish yourself off'. There are even, in Marin County north of San Francisco, what are called New Games Festivals, involving games such as Earth Ball (in which a large number of persons strive to keep a ball aloft), and Infinity Volleyball (in which the object is to knock the ball about till kingdom come). The New Games Foundation organizers are busy introducing such novelties into schools across the USA, hoping to replace competitive sports.

Symbolism to denote winning (or succeeding) is nevertheless important in the sport experiment itself, because Seeing Pressure Overcome Resolves Tension. Spectator sports rely very much on this for their appeal. Public sport experiments that produce no winners settle nothing and satisfy nobody – which is why anti-competitive adaptations seem inherently ridiculous. Audiences pay attention (and money) to see an experiment with an outcome, which 'proves' or demonstrates something about stress, not an experiment which sets them worrying over infinite possibilities and imponderables. Their lives are sufficiently messy and meaningless already, without the need for further demonstrations of mess and meaninglessness. They want the dinosaur painted on the wall – and painted as vanquished – not rampaging through the terraces. 'One of the realities of the human predicament is that we frequently have to make decisions before all the facts are in ... The Child in us demands certainty.'[11]

Indeed, it has been shown that audiences may be deeply disturbed and unsettled by postponements and the continuing occurrence of 'draws', and uncertainty about which subjects have been successful in their performance disturbs the participants themselves.[12]

It may be that the contrivance of 'winning draws' in football pools coupons is aimed at providing some public satisfaction over this frustrating phenomenon. It may equally be that the high incidence of hooliganism in the stands of team sports in which draws are common may be due to spectators being predisposed to take the score into their own hands. The Brussels riot in 1985 in which 38 people died broke out before the match started. Soccer is a low-scoring game, and often there is no score at all. The ball is manoeuvred agonizingly from one end of the pitch to the other, with spectators' voices rising to a crescendo and then breaking off with strangled moans as goals fail to materialize. When Northern Ireland advanced into the World Cup Finals in 1985 after a scoreless draw with England, Wembley fans screamed 'It's a fix!' and 'What a load of rubbish!' This is the stuff of which martyrs are made. One of the worst riots in soccer in 1978 occurred after the UEFA Cup clash between Manchester City and AC Milan. Milan had three goals disallowed for offside. The final score was 2–2, and outside San Siro Stadium police and troops used tear gas and rubber bullets to disperse rival supporters bent on annihilating one another. There are other examples. The traditional tactic of 'playing for a draw' in cricket has been known to make spectators in the West Indies and Australia cross and occasionally causes spectators in India and Pakistan to set fire to their seating arrangements.

'Sudden death' in play-offs is a crude example of what we could call termination symbolism. In extra time, an experiment which has failed to produce a result is said to have concluded when one or other side has nosed ahead, however marginally. That side are designated 'winners'. Photo-finishes are similar emergency procedures. In 1973, Brendan Foster and Frank Clement tied for first place in the 1500 metres at Crystal Palace in London. Their time was 3 min. 38.5 sec., and since they were both British and had paced each other through the race, it was apparent that they had agreed to finish together. However privately satisfying this may have been for the two subjects concerned, something had to be done for the sake of the experiment. A photo-finish decision awarded the first place to Clement. It is, of course, possible for sports subjects to sabotage experiments, and prevent a valid result being obtained. This is the subject of several books on sport, including Alan Sillitoe's *Loneliness of the Long-Distance Runner*.

More usually, winning and losing is ensured by some agreed restriction on the distance or duration of an event and the simple expedient of 'scoring'. A higher score by one side is agreed to signify a superior performance under competitive conditions;

hence these are the 'winners', even if the other side is still physically alive and kicking. Cheating is condemned: it distorts the 'findings'.

It should not be supposed that restrictions on the duration of a sport experiment have anything to do with compassion for the subjects, although economic factors may be at work (players can be very expensive to replace). While it is true that the same players can be used over and over again by merely representing their termination rather than actually showing it, there is no evidence to suggest that this is what the observers would prefer.

And the Philistines stood on a mountain on the one side, and Israel stood on a mountain on the other side: and there was a valley between them. And there went out a *champion* out of the camp of the Philistines, named Goliath, of Gath, whose height was six cubits and a span. . . . [I *Sam.* 17 v 3]

Various claims have been made concerning the relationship between the sports subjects themselves and the mass of spectators observing their behaviour. Some of these claims are made by psychologists, sociologists and politicians disturbed by the power of sport to hive off, purge, excite or otherwise influence public emotion. Sport has an enormous vicarious following, and sportsmen have been accused of setting a bad example to spectators by displays of primitive behaviour. One critic thought spectator sport a reversion to barbarity, and that sportsmen themselves showed signs of 'predatory temperament' and 'arrested spiritual development'.[13] Another sees them 'indoctrinated with grotesque conceptions of national prestige' and mere puppets of a warmonger philosophy.[14] Another thinks sports fans are subjected to exhibitions of 'violent aggression . . . corporate obedience . . . obsession with personal success . . . and mechanical efficiency'.[15] Sport reinforces these values not only in the sportsmen but, Nelly bar the door, in the spectators too. Still another claims 'sport draws people together in a communion that is bizarre and unnatural' in order to 'witness, identify and participate in a contest where the predominant perception is of people struggling against one another'.[16] This critic believes the fans are being exploited by national and corporate powers, and deceived into accepting sport's 'meaningfulness and validity'. Others see 'the growing passion for sport' as 'a sad commentary on the inadequacy of the societies we have created', and find it depressing that large numbers of people, alienated at work and ineffectual in their lives, 'identify themselves so passionately with the participants in some sporting ritual'.[17]

These critics seem generally to miss the whole point of sport experimentation, and its undertaking to investigate stress. This is, surely, a most important public preoccupation, on which man's survival may ultimately depend. They also overlook the possibility that the masses who watch sport are actually studying what takes place, as well as experiencing strong feelings about it. Results of sports contests do receive most careful consideration. Matches are analysed both in the sports pages of every available newspaper, and in 'post-mortems' held by the spectators themselves. Sports analysis, however badly informed on many issues, is a burgeoning industry, and another industry (equally burgeoning) handles public speculation on the most likely results of forthcoming fixtures, based on their knowledge of 'form' and 'odds'.

Those who believe spectators are being exploited, or corrupted by the behaviour of 'moral primates' on the field, may also overlook something else. The powerful feelings whipped up by sport depend very much on the development of pressure situations. The spectators are particularly interested in these, and they are rarely persuaded to attend any contest in which pressure situations are not forthcoming. They may even, in the absence of any pressure they can perceive, try to create some themselves, by booing, baiting, and interfering with the progress of play. The sportsman's role, too, is often supposed more congenial than it is. Spectators may indeed identify very strongly with certain individuals and teams and shower them with affection, but the fans' allegiance is notoriously fickle. It lasts for as long as the fans feel they are being 'championed' and represented in the battle with pressure they see before them (either in a winning or losing capacity, depending on how the fans view themselves; they may choose to support an underdog, if they feel this represents their particular cause). Should the sportman once fail them in this role, ties are very quickly severed. Sportsmen who remember nothing else about the fans are likely to remember their caprice and callousness in this respect. To the spectators, the sport experiment is more important than the subjects. Man has always sought, by any means he can discover, to pry into the nature of a thing. The small boy who pulls the spider's legs off is both cruel and curious, and the thousands of people who wished to see Nastase lose his sanity in his match with Hans Pohmann at Forest Hills, or who clamoured for the Italian

Grand Prix to be restarted after the Monza pile-up from which seriously injured racers were carried to hospital, were cruel and curious too.

The emphasis on *emotion* at sporting events (as opposed to observation in the widest sense, which is surely what the experiments involve) has led several theorists to suggest the purpose of sport is to act as a social safety valve. According to these theorists, sport helps to prevent public disorder by 'purging' both players and spectators of harmful emotional excesses. They refer particularly to aggression, and to sexual energies expressing themselves in unorthodox ways. Unfortunately, since sporting events are occasionally associated with riots, this cathartic theory still has a lot of explaining to do. (There are two widely accepted theories of aggression. One holds that aggression is purged by display, the other that aggression triggers more aggression.[18])

Other commentators suggest that sport is a masculine initiation rite; that it celebrates social stereotypes; that it symbolizes the struggle by man for survival, the struggle for competence, or a struggle to impress the opposite sex; or else that it shows the re-enactment of psychological or social conflicts. According to some, it symbolizes social interaction, self-actualization or self-evaluation, and according to others, the pursuit of excellence, achievement or superiority. Still others point to the celebration of national ideals, political ideologies of various kinds, Russian communism, British colonialism, militarism, commercialism, corporationism, and the plight of the American Negro. It is argued that sport prepares and conditions the populace to do various things: to amass fortunes, kick cats, develop hernias, build businesses, drive Sherman tanks, emulate wild boars, covet, compete and annihilate. It is proclaimed that sport uses the language of war (which of course it does) and the language of sex (which of course it does too), and that this use of language proves that sport symbolizes these subjects (which, among other things, it may well do).

The truth is that the experiments crystallize the stresses of life, which they are designed to investigate, and these may be seen to include just about anything under the sun, provided it can be symbolized. Although sport may indeed reflect the values of a particular society in a particular place at a particular time, it is not circumscribed or limited by these values, and will quickly slough them off when they cease to be of relevance. Nor can sport, any more than art or science, be wholly appropriated to a particular cause. The ease with which it has traditionally thrown off transitory restrictions politics and governments have imposed on it (Henry II's attempts to ban soccer, like Hitler's attempts to beat Jesse Owens came to grief) testifies to its agelessness as a social sacrament.

In every age, man has crystallized the stresses that haunt his life, in cave paintings, stained-glass windows, poems and plays, rites and rituals, *mimeses* and speaking pictures of every kind. Sport is one of these crystallizations. Its enormous evocativeness has attracted, not crowds, but the largest massed audiences in the history of mankind. Why do they come? Out of cruelty and curiosity, but also out of concern, to see the subjects champion them in their battle with stress. Stress haunts their lives, and to see the monster vanquished, even under controlled experimental conditions, in an arena full of lights and rules and whistles and referees, gives each spectator hope. The real monster, at large outside the stadium, may somehow be vanquished too. And if some of the subjects, who are supposed to be champions in this cause, are torn to pieces by the stresses let loose in the arena, and injured physically and emotionally for the rest of their lives, well, life is cruel, and sport is cruel too.

Sport's cruelty, and its breathtakingly clever techniques for dislodging competitors from their mental stability in front of observers, has been viewed around the world with varying degrees of clarity by nations seeking to train athletes for competition. The West has, until very recently, lagged behind for want of an honest appraisal of sport's real requirements. The stern coach who bellows at his team in the locker-room before a match, cuts, to the Communists, a comical figure. Their sportsmen have no need of such last-minute 'psychings-up'. The Communists consider that a team with only eleventh-hour psychological preparation might as well stay in the locker-room anyway, for all the good they will do when the crisis comes. They believe, and with some justification, that under sufficient competitive stress, the Western sportsman cracks. And because in most cases he is psychologically untrained for competition, and uninformed, other than by his own five senses, of the fierce and frightening pressures that sport involves, the Western sportsman very often does.

Roger Kahn, a keen amateur baseball player and later a best-selling sports author, was assigned as a rookie reporter to cover the legendary Brooklyn Dodgers of the 1950s. Kahn was invited to stand in as a batter, to give one of the Dodgers a little pitching practice. His account illustrates rather vividly the difference between the game he thought he had played as an amateur, and the sport experiment itself. 'I began to sweat, and then the shock of standing in gave way to something deeper. This was not my game, I knew. All the baseball I had played was irrelevant to sinkers that hissed like snakes and curves that paralyzed. . . . This wasn't my game, that the Dodgers played. I didn't want to play this other game. It was too full of menace. It was the knotting of young muscles and killing self-demands. A fast ball would shatter the human temple. I didn't want to play this game. I had never wanted to play *this* game.'[19]

Rarely does a player trained in Britain, or to a lesser extent America, produce his best performance on the day. On the day, he finds himself suddenly a stranger in his own sport. He comes believing it to be a game, and finds it is something else. What happens? For a start, he finds his whole identity is involved in a sort of side-bet, and that everyone is looking at him in a meaningful way. His arms turn to sausages. His knees sag. His hands swell up like soft crabs. He can't hear properly, or see straight. His skill deserts him. His mouth goes dry. He loses.

The Western athlete who goes into the sport experiment believing it is merely a question of technical skill may find himself suddenly very uncomfortable indeed:

I don't get frightened when I am driving because if I am in a nasty situation I'm too busy sorting it out. It's cold calculation. If you're frightened you're not capable of looking after yourself, you're not in control. . . . I'm frightened when I sit at home and think what can happen. *Then I get scared*. It's very worrying. I have to live with this thing. It's a big pain in the arse because I have a hell of a nice life. I'm in my prime now having a hell of a good time, and there's this bloody great cloud hanging over my head. A real pain. [James Hunt, talking to author Ronnie Mutch][20]

When Roger Maris hit sixty-one home runs in 1961, the pressure of constant interviews so upset him that he began to lose bristly clumps of hair. [From Roger Kahn's *The Boys of Summer*][21]

In the Neath match the first sound I heard at the kick-off was a war cry, 'Charge,' coming from their pack. Within minutes there was a viciousness about the game which frightened me. The boots were flying in, fights going on off the ball and I honestly thought someone was going to be killed. [Gareth Edwards][22]

Cliff knelt down in front of Arthur, who was sitting stiff and scared in his chair. Speaking quietly and earnestly, Richey tried to drum into his colleague the need to stay back and rally, to wait for the openings. . . . Ashe just nodded. When he's really nervous, Arthur literally scares himself rigid. . . . He all but goes into a trance of fear. [Marty Riessen talking about the 1967 Davis Cup][23]

I was out to a loose one, and England were 54 for 5. When I got back to the dressing room, there was a deathly silence. I sat in the dressing room through lunch nearly in tears. I missed the Fourth Test, then went to Melbourne where I bowled thirty-three overs against Victoria. By now my [injured] leg was dragging as I ran. Finally at Geelong I felt something completely snap. I collapsed, couldn't get up and had to be carried off the field. I lay on a table for the rest of the day sick and feverish with ice-packs being applied to my head. And at the end of it the senior players gave me a solid cursing. There were one or two occasions on that tour when I felt so completely out of my depth that I even contemplated killing myself. [Brian Close][24]

During the match Ilie's language had also been a disgrace. I was sitting on the side of the court taking photos when something caught his eye in the crowd and he yelled over my head, 'Go fuck yourself!' Apart from being vulgar and embarrassing it was unnecessary. But such was his state of mind that he didn't care. Inside, he was threshing about with his own emotions, scared, angry, unhappy, and, as a result, vindictive. He wanted to strike back at a world he was rapidly losing faith in. Pressures he often didn't understand and could rarely control were becoming too much for him to handle. The more he struggled, the tighter the web of disaster clung to him. [Nastase, although Romanian, never came in contact with the Communist sports scientists or their training methods][25]

Left-hander Roger Moret, hospitalized in a psychiatric facility since he went into a trance in the club-house 12 April, is due to resume work-outs today on an out-patient basis with the Texas Rangers. . . . The 28-year-old reliever hurled four strong innings of relief April 10 and gained a save against the New York Yankees. Two days later he was found standing motionless in a trance-like state for more than an hour. [newspaper report, 1978][26]

Arnold Beisser, an American psychiatrist, has written a book, *The Madness in Sports* (see page 239ff.), about his patients, many of whom have been professional sportsmen. A number of prominent athletes have sought psychiatric help, and many others have abandoned promising careers, publicly stating that to continue would have caused a nervous breakdown. Baseball player Jim Piersall, in his autobiography *Fear Strikes Out*, describes how his parents pushed him into sport, and how he eventually broke down under the pressures of achievement. Football player Lance Rentzel went into psychotherapy with a professor of psychiatry at UCLA, Louis West. Rentzel was in despair, having apparently lost all control over his own behaviour. Soccer's own Jimmy Greaves reveals in his autobiography *This One's On Me*, how a superb athlete ended up in the alcoholics' ward of a mental institution. Argentinian tennis player Guillermo Vilas hurried home from Wimbledon in 1976, after a lifeless display in the quarter-finals against his friend Björn Borg, reportedly to see a psychiatrist in Buenos Aires. During the change-overs of that match he sat staring at two identity bracelets on his wrists, pale and shaken. After his victory in the Masters tournament at Kooyong he withdrew from the circuit for several weeks, apparently suffering from 'nervous dyspepsia'.

While it is true that sport may attract individuals seeking to resolve inner conflicts (Seeing Pressure Overcome Resolves Tension) it is also true that for many people otherwise well-integrated, sport has evoked stresses beyond their capacity to handle. Considering its purpose and design, this is not surprising. Nor is it surprising that those sportsmen who have suffered most from its psychological pressures should be the ones least apt to communicate their difficulties. Most athletes believe that it is part of their job to be courageous: they have no business letting pressure get on top. They are ashamed to be in need of help, and afraid this may reflect on their competence. The taboos surrounding 'nerve' and 'nerves' in sport are many, for the sportsman is often cast in the role of fear frontiersman. His confrontations with tension, panic, fight-or-flight crises and adrenalin build-up are part of this role; many of the studies carried out by sports psychologists have broadened our general understanding of such things as 'stage-fright' and 'arousal', because athletes exhibit them to a marked degree. It is as much a requirement of the pro sportsman's job to swallow his anxieties, as it is to polish his skills.

Nevertheless, partly because of the growing volume of personal testimonies from sportsmen who have suffered breakdowns, and partly because of the ferment of interest generated by East European research, there has been an increasing concern with sports psychology in the West. A growing number of psychiatrists and psychologists (most of them, sadly, of a behaviourist persuasion) have begun sifting and analysing all available information on sports stress, both from the players themselves and from comparative research with children, war-time pilots, Vietnam veterans and volunteers in laboratory experiments.[27]

As will be seen from the final section of this book, field tests and laboratory experimentation into the nature of fear, pain, will-power and co-ordination are already being systematically carried out on sportsmen around the world. The reader who considers the foregoing allegations about sport's real purpose far-fetched will find ample evidence to substantiate them in the last chapters. If anything, they are not fetched far enough.

2

The Brain Game – Cricket

In 1870, for the first time, they dragged out the heavy roller at
Lord's. Keats had been dead for fifty years but his 'Ode on
Indolence', written while he was recovering from a blow over the
eye with a cricket ball, was charming all Victorians except
Matthew Arnold. This was a gentlemanly age, and the heavy
roller, it was believed, would iron out any dangerous lumps in the
pitch and ensure the safety of English cricketers everywhere from
uncertain bounces and flying red leather. In June of that year,
1870, an MCC side that included W.G. Grace played
Nottinghamshire at Lord's, and Notts. were set 157 to win in their
last innings. A wicket fell, and in came George Summers, a slender
man of 25, to face. He had no reason to suppose his team would not
trounce the MCC, of whom some were bad eggs, and others had
been able to accumulate runs solely because of their bodily cor-
pulence in front of the wicket. The bowler, however, was a whippy
little fellow from Derbyshire, John Platts. He was certainly short
for a fast bowler, Summers thought, but also very quick, and in he
came. The ball got up sharply and struck the batsman in the face.
He wavered for a moment, 'reeled like a teetotum', according to the
wicket-keeper, and fell. Four days after the match, Summers
was dead.[1]

In February, 1975, an MCC side met the New Zealanders at
Eden Park, Auckland. The New Zealanders always lost to the
MCC, and here they were again, still needing 127 runs to save
them. They had lost all but their last wicket when tail-ender Ewan
Chatfield came in. Although not a recognized batsman, Chatfield

proved difficult to winkle out and on the Tuesday morning the bowler, Peter Lever of Lancashire, decided the time had come. The next ball to Chatfield was short, lifted, glanced off the batsman's glove and flew in his face. One of the fieldsmen, Dennis Amiss, noticed with some horror that the batsman's eyes flickered before he fell down. What followed was very frightening indeed. 'As he lay there with his body convulsing Chatfield's tongue became lodged in his throat and he started to choke. His face began to go blue,' says Amiss, and 'we realized that here was a fellow cricketer dying in our midst, and we were apparently powerless to help him'.[2] Fortunately, while others stood wringing their hands, a St John Ambulance officer and Bernard Thomas, the MCC physiotherapist, rushed on to the field, prized out Chatfield's tongue and gave him the kiss of life.

The New Zealanders never forgot the bouncer that felled Ewan Chatfield. In 1978 they set about redressing the balance of 48 years and beat an England XI for the first time in a Test match. The unsuspecting Englishmen, captained by Geoff Boycott, arrived in New Zealand expecting the usual spot of batting practice and found instead ugly crowds, grinning umpires and bowling of such savagery that Boycott, sporting a black eye, said afterwards: 'I've heard of fellows getting 3 million dollars for going three rounds with Muhammad Ali. . . . I think I'll be writing to the Test and County Cricket Board.'[3]

At the beginning of 1979, a 'lifter' from Bob Willis, on the first day of the Fifth Test in Adelaide, struck 21-year-old Rick Darling under the heart. Like Chatfield, Darling swallowed his tongue, as well as his chewing gum. Like Chatfield he was saved by a physiotherapist, Michael Mason, hooking them out of his throat, and by a punch on the chest by England spin bowler John Emburey, which apparently re-started his breathing.

The accidents to Summers, Chatfield and Darling are an integral part of cricket wherever it is played under pressure, because bowlers are obliged, under pressure, to be dangerous. The ball that struck Summers is supposed to have pitched on a small pebble,[4] (rather than the famous Lord's 'ridge') but it is common practice for a pace bowler to 'dig one in'. Indeed this is hardly surprising, considering the implications of his job. His team and his supporters pride themselves on his ferocity and his ability to 'part the batsman's upstanding hair'. Without the bouncer in his armoury, a fast bowler considers himself undressed, if not unmanned, and much of his behaviour on the field, including mile-long run-ups and out-rageous appeals for l.b.w., are to make the batsman quiver, or, if possible, fall over backwards on top of his wicket out of sheer fright. This is how the fast bowler sees his job. 'I don't think people realize the pressures involved,' Bob Willis told me shortly after-wards. 'If a batsman knows he's not going to get a bouncer, he's 50 per cent more relaxed.' That makes the fast bowler's job 50 per cent more difficult.

There are many battles on the cricket field, but none of them rivals the one that takes place between the immovable batsman and the irresistible bowler and the latter is often, though not always, fast. Understood by all the players, by every man and boy in the stands, and by all those watching the match on television or rattling to the back pages of the newspaper, is this ancient rivalry between bowler and batsman – a primitive confrontation redolent of castles and sieges, of big bad wolves, huffing and puffing, and houses belonging to piglets. This imperishable rivalry makes cricket a very serious and passionate business, less often referred to as a game than most sports, and in some areas such as Yorkshire, regarded with hostile reverence. 'Without in any way wishing to sound melodramatic about it,' says Brian Close, 'it is no exaggeration to say I would have died for Yorkshire. I suppose once or twice I nearly did,'[5] he adds, referring to those occasions when he returned to the pavilion black and blue from 'fielding' balls that hit him on the head and flew twenty yards into the hands of a slip fieldsman.

In view of all this violence, calling cricket the Brain Game may appear odd. Why not call it something else: the Brawn Game might be more appropriate, or the Brainer's Game, perhaps. The answer is simply that the confrontation between batsman and bowler is first and foremost psychological. Sir Don Bradman reportedly summed up his philosophy of batting like this: 'I am trying all the time to find out what is in the bowler's mind as he delivers the ball. It is a constant battle, one man against another – I to hit him, he to beat me.'[6]

Consider the symbolism. Three sticks in the ground delicately supporting two bails, are the batsman's castle. If they fall down, for whatever reason, he is done for. The batsman is essentially alone (although there are for the convenience of play always two on the field at the same time). Everyone is out to get him. The bowlers, the fieldsmen, the opposing skipper, everyone. They use a ball for this purpose. They aim it at his castle, and if he is in the way, they aim it at him. He has a weapon with which to defend himself, called a bat. With this he can deflect the missile to different parts of the field. The time that this gains for him (while they fetch the ball) enables him to run. He runs and runs, and this is all he can hope for, actually, until somebody knocks his block off. The number of times he runs is his score, and the better the score, the more running he was able to do before his castle fell down.

It is not difficult to spot the analogy with man's predicament. His score is his age (the metaphor concerning 'centuries' and 'innings' when referring to age is colloquial), the falling of his wicket is death, and running and running is his glorious achievement – all the more glorious because of its ultimate doom, according to some schools of thought. There is also a kind of honour attached to the batsman's task. If he hits the ball well enough, and far enough, for it to go over the boundary rope, the fielding side give him a small respite and pretend he has run four or even six, depending on whether or not the ball touched the ground on the way. In this event, he doesn't have to exert himself physically and the spectators, if there are any, acknowledge this with applause. If on the other hand he hits the ball in the air and it is caught, this signifies a failure, as it leaves him no time to run anywhere at all. For this he is punished by dismissal.

So the role of the batsman is inherently fugitive. But the psychological battle becomes increasingly apparent when we realize that the batsman could, theoretically, use his body as a shield to defend his wicket, and block out the incoming missiles with trigonometrical ease. This is physically possible (though dangerous); the wicket is smaller than the batsman, and could not logically be broken with his body in the way. Colin Cowdrey used this method successfully against the West Indians once, when there was an ungodly amount of short-pitched bowling (in the Third Test at Sabina Park, Jamaica on the tour of 1959/60). Wes Hall and Chester Watson would come thundering in, teeth blazing and crucifixes flying, and hurl everything except the kitchen sink at Cowdrey, and Cowdrey, who was wearing a Dunlopillo vest for this special purpose, simply took the blows on his body. He found the method more or less foolproof. Playing the good-length balls, he also made some runs, 114 and 97, because his mind was relaxed and clear, and he knew that he had taken the initiative. Whether or not the same Dunlopillo ruse might be effective against Messrs

Marshall and Garner in the 1980s remains a matter for speculation.

However, the reader will realize from the opening chapter of this book that the rules of all sport experiments are designed to a nicety to increase the pressure on the participants, to see what they will do, and a batsman cannot be allowed to get out of it by mere physical courage. Cricket, and particularly Tests (advisedly so called), would be ruined. Batsmen could come clanking out of the pavilion in suits of armour, or mattresses, and stand doggedly in front of their three sticks all the hours that God sends, without feeling anything else incumbent upon them. So to increase the pressure on the batsman the rules are such that (a) he may not shield his wicket with his legs (the l.b.w. law) and (b) he is cruelly obliged to score.

It is not enough for him stoutly to defend his wicket (in spite of exceptional stalwarts such as Trevor Bailey made heroes in the memory). He must make runs as well, and he must make them fast, or the spectators and selectors (two other sets of persecutors not enumerated before) want to have a word about the matter. Be he never so difficult to get out, if he returns to the pavilion without a tolerable number of runs, a pall of gloom descends. He will not be applauded. He will not readily be trusted again. Team-mates may crack the odd joke, but his competence and even his manhood may be held in question, especially by spectators on Sydney Hill. If worst comes to worst, he begins to feel a failure, and becomes a failure, and then a loser, and then the team is obliged to find somebody to replace him, because his nerve has gone. This is the batsman's dilemma. He must take risks, and yet not take risks. He must be watchful and stoical, but he must also run. He must defend his wicket, and yet 'go after' the bowling. He must convince the opposition of his intentions, even if he doesn't know what they are. He must make 50, or 100, but he must not be concerned about these milestones. He must be carefree, and full of care. He must think of his team, and yet cover himself with glory. And he must reconcile all these apparent contradictions in his mind while the bowlers come pounding in, and the bouncers, beamers and boxers assail his person. If ever a job was designed to induce schizophrenia, it is walking out to the middle in a Test match, and many a brilliant and gifted batsman has made himself ill trying to do these things, as we shall see.

It is probably not true that the bowlers want to kill him, although some have used the technique of expressing this intention. South African Peter Heine told Trevor Bailey, 'I want to hit you, Bailey – I want to hit you over the heart.' Laker's impression was that he meant every word, though I think this unlikely. Jeff Thomson of Australia is by nature a diffident and rather quiet fellow who in June 1974 somehow gave the impression of having told a journalist, 'I enjoy hitting a batsman more than getting him out. It doesn't worry me in the least to see a batsman hurt, rolling around screaming and blood on the pitch.'[8] Fellow-Australian Dennis Lillee made similar murderous boasts, both in *Back to the Mark* and *The Art of Fast Bowling*. Dennis is a hospitable chap, who worked himself into a mood of hatred by ingenious techniques and by listening to the Australian spectators chanting (after a few Fosters) 'Kill, Kill, Kill.' He drew the line at hitting a batsman on the head – 'because I appreciate what damage that can do'. Thomson has been timed, by the use of photosonic cameras, at 99.688 m.p.h. on release.[9] His slingshot action, with the bowling hand concealed until the last moment behind his back, makes him a very difficult bowler to anticipate or 'pick' as the batsmen say. They do not know what he will do with the ball, but they know that, whatever it is, it will be done quickly. By the time the batsman's central nervous system has processed the information about the delivery he has approximately half a second to determine what his response should be. If the ball deviates after pitching, as it often does, he has considerably less than half a second and it is possible, by the use of logarithms, to produce figures proving conclusively that he should begin playing his stroke before the ball is bowled, and even before he can see the seam (0.162 seconds before, according to one national newspaper). In other words, he should answer without knowing what the question is. Many technically accomplished batsmen, under this kind of pressure, have failed for want of psychic gifts. Others are presumably able to make educated guesses, based on what has gone before and minute changes in Thomson's movements prior to delivery.

Dennis Lillee, having made a comeback from vertebral stress fractures which threatened to end his career sooner, was timed at 86.39 m.p.h. on release (on a bad day, according to him). Dennis made no bones about bouncers. 'You *are* trying to hit the batsman,' he said.[10] The bouncer or bumper is aimed at the area between the batsman's chest and just above his head. Lillee had made it quite clear on a number of occasions that this is the target area for all bouncers, even if the bowler does not admit it. And he said of his attitude to the batsman, 'I try to build up a sort of hate feeling.'[11] He had, by discipline, no sympathy for his quarry, because ruthlessness was part of his job. 'There is no room for conversation with the batsman, for example. In fact, I make it my business to say nothing to him unless it's to give him a piece of my mind when I think he deserves it. And I'm not interested in any replies from him.'[12] Interestingly, these disclosures come from *The Art of Fast Bowling*, an instructional book obviously intended for children.

The greatest fast bowler of the author's lifetime, Fred Trueman, used to come home from a spot of bouncing to find his father still up and sitting at the kitchen table. 'You've been at it again,' his dad would say, and though Fred admired his father beyond description, the requirements of his job were such that he had indeed been at it again, and that he would continue to be at it again for as long as his bow legs could be made to trundle in. Not that Fred ever tried to 'build up a sort of hate feeling' for the batsman. It came quite naturally. The sight of a man with a bat in his hands filled Fred with such murderous loathing that it was all he could do not to accompany his deliveries down the pitch towards the object of his ire. His run-up was more than once likened to the quiet, swaying charge of a bull.

All this talk of violence on the part of fast bowlers tends to reduce our primitive confrontation to a mere coconut-shy, or bun-fight, which it certainly is not. A batsman who is carried off the field, provided he did not fall on his wicket or give a catch, goes down on the score card as 'retired hurt'. The bowler receives no credit for the wicket, which theoretically is still intact. If necessary the batsman can come back and continue where he left off, plaster casts and all. The bowler's success lies in wicket taking. This is his job, and this is what he must do in order to justify his place. So the bowler cannot make a living by maiming batsmen: this is a mere embellishment of his purpose. Wickets do not necessarily fall to bowlers who can knock batsmen about, but wickets *do* fall to bowlers who have in their repertoire this psychological threat, of dreadful violence just below the surface, of implacable hatred and callous rage. That these may not be their real feelings does not matter in the slightest, so long as the batsman believes them to be real. For the fast bowler's purpose is not to break the batsman's bones, but to break his *nerve*. This is the Art of Intimidatory Bowling, and it may easily be seen that this is a far more sinister and malevolent design than mere physical hooliganism.

If we look more carefully at the fast bowlers' boasts concerning bouncers, this note echoes in them all. To start with, seriously injuring a batsman does not generally fill them with pleasure. Usually they are overcome with remorse, particularly if they think the injury may prove fatal. Bob Willis looked away when a batsman was injured. It upset his rhythm, apart from anything else. Fred Trueman felt 'sick to the stomach', whenever it looked as though he might have 'done' a batsman.[13] Platts, the bowler who inadvertently killed George Summers, broke down when he saw what he had done. W.G. Grace said of him, 'I shall never forget his mental distraction.' Peter Lever, who struck Chatfield in the face, sank to the ground and wept inconsolably. He said, and this is a nervous subject for most fast bowlers, that he never meant to hit Chatfield 'on the head'. In the next Test match his bowling was obviously affected: his early deliveries were wide, and he has never bowled with the same venom or accuracy since. Bob Willis believes that one day, because of the fast bowler's need to resort to bouncers, a batsman will be killed 'and the memory will scar the particular fast bowler for life'.[14] Historically, the fast bowler has often been a figure of tragedy rather than brutal glee. Eddie Gilbert, the awesome Aborigine, has spent twenty-three years of his life in a mental home. Tom Richardson, the huge moustachioed gypsy who in 1895 took 290 wickets, would ease off whenever he hit somebody, for fear of finding out his own strength.[15] Merritt Preston who in 1883 sent down the ball that killed batsman Albert Luty, was never the same man again, and when he died his grave was within a pitch-length of his victim.[16] Of the thirty fast bowling contemporaries enumerated by the legendary 'Plum' Warner in his autobiography three, or ten per cent, committed suicide.[17]

Even taking a batsman's wicket in a Test match, without causing him actual physical harm by bowling bouncers, may be traumatic to a bowler unused to his own devastating powers, especially if he has been 'bayed on' by bloodthirsty spectators. Rodney Hogg, the remarkable Australian who emerged as the bowler to fear in the 1978/9 England–Australia series, was so overwhelmed at taking the wickets of Boycott and Brearley in one over at Melbourne, that he suffered an asthma attack. A week later he said he could still see Boycott's dismissal in his mind's eye, as if he were in a car accident and about to collide with a tree.[18] In Adelaide, Hogg had sent Clive Radley staggering from a blow on the head.

Why do so many fast bowlers 'dig one in', knowing what damage it can do, both to the batsman and themselves? Harold Larwood, the bowler at the heart of the notorious Bodyline rumpus, says in his autobiography:

> I never bowled to injure a man. . . . Frighten them, intimidate them, yes.[19]

Bob Willis (telling me before his retirement how he broke Rick McCosker's jaw):

> I aim at the batsman's chin so that he'll hook up and sky a catch. But it is part of the fast bowler's job to be aggressive. He's got to have 'devil'. He doesn't want to see the batsman badly injured, but he wants to tickle his ribs with a fast one. And if you sense they're scared, you give them another.[20]

Richard Hadlee of New Zealand:

> Listen, I never bowled a ball in my life that was intended to hurt a batsman. Shake him up a bit, terrify him a little, sure. But at Test level, the batsman is there to be tested.[21]

Note the assumption on Hadlee's part – and he is quite correct – that Tests are for testing the batsman's nerve. Sport experiments are not usually seen with such clarity by the participants.

To intimidate, or strike fear into the batsman, is to increase the psychological pressure on him to the point where he is muddled, self-conscious and no longer able to make rational decisions. The implied threat is not to his physical person, so much as to his sanity – and sometimes this is a very real threat indeed under Test pressure. The bouncer is not merely for blacking the odd eye or bruising the odd rib. It is for inducing a state of mental anguish in which the batsman is likely to panic and drop his bundle. It is, as Larwood says, 'a ball intended to intimidate, to unsettle'.[22] Splitting minds, rather than heads, has nothing to do with thuggery, which by comparison is an art abject in its naîveté. Splitting minds in Test matches is a highly skilled job, involving the fast bowler's entire repertoire: inswingers, outswingers, cutters, yorkers, beamers, bumpers, knuckle balls and palm balls: anything, in fact, which can contribute to breaking the batsman's confidence, and making him uncertain and scared. This is the fast bowler's brief, and to be seen to be doing it, in front of thousands of witnesses, is his chief joy.

Fred Trueman's bouncers were often condemned as assault and battery. This was not so. Fred's bouncers were for breaking and entering the mind. 'If the odd bouncer helped to break their concentration – and that is what I was trying to break, not their skulls – then I considered it a fair weapon.'[23] Fred was frequently accused of being too aggressive, to which he replies that first of all, short-pitched bowling was imperative on lifeless wickets, and second, that 'If I could get one to lift round their head now and again it served two purposes – to liven things up a bit for bored spectators and, more important, to sow a seed of doubt about the state of the pitch in the mind of the batsman and perhaps push him into a mistake.'[24]

Although Fred was obliged by his job to look as though he intended to 'do' the batsman, he never set out to inflict serious injury: the sight of it made him feel quite queasy and upset. Of course, such feelings could not be revealed at the time, or they would have compromised his psychological power, for the spectators, his own team, the selectors, and all the batsmen still waiting in the pavilion for 'their bloody lot'. Having injured somebody with a delivery, Fred would stump back to his marker, and even sit down in a casual fashion, as though mildly annoyed at this interruption of his bowling skills. Fred was always very good at psyching. He says he was psyching opponents before Muhammad Ali had the strength to knock his teddy bear over. Even though he frequently didn't know, for example, which way the new ball would swing, or if it would swing at all,[25] he never let on. The batsman was not to see behind Fred's omnipotence. It is not uncommon for a quick bowler to be unaware which delivery he will produce. Mike Hendrick was fast-medium, and he didn't know if the ball would move in or out.[26]

In 1978, in the First Test at Edgbaston, a delivery from England fast bowler Bob Willis struck Pakistani tail-ender Iqbal Qasim in the mouth. A furore followed, involving such headlines as 'TEST SICKENER', and accusing 'Willis the Bruiser' of staining England's victory with Pakistani blood. Just as the sports press generally fail to grasp the implications of a batsman breaking down under the extreme pressures of his job (as we shall see from the cases of Barrington and Boycott), so it makes a pig's breakfast of dealing with a fast bowler trapped in the requirements of *his* job. The state of sports journalism in this country in its criticism of players echoes the joke about the two eggs boiling in the saucepan. One egg says to the other one, 'My God, it's hot in here,' to which the second egg replies, 'That's nothing. Wait till you get outside; they smash your bloody head in.' The fact that some of the journalists writing about cricket are ex-players themselves serves only to highlight the reluctance of those involved in sport experiments to acknowledge what their five senses have told them about the experience.

The hue and cry suggests two things: had Iqbal Qasim's batting-average been rather better, the injury would have been passed off as a professional hazard, and Willis must have been a thug to behave in this way. Anyone who has even a passing acquaintance with Bob Willis's career and character is aware that he is very far from being a thug; he was in fact trying to do his job as a fast bowler, with all the pressures that this implies. Willis, or 'Goose' as he was called, took a record twenty-seven Australian wickets during the previous summer series. Mike Brearley, the captain, pointed out that the England side were wary of tail-enders who could make a lot of runs (as they had done in India), and that both Thomson and Max Walker were in fact good drivers of the ball, so it was important to keep the initiative away from them by bowling short. 'Willis, in particular, who had been hesitant to do this, was encouraged to dig a few in just short of a length to them'[27]. At Old Trafford, for some reason, Willis was similarly unwilling to bowl bouncers at Greg Chappell, a magnificent batsman who had announced his retirement. Dennis Amiss, according to his captain, coaxed Willis to send down a few. 'When you bowl to him, Bob, you seem a different bowler. After one early bouncer, he knows he won't get any more, so he moves confidently onto his front foot. All top batsmen,' Amiss apparently continued, 'go through a period of timidity sometime in their careers. Give him a bombardment.'[28] It is true that Brearley did not actually order Willis to bowl bouncers at Chappell or anybody else, partly because Brearley was a very good psychologist, wary of upsetting a man's delicate rhythm and confidence, and partly because he remembered John Lever telling him in Melbourne that a fast bowler did not like to be *told* to bowl a bouncer: it has 'to *feel* right to make it worthwhile'. Having been generally encouraged, though, when Willis thought it 'felt' right, he sent down a bouncer to remove Iqbal Qasim. He still thinks it was perfectly justified. In December 1978 the TCCB, considering the possible tactical advantages of the nightwatchman ploy to the batting side, ruled that in future a bowler would not be prevented from bouncing nightwatchmen.[29]

One irony of this incident was that Willis was one of several cricketers (Tony Greig was another) who favour the use of crash helmets for all batsmen, irrespective of their skill at making runs. When the accident happened the press, while condemning Willis, were busily conducting a campaign against these helmets on the grounds that they looked unsightly. This interesting paradox is central to the psychological dilemma in which the batsman characteristically finds himself.

The question of protective headgear is not new to cricket. One of the possible origins of the word 'daft' was the aftermath of that MCC–Notts. match in 1870 in which Summers received his fatal injury. C.I. Thornton, one of the people who carried Summers down to the Tavern parlour, said: 'I shall never forget Richard Daft coming in next, with a towel round his head covered with a scarf tied under his chin.' C.E. Green, who had been fielding at long-stop, observed that Daft, a gent 'always dapper and rather full of self-importance', now looked 'ludicrous' in his improved head-protector.[30] The fact that this ludicrous-looking batsman proceeded to set about Platts' bowling was perhaps less memorable than his visible daftness.

In his early days, G.L. Jessop – the Croucher – used to be a bowler, and a quick bowler at that. A Cambridge bard was moved to celebrate his exploits:

> 'There was a young Fresher called Jessop
> Who was pitching 'em less up and less up
>   'Till one of the pros
>   Got a blow on the nose
> And said, "In a helmet I'll dress up." '

David Frith, quoting the song from Gerald Brodribb's biography *The Croucher*, points out that there was a variant of the last line: 'And a man with a mop cleared the mess up' – which readily illustrates the general good humour on the subject.

In the early 1930s Patsy Hendren sat up in bed after being struck on the head and designed a very remarkable cap with three peaks, which he wore for the 1933 Series against the West Indies, to the chagrin of many of the England camp. When a newer controversy arose concerning modern plastic helmets with face grids, Ian Wooldridge, never a man to miss out on a possible sporting comedy, phoned Harold Larwood in Sydney to ask what the principal

Bodyline bowler thought of this new-fangled device. Larwood said the Australians who faced his bowling in 1932/3 would never have worn such a thing. Why? 'Well they were men.' Apparently they stuffed wet towels down their singlets, but didn't go so far as to protect their heads. 'They would have seen that as an admission of weakness, and so would I.'[31]

The reader will gather from this discussion that there are psychological laws which govern the batsman's attempts to protect himself, and which have nothing to do with practicality or mere good sense. The rules of cricket are designed to increase the pressure on the participants, and any attempts to circumvent these pressures are met with the greatest disapprobation. It would seem, to the disinterested observer, that the history of frightful injuries to batsmen's faces and heads would have ensured the introduction of helmets long ago: after all, many American baseball players owe their lives to such equipment, and of all sports injuries, those to the head and face are unquestionably the most dreadful and dangerous. India's Nari Contractor, whose skull was fractured by Charlie Griffith in Barbados in 1962, recalls how the delivery appeared ('got big' as batsmen say) about three feet from his head, and that he just had time to avert his eyes. 'I can remember the ball hitting me and dropping at my feet, then blood coming out of my ears and nose.'[32] Contractor would certainly have died had it not been for six hours of major brain surgery; and he is not the only one. Yet when the first commercially manufactured helmets appeared at last, and Mike Brearley and others came out to bat in white bone-dome Amiss Mark IIs, journalists and ex-players everywhere were face-down in their cereal the following morning, unable to bear the ignominy of it all. Brearley was cruelly photographed in the offending item with a fish-eye lens for maximum effect, and variously described as a 'flannelled Evel Knievel', a 'Martian' and a 'caged commander'. Said Denis Compton on television, 'I think it was most embarrassing to see the England captain go out to bat in a crash helmet.' Compton was one of many who considered it 'looked so unmanly'. Brian Close said he never would have worn a helmet. 'I was brought up that cricket was a man's game.' 'Going soft,' proclaimed the irritating Alan Thompson in the *Express*,[33] and Tony Lewis prattled on in the *Sunday Telegraph*[34] about the coming of a sub-epsilon state of faceless men. Even the normally sensible Richie Benaud and Jim Laker sat in the BBC TV commentary box prior to the Lord's Test and pretended the helmet in their midst was too small to go over their heads. Benaud said that perhaps 'transparent' helmets would be better as they 'wouldn't offend the sight'. Jim Laker promised, 'You wouldn't get me to wear one of them,' and the helmet ended up on the head of Peter West, a man of enormous natural dignity, to show viewers what it did in fact look like.

On the third day of the England–New Zealand Test at Trent Bridge, Ian Botham, one of the bravest and most remarkable crick-eters to emerge in recent years, took off his helmet and stepped up from his close-fielding position to bowl. The umpires declined to hold the helmet, which was passed among the fielding side like a bomb until Clive Radley deigned to put it on his head. Since that day, both Radley and Botham have been 'skulled' by balls which could have killed them, and Ian Botham was saved from serious injury by wearing a helmet to field at short leg. The latest develop-ment has been that the TCCB are looking into a possible ban on the crash helmets for close-in fieldsmen, on the grounds that they are encouraged by the headgear to stand close to the bat – as though cricketers have ever needed any encouragement to do that. Even-tually, after the spectacle in Australia of four batsmen staggering sideways from head injuries, a bulk order of head protectors was freighted in for the Australian and England Test teams. The mini-helmets were made of fibre glass and designed to look like caps. This seemed to satisfy most sensibilities. In 1984 Andy Lloyd, in the first Test against the West Indies, was hit on the head by Malcolm Marshall. He missed the rest of the season. Had he not been wearing a helmet he might well have died.

The upshot of the scandal against virility in 1978 was that poor Mike Brearley, already in miserable form with the bat, slumped to virtual paralysis, moved down the batting order, discarded his white helmet in favour of the wax pie-mould he had worn the pre-vious season, and blamed several of his dismissals on being 'unsighted' by the visor: a phenomenon to interest opticians everywhere, since he could presumably have moved his head to accommodate a better view of the ball fairly easily. Other more pragmatically minded batsmen persevered, to the general oppro-brium of their more 'masculine' peers, but Brearley, a sort of crick-eting Ashkenazy, blamed every pressure on himself. There are many batsmen like him, for the job attracts gifted people of unusual complexity. Brearley told me at the time that one of the worst pressures of the captaincy had been conspicuousness. 'If I go and play a county match and wear a helmet, it's news, whereas there may be people in the opposing team who have been wearing them for half the season. I can't go away to some corner and mark off my little patch of land and play my little innings.' Much was said and written, certainly, about Mike's batting slump. He does not know why his bad trot should have come – he believes it may have been partly bad luck and partly a tightening of his right-hand grip. Many people offered him a variety of technical advice, but perhaps the key to understanding his poor form lies somewhere deeper than that. What, after all, are the pressures of Test cricket like? 'The biggest pressure is the one of exposure. No one likes to make a fool of himself in public. And this is fairly ruthless exposure, cricket. It goes on for a long time, there's a lot of television coverage, a lot of press coverage, there are action-replays, there's a *long* time for you to feel embarrassed, and a fool, and incompetent, and there's a certain amount of physical danger too'.[35] The worst pressure of all, Brearley discovered, is having to fight for one's privacy. This is the lot of almost every professional sportsman who earns (by his talent) the attention of sport's observant multitudes. There is no escape from this attention, and the latest cricket hero to be roasted in its glare was Ian Botham, hounded by the press and suspended by the authorities for drug confessions. Brearley was not the first captain to suffer 'ill luck' with the bat, either. Peter May, Ian Chappell, Greg Chappell, Mike Denness and David Gower have all been affected, and Botham's batting average as captain was 13.14, compared with 40.92 when *not* captain.

Threats to the batsman's life and limb, though serious, are perhaps less cruelly devised than the threats to his emotional stability, which are part and parcel of the professional sportsman's lot, and which he is indirectly paid to undergo for the sake of public enlightenment. Many batsmen who are 'Tested', that is, required to perform in Tests, have made themselves ill trying to resolve the contradictory pressures of their job. Some are struck down by mysterious physical maladies which clear up as soon as the crisis is passed. They are not malingering; they are simply ill. Peter May, Colin Cowdrey, Mike Denness and several other batsmen upon whom the additional responsibility of the captaincy has been thrust, suffered constitutional breakdowns which seriously affected their health during Test crises. May was forced to return to England during the riotous tour of West Indies in 1959/60 because an 'internal wound' would not heal. Denness was laid low by a mysterious virus at the start of his disastrous Australian tour and stood down after the Third Test. Cowdrey, who always seemed to have the captaincy thrown at him rather than conferred, was frequently either ill or injured. He declared himself unfit for the crucial Oval Test against South Africa in 1955[36] and he felt so ill on his way to the Manchester Test against Benaud's Australians in 1961 that he was forced to pull out. In his marvellous autobiography he describes the lifelong temptation to deal with unbearable pressure by being injured or sick.

Many batsmen (though not all) suffer from that unpleasant stress disease endemic to all sport experiments: split mind. Len Hutton was evidently mentally exhausted when he stepped down from the England captaincy. His whole personality, intelligent and complex, had been put through every degree of anguish during his triumphant tour of Australia, and in view of Sir Len's own comments to Ken Barrington about having endured a crisis similar to his, was perhaps fortunate that he withdrew from the pressures of Test captaincy when he did. Cowdrey, batting opposite him, saw one of the greatest batsmen in the history of cricket fumbling and disorientated, trying to do his job as though in a trance. 'He tied himself into all imaginable knots,' Colin says.[37] It was all Cowdrey could do not to run him out on occasions, because Hutton would omit to 'call' (compare Geoff Boycott's troubles in this department). Although the young man thought this part of his captain's tactical repertoire, such an explanation seems highly unlikely. I have seen several other great sportsmen affected in this way by intolerable pressure, who have afterwards confessed to being ill. There is more to sports performance than technical skill, and there is more to pre-match tension than butterflies in the stomach. As former England fast bowler John Snow says in his brilliant little poem, 'Lord's Test':

'Tomorrow starts the night before
lying looking through the blackness. . . .'[38]

A few unlucky batsmen of Test standard – which means the very best – have become emotionally disturbed to the point where they have withdrawn from the Test arena to play quietly in some cricketing backwater, trying to recapture their sense of self and their feeling for the game they loved. One or two remarkable men have actually come back from the brink of nervous breakdown to play at the top of their form again as Test batsmen. One of these was the late Ken Barrington.

In his autobiography, Barrington half-apologizes for talking about 'nervous tension and all that',[39] and after describing his harrowing experiences of 1966 says, 'Before we go any futher I'd better tell you a bit about myself as a person. If I don't, some of you might write me off as a crank!' The reader is asked to reflect on the implications of this statement from a professional sportsman made ill by sport. Instead of Barrington coyly apologizing for bringing the subject up, one wonders if we sports enthusiasts should not have apologized to him. The spectacle of a professional sportsman, gifted and full of courage, made to feel ashamed of succumbing to the pressures of sport – pressures quite deliberately imposed on him, and under Test conditions – strikes the author, for one, as ludicrous indeed. It is rather like some innocent knocked down by a car offering to get the mark off the paint, in case the driver was going anywhere special.

Barrington's illness began in 1964 at the time of his Surrey *v.* Yorks. Benefit match. Benefits are traumatic occasions for all cricketers because of the sentiments and social activity involved. It is not unusual for them to upset a batsman's equilibrium: Boycott, Amiss and Brearley are cases in point. What precipitated Barrington's illness was a disputed catch by Fred Trueman dismissing him for a mere 8 runs – although it might equally have been triggered off by some other incident threatening his efforts with meaninglessness: tennis players are often deeply disturbed by apparently unjust line-calls for the same reason. Ken had pinned all his hopes on a good innings in this match because one's Benefit is a sort of personal testimony, a signal of one's worth as a player over the years. The following day Barrington woke up in a state of mental paralysis not unlike Keats's 'drowsy numbness' that 'pains the sense' with, as he says, 'no life in my mind'.[40] Though he had always been a deeply conscientious player, he didn't care about a second innings. In fact he didn't care about anything at all. He took no further part in the match, and his indisposition was reported as a chill.

Though this might well have served as a warning, Barrington continued to play, and to play in Tests, which are purpose-built to exacerbate psychological frailty of any kind.

There are barriers in every sport: match-point in tennis; the last hole in golf; leading on the last lap in a Formula One race. The barriers are not visible to spectators, any more than a sound-barrier is visible to a pilot, but sportsmen know that they are there, and that intelligent beings pass through them at their peril. Not knowing what voltage such fences may pack, many technically capable sportsmen steer well clear of them, while others, after a few close calls, settle into a state of anguished expectancy for the rest of their careers. For most batsmen, 100 is infinitely different from 99. In Tests since the end of the 1979 series in England 57 innings ended in the nineties, with eight players falling just short of a century twice, and three (D.L. Haynes, C.G. Greenidge and K.T. Hughes) being pipped at the post three times. Barrington had always had a sensitive and superstitious mind and a Home Test Century, that cricketing icon, shone like a beacon in front of Ken's eyes for nine years and thirty-nine Test innings. Cricketers often refer to the 'nervous nineties', but Ken never reached even that state of initiation: he was more of a nervous eighties man, scoring 80, 80, 87, 80, 83 and 80 on various occasions. Ken attributed this to his being a back-foot player; others blamed his two-eyed stance, but the barrier phenomenon is so widespread in sport that technical explanations seem inadequate.

In 1964, in the second innings of the Leeds Test against the Aussies, Barrington looked up at the scoreboard. He was on 85. Suddenly, as Dexter was out, Ken felt burdened with the responsibility of steadying his side. Up went the Great Wall of China in front of him, and runs trickled to a halt. He was out padding up outside the off stump – another disappointment.

In the Fourth Test at Old Trafford, Barrington looked up during his innings and this time the scoreboard said 90. Up went the Great Wall again. For the life of him, Ken just couldn't push the score along: 'I stuck, as though immobilized and runless for ever, at one stage. Chaps being called by their wives from the "telly" to the meal-table said "OK, I'll just wait to see Barrington get his hundred," and were destined to find their meals dried up.'[41] Ken eventually crawled to 99 and then a hard top edge flew past McKenzie's hand and went for two. He'd made it. The trouble was, he now seemed trapped in the innings in that 'defensive groove' for an eternity. He went on scoring and scoring in a sort of limbo, past 150, past 200, past 250, until he was at last mercifully out for 256. He felt 'like a drugged man', and these other barriers were passed through without the slightest exhilaration. He didn't even notice his 200, which is usually Christmas morning for a batsman. The innings was roundly condemned. Barrington was attacked for not batting more attractively. It was a 'selfish display'. That he may have been paralysed by the pressures of his job seems scarcely to have crossed anyone's mind.

As Barrington's is a fairly accessible case, let us have a look at the circumstances. First of all, Australia had declared at 656 for 8, which meant that Ken's innings was meaningless. His efforts were a mere formality, and this is always a dangerous passage for a sportsman. What batting commandments did Barrington carry in his head? The most important was: Thou shalt not get out. Getting out is a cardinal sin for any batsman, but for one of Ken's spartan and meticulous discipline, it was anathema. The next commandment was: Thou shalt make runs, 100 if possible, as you've never managed that before in England. Now, Ken, as we have seen, resolved these two in his mind by making runs *carefully*. Then came another commandment: Thou shalt move thine arse. This is a particularly important commandment when trying to please spectators and selectors, and obviously conflicts with the earlier one about not getting out. But Ken had another commandment in his head, which had been there all his life: Thou shalt not play a reckless shot. If Barrington couldn't make runs 'properly', he couldn't make them at all. This was the real killer, because it meant that he couldn't just hit his way out of his paralysed slowness as another batsman might have done. The result of all these conflicting directives, and the agony of trying to obey them, was the 256 that Barrington scored in that innings. He was under terrible pressure, and he did his best.

The same torpor that seized Barrington's mind that morning during his Benefit game had taken hold of him again, in a Test match. It was a chastening experience, but worse was to come. At the start of the 1965 season, *Daily Express* journalist Crawford White phoned Barrington and asked for a commitment on 'brighter cricket', partly because of the recent dour MCC tour of South Africa, and partly because of Barrington's reputation as a 'crawler'. Mr White wanted a few quotes, and Ken rather foolishly gave them to him. Next morning, the story appeared: Crawler Barrington was about to flay the bowling to all parts of the ground. 'For me,' said the piece, 'careful cricket is now out.'

Poor Barrington. Another comandment was all he needed to wreck his form completely. By the First Test against New Zealand at Edgbaston, he had scored (for Surrey) 41 not out, 23, 21, 3, 7, 5, 6, 3, 0, 15, 18, 35, 1. Suddenly everything was wrong with his batting, and on the morning of that fateful Test, somebody had even snatched his lucky place in the dressing-room. 'I hadn't the nerve to ask him to swap.'[42]

The innings started fairly respectably: his 50 came up in two hours. Not glittering, but not too bad. Then the trouble started. The first day he made 61 in three and a quarter hours. 'The second,' says Ken, 'was sheer agony.' Paralysis set in, this time with a vengeance, and this time he couldn't get out. At 85, the place where he had stuck at Headingley the year before, he froze for an hour, unable 'to hit the skin off a rice pudding': 'Understand, too, that I was *trying* to score during that terrible scoreless hour: trying desperately. It was real inner torment, I can tell you. I craved despairingly for ones and twos which never came. Once I was so annoyed with myself that I threw my bat to the ground. Many times I was tempted to lose control and have a swing, but in moments like that I'd walk away from the wicket to regain concentration. . . .'[43]

At lunchtime, Mike Smith had a quiet word: 'Try and push it along this afternoon.' Barrington felt abject. 'I tried to apologize to him for batting so badly. "I'm sorry, Mike", I said, "but I just can't hit the blasted ball." '[44] His 100 took six and a quarter hours, his 137, seven and a quarter. It was a sad day for cricket, because Barrington was one of the bravest and most rugged little batsmen England had produced, and no one could understand what was the matter with him. The selectors dropped him, 'as a disciplinary measure', according to the press, and of course the press went to work, as they usually do. The *Daily Express*, which under the circumstances might decently have kept silent, ran a scourging piece by ex-all-rounder Keith Miller – the man who boasted that he once bowled eight bumpers in an over at Arthur Morris.[45] 'Barrington set the cricket clock back to the Dark Ages,' proclaimed the Australian. 'His innings was a selfish exhibition, the worst I have ever seen in this respect.'[46] Doug Insole, the chairman of selectors, told Ken, 'I can only say that to me and the other selectors it appeared as though all you wanted was 100 – which looks very selfish.'

The following season, 1966, on the way to the Trent Bridge Test in Doug Insole's car, Barrington, who had always been admired for his fine temperament, asked to be left out of the side. He felt very ill indeed, his mind was overwhelmed with tension, and he didn't care if he never played for England again. All the usual stories circulated: Barrington was scared of fast bowling; Barrington was frightened of Charlie Griffith; Barrington had raked the money in from his Benefit year; and so on. But the real reason was that under the pressure of Test matches, Barrington had become afraid of himself. The fact that he eventually returned to the Test arena to bat more glamorously than at any time in his career, shows a kind of courage that many of us never have cause to discover in ourselves.

In 1969 Ken Barrington suffered his first heart attack. To this day Fred Trueman believes this was brought on by the prospect of facing Charlie Griffith's bowling.[47] Ken died in 1981.

A similar fate to that described by Barrington in his 'paralysed' innings of 256, befell Geoff Boycott at Headingley in June 1967 (see pages 153–4) and with similar repercussions. However, unlike Barrington, who was rugged and unorthodox, Boycott is a batsman of a class rarely seen, and one of a handful of cricketers to whom the term 'genius' has fairly been applied. Boycott, when he is not at the crease, is in the nets, never trusting his skills, never satisfied with his aggregate, and driven by an obsession with batting embarrassing to many of his colleagues. Somewhere in his mind's eye there is a vision of the perfectly executed shot, a whole cascade of perfect shots, and Boycott tries to come as close to these as humanly possible – which takes a sportsman's lifetime. Like all great cerebral batsmen, who make runs by intellect alone, Boycott is often very slow to score. He lacks the instinctive graces of a Sobers or a Gower. He taught himself technical perfection, to the exclusion of practically everything else in life, and he has to remind himself daily how this is achieved, by long hours of practice. It is therefore very hard for him to score quickly, however he may envy those who do. The more he is criticized for slow scoring, the more carefully Boycott tries to reproduce the shots in his mind, and the more elusive those model strokes become. Whenever his confidence has been undermined, paralysis threatens. What often follows is that he snatches perilous singles, in an attempt to push the score along, and this habit has led him, on some occasions, to run out his team-mate at the other end, or himself, quite stupidly.

Losing his wicket is, to Geoffrey Boycott, a thing of magnitude few of us can comprehend. 'Unlike most, a ball player must confront two deaths,' says baseball-writer Roger Kahn of a sportsman's retirement.[48] In Boycott's case the deaths are rather more frequent: they occur every time he is out.

In 1978 the critics of Boycott's run-rate grew more numerous and noisy than ever. Vice-captain Boycott had taken over the England captaincy, after many years of dreaming about it, for the last part of the 1977/8 tour of Pakistan and New Zealand. Mike Brearley had broken his arm and gone home, and Boycott did his best to steady England's batting, by his usual method of thoughtful, slow gathering of runs. He received a black eye for his trouble (from a bouncer) and he also lost one of the New Zealand Tests, to the chagrin of his countrymen back home. Angry references were made to Boycott's decision, at the end of 1974, to withdraw from Test cricket 'for personal reasons', which many people believed concerned either ambitions about the captaincy or plain fear of fast bowling. Critics wondered how England could have entrusted him with the captaincy, or the vice-captaincy or anything else, on his return to the Test arena.

His contribution to the Ashes-winning performance of England in 1977 was quickly forgotten: critics called to mind that, after all, he had been 'very lucky', with dropped catches and so on, to make those runs at all. (At this time Boycott had amassed almost 33,000 runs in first-class cricket, an unusual tally.)

There followed a series of disasters. In July 1978, in a county match at Northampton, Boycott's vice-captain of Yorkshire, John Hampshire, staged a run 'go slow', apparently to demonstrate his disapproval of Boycott's slow scoring. Hampshire was disciplined for this by the Yorkshire Committee, who nevertheless saw his point of view. At the end of the summer, Geoff Boycott's widowed mother, with whom he had lived all his life in a small mining town, died. A couple of days later, the Yorkshire Committee informed Boycott of his dismissal as Yorkshire captain, after eight years. They had decided this was in the best interests of the Club, because, according to a statement, Boycott was self-involved, indecisive, and lacking in leadership qualities. They evidently felt that they had put up with these shortcomings long enough, and that such an important Committee ruling could not be postponed simply because his mother had died. John Hampshire was named as his successor.

Shortly before this, the England party to tour Australia had been announced. Boycott had lost the vice-captaincy, to Bob Willis. Boycott therefore went out to Australia as a batsman and nothing else. He was to be the backbone of the England innings, should others fail. The size of his responsibility was illustrated by the fact that Australian bowlers prized his scalp above all others. One 20-year-old from New South Wales, by the name of Lawson, sent down four successive bouncers, and in a one-day Test Alan Hurst delivered five on the trot, to see if his scalp could be separated from his head. Queensland players were told by a local firm that they would pick up £750 if Boycott were dismissed for less than 20 in either innings, and perks like this encouraged a new level of bouncing on the pitch and braying in the terraces.

In spite of one match-saving innings in the Perth Test, Boycott's batting, which was all he had left, began to quaver. In the Fourth Test in Sydney he suffered the ignominy of a 0 against his name, the first time in a Test match that he had sunk so low since 1969. He was angry about one or two l.b.w. decisions that went against him, and he had also received news from England that a campaign to restore him to the Yorkshire captaincy had failed. In Perth, during the match with Western Australia, Boycott was obliged to apologize to officials for a remark he had made during the course of play to Ian Botham, which Boycott was asked to repeat to the umpire. He had apparently called umpire Don Weser 'a — cheat', and the *Sun* ran an article, 'Play the big boy, Geoff,' in which it was suggested that Boycott should be wearing 'a dunce's cap'.[49] Hours after this incident, Boycott was once again passed over for the job of captaincy, this time in a minor one-day fixture at Albany, in the absence of both captain and vice-captain. The office went to Bob Taylor, the wicket-keeper.

Geoff Boycott's future as a cricketer is uncertain, to say the least. His batting average during the Indian summer of 1979 was sufficient to silence most of his critics and he was second in the first class averages even in 1985. But with a three-year ban for playing in South Africa having put paid to his long Test career, nobody knows if we shall ever see Boycott the batsman again, whatever ghost might walk out to the crease and accumulate runs against his name.

3

The Fast Game – Formula One

The Formula One car cannot speak. It has hundreds of moving parts, delicately interdependent, all of which can and sometimes do go wrong. It is an inbred, snorting, snarling strain of motoring genealogy, whose fuel consumption is prodigious, whose noise is deafening, and whose bodywork has more to do with origami than common roadworthiness. Standing idle in the pits it reminds the cynical observer of a grounded pterodactyl, unadapted for anything outside its own loony world. But, set in motion, it becomes the fast and terrifying god that all men recognize, and little boys dream of imposing their will upon.

The cars have killed by mechanical failure, though perhaps less often than is commonly supposed. The attraction towards them has partly to do with the danger, partly to do with the conquest of speed, and partly to do with the extraordinary, imposing beauty of the cars themselves. Most of the men who are honoured to race these strange cars have very strong feelings about them: curiosity, anger, wonder, resentment and other very private and mysterious feelings not all to do with grommets and widgets. Many of them talk to the car in moments of crisis, which is scarcely surprising, considering they spend so much time alone with the creature. 'Car, please finish, please finish, don't break down,' whispered Niki Lauda through his buck teeth. 'This car really sends you messages I tellya,' said 1978 World Champion Mario Andretti. 'Man, you can really talk to that car. She's handling like she's painted to the road.'

In 1974 before the Monaco Grand Prix, Lauda was sitting in his

Ferrari on the grid when a group of top-hatted swells came up and started posing for TV cameras and resting their hands on the car. Lauda's little fist came down like a hammer. It incensed him so much that he records the incident in some detail in his book *Formula 1* as an example of a rare emotional outburst. Lauda called each of his new Ferrari engines '*mio nuovo figlio*', my new son, and if he accidentally crashed a gear or hopped over a kerb he was so remorseful and disgusted with himself that he felt like coming back into the pits and chucking up the whole game. Lauda always prided himself on his gentleness with the Ferrari, which was undoubtedly one of the reasons for his success. It seemed he would rather come second and spare the engine, as he often did, than come first and flay the daylights out of it. After his horrifying crash on the Nürburgring in 1976, when Lauda received the last rites in Mannheim University Clinic, he cabled Enzo Ferrari from what had seemed his deathbed. Five days after being pulled from the flaming wreckage of the Ferrari, Lauda wished to thank the Old Man of Maranello, whatever their differences, for his decision not to compete in the Austrian Grand Prix. The cable said, 'to know that someone else was in my car would have been a nasty shock for me'.[1] Yet this was the very car that, according to the entire motoring press, had nearly killed him on the Ring – because a wheel fell off, or the rear suspension broke, or the car was a fire hazard, or so they said. Lauda himself has no memory of the accident and in spite of all prompting, by means of interviews and amateur ciné films of the crash, and despite switching to Brabham Alfa Romeo and then McLaren and going in and out of retirement, he resolutely refuses to blame the Ferrari for his accident. He insists he doesn't know what happened and that nobody else will ever know. In this Lauda distinguishes hmself from most of the members of his profession, who tend to hold their cars in less reverence, and frequently blame them for misfortunes on the track.

South African Jody Scheckter, runner-up for the 1977 World Championship in the Wolf, was a racer of enormous natural talent who hitherto narrowly missed fulfilling his potential. In 1977, when he came so close, he was forever complaining about the Wolf. After the Long Beach Grand Prix of 1977 in which he finished a disappointing third, Jody softly pounded the wing of his traitorous motor and repeated, 'had a puncture, had a puncture'. The Wolf was usually either understeering or oversteering or both, or else it manifested some other more peculiar malfunction during the race to rob Jody of a crucial victory. The malfunction was all the more exasperating because Jody could not always quite point it out to the designer or mechanics. The phenomenon continued into 1978, at the end of which Scheckter switched to Ferrari. In Brazil 1978 the Wolf had 'a little problem at the back end now, I don't know what it is'. There were other little problems throughout the season. In 1977, the year Jody almost seized the World Championship, it was some mysterious fuel pick-up trouble. The Wolf team were so puzzled, they called the Cosworth engine wizard, Keith Duckworth, for help. Duckworth examined the car's fuel system and said, 'Well, if your fuel system isn't working I can think of about eight others that shouldn't do either.'[2] It was a curious business. At Watkins Glen towards the end of that crucial season, Jody was at the back of the starting grid because in practice, where grid positions are determined according to fastest laps, he was unaccountably slow. Peter Warr, the team manager, was frankly at a loss to explain why. 'Jody says the car is well balanced, braking well, and the speed trap times are no better or worse than anybody else's, yet he is one and a half seconds off the pace.'[3] One and a half seconds, in F1 racing, is the difference between a car and a kart. Ambient temperatures and 'tyre convulsions' were suggested, or it might have been 'a sluggish engine'. Nobody knew. One of the things *not* suggested as a cause was that at Watkins Glen the previous year Scheckter had felt sick in the car and slackened his pace at the sight of Jackie Ickx's Ensign on fire. Ickx was in fact unhurt in the crash, but when Jody saw the flames he was convinced that the driver was dead. In 1973 Scheckter had seen François Cevert die on this track, near the notorious bridge.

So the 1977 season that had promised so much ended in disappointment for Jody Scheckter. For its own part the offending Wolf, which had won every motoring accolade only twelve months previously, maintained a sleek black silence. It could scarcely defend itself. Scheckter won the World Championship in the Ferrari in 1979. Was it just the car that had held him back?

The F1 vehicle of the year in 1977 was the splendid JPS Lotus 78, a black crow of a car that had the motoring world all agog at its design, its power, its 'wings' and its uncanny cornering ability and adhesion. Lotus dominated F1 racing in 1978 with the Lotus 79 and a religion grew up around the car. It became a legend in its own time; the 'ground-effects' car with skirts around the wing pods to increase downthrust and 'suck' the car against the road surface, thus improving cornering and handling. It could make a driver World Champion if he so much as sat in the cockpit and faced the front. But cars do not win world championships by themselves and in 1978 Colin Chapman's Lotus had the benefit of two of the greatest drivers in recent history to take it down the ten-ten line – Ronnie Peterson and Mario Andretti. During that year of Lotus domination, Peterson died and Andretti became World Champion.

Many people in motor racing believed that Andretti would win in 1977, when the Lotus had so clearly demonstrated its superiority through the season. Andretti, an enormously likeable Italian-American who, to borrow Ali's expression, can 'throw the jive', drove the car 'on rails' (smoothly, without drifting the tail out) – the only way, because of its differential set-up, that it is capable of being driven – and had the Championship within his grasp. He won four Grand Prix, only to have five Cosworth DFV engines unaccountably blow up on him; and the Championship flew out of the window. How this disappointment could have happened, nobody knew, because as Mario very angrily pointed out, he was never unduly aggressive. In Austria, a comfortable leader till lap 11, Mario, Lotus and all, blew up on the Bosch curve. 'Man, I was drivin' like it was an economy run, *nice an' easy*. Damn it, no way do I mistreat engines!'[4]

In 1977 Andretti's aggression astonished even his forceful rival James Hunt. In the Dutch Grand Prix the pair had a disagreement over Tarzan, one of the rare overtaking points on the track. Beaten away at the start by Hunt's McLaren, Andretti ate his heart out for five laps and then, unable to stand the humiliation of second place any longer, attempted to overtake Hunt on the outside. The two cars clanged wheels. Hunt's was written off, and Mario charged ever onwards. Well, almost. The Lotus engine blew up nine laps later. After the race there was a terrible row as to whodunnit. 'James Hunt thinks he's the king of the goddam world,' said Mario. 'There was no need for him to ride me out there, the jerk.'[5] James, for his part, was amazed at Mario's impatience. 'I don't know what Andretti was doing. It was his race. He had the best car. Sooner or later he was going to get by me.'[6] Lotus chief Chapman was familiar with the problem. In Italy Mario miraculously avoided overtaking Hunt at the start of the race. He told Chapman, 'Well, I could have had Hunt, but I figured to hell with it. Y'know it was one wheel on the grass, and I figured. . . .' Chapman, almost overcome with delight, interrupted, 'He's learning! At thirty-seven years of age he's actually learning.'[7] Unfortunately graduation day in 1977 was not to be, because Mario's engines kept blowing up all the time. 'Engine. Again. My fourth. I can't believe it. Honest. I can't believe it,' said Mario[8] indignantly. Despite its so-called 'locked' differential set-up and its 'wings', and despite its envied adhesion on every track, the car's miserable innards had somehow let Mario down. 'Few would argue that only [sic] bad luck has kept Andretti from the World Championship this year,' said a prominent motor magazine.

F1 racing is one sport in which virility is indisputably at stake. There's no beating about the bush. Divina Galica, one of two women attempting to breach the walls of this male citadel, was interviewed by motoring editor Mike Doodson at the beginning of 1978. 'But surely there are occasions,' said Doodson smugly, 'in the braking area for example, where (if she'll pardon the expression) there is no substitute for *balls*?'[10] Niki Lauda, asked about easing up in the Austrian GP in 1977, retorted, 'Ease up? I didn't bloody easy up. I drove balls out all the time'[11] (technical meaning notwithstanding). Even more than in society at large, a man in Formula One is under constant pressure to prove himself invulnerable to his male peers. It is joked about, without actually being a joke. If a driver misses victory by a whisker, if he crashes a gear, buzzes (over-revs) an engine or misses a braking point and causes a shunt, he is a bold racer who will admit it when he doesn't have to. This is not simply because of the enormous practical cost and trouble involved in mistakes on the race track, or the inter-team rivalry, or the fact that racers are always professionally looking over their shoulders, but because the driver, if he races, subscribes to the idea of invulnerability. To admit to a serious mistake in front of his peers, his fellow-racers snapping at his heels, to admit it to his team manager, his designer, his mechanics, his sponsors, and the entire motoring press all ga-ga over his talent, is prodigiously difficult. And even more difficult, for a man who earns his living on the ten-ten line between life and death, is to admit his vulnerability *to himself*. In a way, this comes under the heading of negative thinking. Objects of concern to the imagination, items to cause fear, are shut out of the racer's consciousness. Indeed, there is a lot of pressure on the racer to blank out worrying details from his mind. Mistakes are worrying details. Much better, all around, to blame the car, whose umpteen moving parts can encompass a multitude of sins, if there is the least doubt as to who was responsible. Derek Warwick has been openly critical of Renault, complaining to the effect that 'they have a group to look after the engine, another group in charge of the chassis, another bunch to look after the wheels' and that they never seem to get the car together.

When you crash on the race track, according to Lauda, 'Eighty per cent of the time you know immediately why. . . . But for the first ten seconds after the shunt, you think, "What can I do to make things look better? Let's look for an excuse." You look at the tyres; they're flat. But the rim is broken, so you can't say it's a puncture. Damn. After a moment you have to shake yourself mentally and say, "Listen, you idiot, what are you doing? You made a mistake, think about it." Then it's quite hard to be realistic. . . .'[12] Lauda's candour here is that of a triple World Champion who has had the advantage of one of the best sports gurus in the world, Willi Dungl, to help him train his mind and body for competition. Consequently he knows something about the psychology involved, which most racers could not be expected to know. He is aware of the mind's bag of tricks for dealing with competitive pressure in a way that most sportsmen are not. So he is sometimes aggressively honest about failures on the track. When he retired after 1½ laps in the 1976 Japan GP, Ferrari's Mauro Forghieri suggested, 'We'll pretend you've got engine trouble.'[13] Lauda would have none of it, and told the truth, which was that it was too dangerous to continue.

The problem of the racer's honesty with himself (and with everybody else) is compounded by the willingness of much of the motoring press to mythologize the driver and criticize the car. This course allows for more ingenuity, or rather engine-uity, on the part of the journalist able to demonstrate his knowledge of torque, toe-in, spring rates, gear ratios, differentials and aerodynamics. The esoteric hugger-mugger that surrounds motor racing at this level ensures that technical analysis is much better received by the goggling multitudes than a serious discussion of what happens, during the race, in the driver's mind. Besides, the obscure subject of driver psychology was once practically laughed out of court at an FIA hearing involving Lauda's performance at Brands Hatch. The known and accountable variable (car) is much less disquieting to examine than the unknown and unaccountable variable (driver's mind). Karl Kempf, a computer expert who was working with Team Tyrrell, embarked on a tremendously expensive programme of data analysis, using both on-board equipment and portable read-out units (sometimes housed in the team toilets). Kempf is a firm believer in the scientific approach to motor racing ('Show me any scientific approach to a problem which *doesn't* work!' he says with Victorian confidence). Unfortunately for Kempf's programme, and others like it which use data bank techniques, not all of the factors involved are accountable to such research. As he frankly admitted in an interview: 'You're up against three kinds of variables. Firstly, things you can identify, measure and control, such as tyre pressures. Secondly, those that you can identify, measure, and *not* control, such as the temperature on the day. And thirdly, those things which you can identify, but can neither measure nor control like the driver's psychological state!'[14] Well, you can certainly neither measure nor control them with the data-flow equipment of Karl Kempf.

In the mechanical, technological and aerodynamic universe of F1, the driver is squeezed – quite literally – into a tiny cockpit, as though to demonstrate his modest role in the scheme of things. He is semi-recumbent and altogether hidden from view by layers of flameproof underclothing, overalls, gloves, flame-retarding balaclava, helmet and visor. Only his eyes can occasionally be seen, and sometimes a flash of nose. He is not recognizably human, and every attempt is made to ensure that he reacts with the same mechanical precision as the car. According to Lauda, he cannot afford the luxury of emotions, because 'emotions are what get you killed'.[15] This taut state of existence causes many drivers to erupt and explode when they are not actually racing: such disparate personalities as Lauda himself, James Hunt and Emerson Fittipaldi have all punched marshals at one time or another, which Hunt calls 'freaking out'. A racer freaks out occasionally, because he is working under compressive forces that most human beings would find intolerable. At the speeds at which a racer's mind must operate on the race track, for example, fear is an inadmissible interference. A racer who allows himself to feel fear cannot do his job. Fear and anxiety may catch up with him after the race (and often do), but while he is working, fear is shut out of his mind. Driving as close as possible to the car's optimum performance is called 'driving at (or on) the limit'. This is one centimetre away from the guardrail as opposed to ten, forcing yourself to keep your foot on the throttle as the tower of Interlagos looms towards you; saying to yourself go, go, go, on the blind Hella Light bend, and putting your foot down hard in spite of all instincts for self-preservation, knowing you can't see round the corner as you come hurtling in.

There is an element of fatalism in every driver. Scheckter said 'You have a thirteen to one chance of coming out alive, which is pathetic.'[16] Stirling Moss woke up from a coma after his serious accident in 1962, and seeing mauve-coloured flowers by the bed, said to himself, 'They must have thought I was going to die.'[17] Lauda originally had his helmet painted Dayglo red so that rescuers would be sure to find him should he be thrown out in the trees.[18] Jackie Stewart recalls, 'I knew, when the season started every January, I would have two major accidents that year,' and made contingency plans which included having the best medical specialists on hand at every race.[19] Lauda's first thought, after the Ring crash he barely survived, was of the rescue helicopter, 'Then I remember thinking that I wasn't surprised it happened to me.'[20] Some drivers have what appear to be 'premonitions' of serious accidents, and psychologists have suggested that racing drivers have a death wish, which will eventually display itself in some reckless shunt. These theorists point (for example) to the case of Alberto Ascari, killed in 1955. Ascari's behaviour before the fatal accident seemed to many people to indicate that he knew he was going to die, and he even refused to wear his crash helmet. Niki Lauda, just prior to the Ring crash, had a recorded telephone conversation with Austrian journalist Dieter Stappert, in which he several times remarked that something dreadful might happen; that 'if nothing happens this weekend it will be a miracle' and that the main thing was 'to get through it alive'.[21] That drivers may have some prior warning of their crashes does not seem to me to indicate a death wish. What it *does* indicate – and we shall look at this in some detail in a moment – is that a racer's mind is sensitive to things that have gone disastrously wrong in the past, and his fears about these may contribute to things going disastrously wrong in the future. This self-fulfilling philosophy has proven genuine in many other walks of life.

Of all sportsmen, the racing driver is closest to heavenly peace, or most imminently threatened with extinction, oblivion, chaos or frenzy – according to his beliefs. His situation, as Count von Trips once remarked, is not unlike that of the medieval knight. The knight rode off to the Crusades with whatever talismen civilization could give him in the way of 'sacred' armour and equipment. The knight's armour was blessed in a meticulous ceremony. The ritual invoked order and reason: where he was going, there would be neither. Although the modern racer tends to shun superstitious ideology about knights and heroes,[22] his sacred equipment receives the same obsessive attention. The ritual is called 'sorting', and has to do with 'dialling in' the car for a particular track by means of a thousand tiny adjustments, to gear ratios, to springs, wings, scoops and skirts.

One of the practical reasons for 'sorting' concerns the aerodynamic laws that influence the F1 car's performance and elevate it above common road vehicles that do not fly. Contrary to popular belief the F1 car does not specialize in straight-line acceleration, but in *bends*. It corners at prodigious speeds by means of wings, skirts and other secret protuberances from its monocoque structure designed to produce downthrust and hence adhesion. These protuberances also produce 'drag' on the straights. Here is a problem to be solved by means of adding bits on and taking bits off, by small adjustments to springs, toe-in, shock absorbers, castor, camber and anti-roll bars, constant mucking about with tyres, and consultations, sometimes ending in bickering, on the subject of the car's 'handling' (especially understeer and oversteer) between the driver, the team manager, the designer, the chief mechanic, subsidiary mechanics, water-boy and data read-out toilet attendant. At the end of the day, sorting is as sorting does. Former McLaren team manager Teddy Mayer:

Our normal adjustments during setting up in practice are of the order of ten per cent before a driver can detect a noticeable difference.[23]

James Hunt, the year he became World Champion:

I'm not a very technical sorter. A lot of drivers think they've got to go madly technical on a car, but I'm a positive believer in keeping everything simple. . . . There are a lot of drivers who think that the more they say, the more they'll impress everyone. There are some drivers who can move a roll-bar a quarter-of-an-inch and come in with a story that will last fifteen minutes about all the differences it's made to the car. Well, that's all absolute rubbish.[24]

The eagerness of a large section of the motoring press to account for every failure on the race track technically or mechanically – or, more recently, by reference to turbo-charging or the ongoing 'tyre war' – is understandable, since the press is largely made up of male journalists who either have been or would like to have been racers themselves, and who identify very strongly with what they conceive to be the driver's cause. They are inclined to excuse all but the most outrageous shunters (novices and poor Vittorio Brambilla, seriously injured in the Monza pile-up) by hunting down the spanner in the works. 'Take Monza '77, when I crashed in practice,' says Lauda. 'I got out of the car and said, "I messed up." Then a journalist comes up and says, "What happened?" I say, "I messed up." He says, "Puncture?" "Look, no puncture. I messed up." "Oil on the track?" "Look, listen, no oil on the track. I just messed up." They can't believe that you make a mistake. More interestingly, they *won't* believe that you can make a mistake and admit it.'[25] The obstinacy Lauda complains of here has led him to be generally rather abrupt with the press, and to descriptions of him as a 'computer driver', devoid of emotional sensitivity.

Former World Champion Jackie Stewart, doing the commentary for *Competition Cassettes*[26] on the Brazilian GP at the start of 1978, mentioned the effects of the extreme heat on the driver's performances. He said before the race, 'I think it'll be a competition to see who breaks down first, whether it's the car or the driver.' Because the cockpit's air supply is upset by the heat and the turbulence from the car in front, the driver's brain would eventually suffer oxygen debt. 'Mentally it impairs your judgement. You start letting your mind wander. You start losing concentration; you start making slight errors of judgement, and these slight errors can, from time to time, become bigger mistakes. That's the biggest problem,' says Stewart, 'drivers do make errors. They overtax their cars. They occasionally miss gears, they run over kerbs; they can of course make errors while lapping other cars because other drivers are using the track in an inconsistent fashion. So basically, it's a mental thing as well as a physical thing.' Even here Stewart attributes the driver's misjudgements to a physiological cause (oxygen debt) rather than a psychological one (pressure) but at least he acknowledges their importance. Driver error is acknowledged as a factor in the racing teams themselves, certainly. One purpose of having a 'tell-tale' on the rev-counter is to see what the driver has been up to, and most drivers try to be frank with their teams about mistakes in practice and testing, because these insights help their cause. But errors during the race are a different matter, as so much is at stake. In a race, different criteria prevail, including a kind of tacit acceptance of the 'spanner in the works' pursued by the motoring press. As with air crashes, there are of course highly sophisticated techniques for locating mechanical failure from remaining wreckage, and these investigations uncover valuable information. But even when an accident is sufficiently serious to reduce the car to a smouldering ruin, an autopsy performed on what wreckage remains invariably isolates some mechanical failure to account for the crash.

Mechanical mysteries abound in F1 because, in spite of computer technology and sophisticated configurations, specifications and formulations, the sport refuses to boil down to Karl Kempf's 'known' variables. Legal adviser to the FOCA, Max Mosley, formerly of March Racing, told journalists in Sweden in 1977, 'There are so many unknowns in this business, things we just don't understand. At the beginning of 1975, Shadow were in a different league from everyone else, and I'm sure they don't know why. I mean, look at Ferrari,' said Mosley, 'they seem to be absolutely lost at the moment, but a year ago they were on their own'[27] – referring to Ferrari's unaccountable change of fortunes in the space of a few months. Frank Williams, after an unexpectedly poor showing at Brands Hatch in 1982: 'We were very optimistic after practice but then we had a run of misadventures. This happens in racing. We had good luck in 1980 and we've had good luck on other occasions. Brands Hatch was a time for bad luck. If you believe in such a thing!'[28] 'Handling' problems are compounded by the driver's subjective feelings about the car. Teddy Mayer: 'You would think it an easy thing to know, but it isn't. Very often a driver will say the car oversteers too much when this oversteer is actually induced by understeer initially and he hasn't recognized this.'[29] F1 constructor Tico Martini: 'When you have two identical cars you never have two identical drivers, so the problems are not necessarily the same. One will complain about understeer, the other will complain about something else in the same corner on the same circuit on the same day!'[30] Sometimes even *one* driver gives differing reports, depending on his mood at the moment. After the 1978 Argentina GP, Patrick Depailler told an *Autosport* reporter, 'The car understeered all race and was very difficult to drive,' and yet assured an *Autocar* journalist, 'The car handled better than it did at Ricard and certainly better than it ever did in practice. Some oversteer. But very nice to drive. I found it so enjoyable to drive. It was a fantastic car.'[31]

Of all the teams in the circus, perhaps the most psychologically astute is the House of Maranello. Ferrari is reputedly run by crazed Italians, and each season reports abound in the motoring press as to how hard it must be for a driver to work amid their flailing arms and flying spanners, but Ferrari have gone a long way, for example, towards perfecting the driver-proof gearbox, and at Ferrari's Fiorano works race track, every effort is made to examine *all* variables including the driver's behaviour on every lap. The test centre has a bank of optical and electronic measuring and control devices, TV monitors, and photoelectric cells implanted in the track. The data of each lap are fed into a computer for immediate analysis by team and driver. Driver errors are recorded and systematically eliminated. Juan Fangio, according to one source,[32] suffered a nervous breakdown at Ferrari and Enzo himself – the Old Man of Maranello – eventually withdrew from racing after a crisis of self-doubt.[33] The Commendatore believes that racing success is 50 per cent to do with the car, and 50 per cent to do with the driver. It follows that he believes this of racing failure also. In 1974 Niki Lauda, then with Ferrari, was involved in a hearing of the FIA following an incident at Brands Hatch which some considered had cost him a run at the World Championship. It had to do with his getting out of a blocked pit lane after a late tyre change, which Lauda believed had robbed him of crucial points in the race. When the incident happened, the little Austrian was visibly upset; close observers could see that he was crying with anger and disappointment. The Ferrari lawyer said that their driver had been so emotionally disturbed by this incident that for the rest of the season he could not finish a race. Journalists reporting the case thought this a remarkable piece of legal chicanery. His emotional state indeed. All he had to do was to sit in the car and drive the bloody thing. But the Ferrari lawyer had a point. Lauda's season trailed off ignominiously in retirements and failures. The mechanical problems, such as they were, were recondite.

Motoring correspondent Keith Botsford recalls[34] that when Lauda was poised to win the World Championship in 1975, 'countless drivers' remarked, 'Wait till he gets close to the lead in the championship, that's where he cracked up last time.' In 1974, Lauda was by no means the 'computer driver' he later became to the motoring press. Lauda made mistakes, and Lauda crashed, especially on the Nürburgring. Max Mosley, who ran March Racing, the outfit Lauda used to race for, said 'He crashed a lot, trying to do too much, and even when he got it together, he was still liable to make silly mistakes'. Niki crashed on the Ring in Formula Three. He crashed there again in 1973 in a BRM, and in 1974, in a Ferrari. By the end of 1974, after coming so close to the World

Championship, Lauda was a very unhappy young man. There was nothing for it but to go and see Willi Dungl, whom Lauda has since described as 'The miracle'.[35] Dungl, who supervised Lauda's recovery from the Ring crash in 1976, is generally described in the press as Lauda's 'masseur', 'physio' or 'confidant'. In fact, he is one of the better-known sports gurus, an acknowledged expert in sports medicine and psychology, who prior to helping Lauda had worked with other international athletes, including the Austrian Olympic speed ski team. Lauda spent ten days in the Alps at Willi Dungl's behest which changed his whole outlook. He told David Benson at the time, 'I took a good look into myself and found where my thinking was wrong.'[36] He underwent a training programme designed to prepare his mind and body for competitive pressure, and by his own efforts Lauda came down from the Alps and won the 1975 World Championship for Ferrari.

What actually happens to a driver's mind in a F1 race under the stress of competition we do not know, but that *something* happens, we may be very sure. A number of racers have referred to the sport affecting their personalities in some way: James Hunt remarked in 1976, prior to winning the World Championship, that racing had 'hardened him up', and after his retirement, he hoped to 'go back to being a normal person'. He said, 'I have seen people in this business, particularly recent world champions, who have completely lost their original personality. Or they have let the business dictate what their personalities should be.'[37] Jackie Stewart told reporter Dave Kindred that for thirteen years his whole life was 'organized' and 'computerized'. He said, 'I was living in a cocoon. Tunnel vision.'[38] Lauda has described the pressure of leading a race from start to finish, when you have nothing to do but wait and watch the instruments, and your mind begins to play tricks. He also recalls that at Long Beach some time after his serious accident, when he was on pole position, he felt 'tremendous pressure, actually inexplicable' about making the best start, leading, and winning. 'I made another mistake in this race, and perhaps pressure was to blame. You could translate pressure as being in bad form, but I don't feel in bad form whereas I do feel "pressure", and in my opinion it is a noticeable frame of mind which presses upon me. Anyway it wasn't my day. . . .'[39]

One of the racing driver's techniques for overtaking is to attack the concentration of the driver in front by manoeuvring about in his mirrors and making him second-guess his braking points. 'Thou shalt keep thy Opponent under constant pressure,' said Lauda,[40] because this is part of a racer's job. James Hunt has described the anguish of trying to go through the win-barrier for the first time and his own tendency, when leading a race, to suffer from nausea (see pages 115–17). Apart from auditory hallucinations referred to by Lauda, there are also visual hallucinations. John Watson in Brazil complained of what he called 'bent vision', an optical illusion he attributed to the heat. 'Sometimes two marshals became a group, and the corner appears to bend off in both directions.'[41] When I asked John about this he said that at the time he was suffering from one of his recurrent colds, and was feeling under the weather generally. Mirage conditions on flat tracks in high temperatures are not uncommon, as any ordinary driver knows, but Watson's optical illusion is slightly different because he is referring not only to distortion, but to *splitting* of the image he sees. Split vision during a race is not particularly unusual. Other racers have experienced it: one of them was Carlos Reutemann.

Reutemann's fraught career which ended in 1982 in disappointed retirement, was the subject of much speculation in the press, and much perplexity in his home country of Argentina. A moody, sometimes solemn man, Reutemann was a 'natural' racer in much the same way as Nastase was a 'natural' tennis player. Designer Gordon Murray said, in an interview: 'He had distinct dips and peaks when his mood changed, but I'm still convinced that for sheer outright natural driving ability, Carlos is probably the best guy around. His sensitivity to outside influences and his inconsistency are a tragedy.'[42] Carlos is particularly interesting to us here, because according to other racers he was easily 'psyched' and vulnerable under pressure. Andretti, a crafty USAC-trained psycher-out of the very best, was following Reutemann in the Brazil GP in 1977, which Carlos eventually won. Said Mario, 'If I could keep the pressure on him, I *knew* I could get rid of him, I tellya.' Jackie Stewart: 'I still think he's too nervous a driver, with his off-and-on throttle cornering. I don't like that. . . . By playing with the throttle you're upsetting the car and it's causing a change of suspension attitudes under extreme conditions.'[43] James Hunt's 'mental file card' on Reutemann: 'He is as good as anyone else in the world when things are going right. . . . On the other hand he cannot salvage bad situations, and his Latin temperament means that when he is down he gets very depressed. He is also easy to "psych" out, and he doesn't like racing under pressure, especially if it is sustained.'[44] Emerson Fittipaldi: 'Carlos sometimes is not good under pressure.'[45]

Carlos, or 'Lole' as he was called, recently switched to Endurance Rallies. In F1 he has driven some brilliant races. Ferrari do not lightly choose their drivers, and when Lauda left it was clearly hoped that Reutemann would come into his own. What happened was that Reutemann won races, as he had done before, and came close, as he had also done, but failed to win the World Championship, in spite of having the might of Ferrari behind him, and in spite of the alleged advantage of Michelin tyres. There are many possible reasons for this, but if the pressures of F1 racing are in any way comparable with other sports, one of them is undoubtedly psychological, and has to do with making decisions under stress. Take, for example, his use of the throttle. Other racers squeeze the throttle. Keke Rosberg squeezes. Lauda squeezed. Stewart squeezed. But poor Reutemann jabbed. Going into the corners his Ferrari's twelve cylinders played several different tunes, possibly because of a difficulty Lole himself has referred to about deciding on focusing points in the curves. At tremendous speeds it is important for a racer to know where to focus his eyes, because this affects his decisions about braking. In 1977, to take but a few examples, Lole braked too late for the first corner at Long Beach and took the escape road. In Belgium he spun from third place on the fourteenth lap, it seemed through a 'wheel imbalance'. In the British GP at Silverstone he spun from eleventh, at the chicane, when apparently a 'front brake lining leaked fluid from its neck'. In Italy he slid on oil on the track in the braking area for the first chicane, which Lauda, running in front, was able to avoid. At the time of the race Carlos had complained about the difficulty of driving at chicanes: 'the big problem,' said Lole, 'is where to look; at the apex of the next corner, or at the exit of the last'.[46] At Watkins Glen he spun from fourth, and in Japan he complained of lack of grip, an insecurity he attributed to the car's geometry: 'I try everything, everything, but nothing makes any difference. It has a fantastic engine, but I just cannot get any traction. Something is very wrong with the geometry. Every lap is like this' (putting his thumbnail under his chin) '– really dangerous.'[47] In Brazil, where he won, he said in practice, 'For the first time since I was driving the BT44, I'm mentally seeing the exit before I've turned in. That's good.'[48]

Of all the psychological difficulties to beset sportsmen under pressure, indecisiveness seems the most damaging to performance. We all suffer from it occasionally, but a sportsman whose ability to make decisions is impaired by competitive conditions is in conspicuous trouble, which may eventually threaten his career (see pp. 144ff). In many cases it may be traced back to ambivalence about winning, or about competing. Often, once a sportsman comes to terms with his own motives and makes up his mind exactly what he wants, indecisiveness under stress, in all its manifestations, can be resolved. After his 1976 crash on the Ring, Lauda returned to racing and found that he could not put his foot down going into dangerous corners, in spite of conscious effort. He wanted to put his foot down, but on the other hand, he didn't. Lauda's solution was to go away, sit by himself in his room, and ask himself, 'Do you really *want* to race?' The answer came: he did. There was no further difficulty with the foot.

The driver's brain, during a race,is working in rather the same way as a bombarded computer. 'Every bloody lap,' according to Lauda, 'you face a different chaotic situation.'[49] F1 racing has to do with formulae: with a synthesis of data about circuits, corners and conditions, with data about mechanical stress, aerodynamic laws on straights and in bends, design, geometry and mechanical accountability. The car itself is a synthesis, a mechanical formula or crystallization of all the known variables, involving 'compromises' (as they are called) between antithetical requirements and conditions. Equally, the driver's brain is constantly synthesizing, or making formulae, from incoming data during the race: about angle, camber, kerb, speed, gears, revs, distance, turbulence, other cars, own instruments, dials, steering, handling, pit signals, winning and spinning. The driver must decide, and constantly under the most dangerous and difficult pressure, real and anticipated, what do I do now? He operates in a continuum of impending disaster, for the race is one long emergency, one long red alert to all parts of his brain. It is scarcely surprising that he occasionally makes errors. Provided he is conscious of his mistakes and admits them, at least to himself, they appear to have no repercussions. But if he represses and buries them under a stockpile of alibis and excuses about the car, the driver is peculiarly likely to make more – and more serious – mistakes in the future. One of the most dangerous of these is what we shall call, for the sake of a label, '*déjà vu*'. Let us look at a few examples.

In 1976 at Brands Hatch, Jody Scheckter left the opposition

standing in practice for the Race of Champions. In the old four-wheel Tyrrell Jody's margin of two full seconds over his nearest rival (Lauda) was, in F1 terms, staggering. His friend and fellow-South African, motoring correspondent David Benson, commented, 'No one ever looked more certain of victory than Jody Scheckter when he lined up for the Race of Champions on Sunday.'[50] But Jody did not win the race. By the end of lap three, having taken the lead, he had gone straight on at Dingle Dell corner and smashed into the guard rail. The car's fuel ignited and, although he escaped unhurt, Scheckter was bitterly disappointed. Later the same year, the British Grand Prix was also held at Brands Hatch. This time Jody was competing in the splendid and revolutionary new Elf Team Tyrrell six-wheeler. In practice for the race, approaching Dingle Dell, Scheckter went wide, put a wheel on the dirt washed up by overnight storms, and spun off the track, crashing heavily into a bank. So extensive was the damage to the six-wheeler that Ken Tyrrell was 'rather cross'. Said Scheckter, 'It was entirely my own fault. I got out of shape and hit the dirt. I feel an idiot.'[51]

1974, Holland. The late Ronnie Peterson was having a tough time in practice. On the Saturday morning he had a nasty moment right near some skid-marks clearly visible on the track, apparently because 'the large rear aerofoil fell down over the gearbox'. Ten days previously during testing he had crashed on the same circuit, in the same place, and had been knocked unconscious for thirty minutes. The skid marks on the track had been his own.

1974, Canada. During the race John Watson, in a Brabham BT44 and with his usual nasal allergy, hit the spinning McLaren of Jochen Mass. He made a couple of pit stops with handling problems, and had a rear wheel changed. Back in the race, at the sweeping right-hander on Turn 3, Watson arrived at the scene of his previous mishap, and had another. The car careered diagonally in across the apex, showering dirt on the racing line. Apparently Watson had braked for the corner and the right front suspension collapsed. Damage to the car after the off included the right front suspension.

A *trauma*, in psychoanalysis, is an emotional shock that may be the origin of a neurosis (inner conflict). In medicine, it refers to an injury, a stress or shock with which the body cannot immediately cope. A racing driver has a great many of both kinds of trauma. When he crashes, especially during a race which means a great deal to him, the shock is both physical and emotional. If he is able to come to terms with the shunt, it does not seem to affect his driving in the future. Most of a driver's catalogue of accidents are dealt with in this way: otherwise he wouldn't be racing. But sometimes a driver is confused as to the cause of a crash, either because he prefers to blame the car, or because the experience was indeed too shocking and painful to be examined and remembered. A man who is not afraid to race is nevertheless afraid to crash, and many drivers close their eyes when a collision seems imminent rather than watch what actually happens. All drivers worry about the possibility of their cars breaking, and this is only natural considering most of them have had crashes which were the result of cars letting them down. But an accident that is the *driver's* fault, as opposed to the car's, is particularly uncomfortable in the memory, because it carries the implication, 'You nearly killed me.' And this, the author respectfully suggests, is a threat of a different order to that from mechanical failure.

Of course, even if a racer fails to come to terms with a crash that was his own fault, it does not necessarily follow that he will have another. He may (though this is unlikely) trundle happily along for the rest of his career, without the memory surfacing. But if he is extending himself in a race, and arrives suddenly at a scene that looks very much like the scene of his accident, the unpleasant and shocking memory of the former disaster may be triggered in his mind, alerting him to the possibility of another equally terrible accident in the here and now. Under these circumstances, given the intense pressure with which every racer is always trying to cope, his brain may well signal 'overload'. Unfortunately, when the *new* emergency arises as a result of the driver's confusion in the cockpit, the correction that he makes is not for the crash that is about to happen, but for the crash that occurred before. In Gestalt psychology this is called the Zeigarnick effect, after the psychologist who discovered it. The law holds that a person interrupted in the course of finishing some important task will automatically resume it later in preference to any other activity, all things being equal. He looks, as Gestalt theory would say, for 'closure' – for a complete pattern. For the same reason, when prompted he is more likely to remember an incomplete task than others he was able to complete.

Let us look, now, at a sequence of accidents, leading up to Lauda's shocking crash on the Ring in 1976, to see if they tell us anything *other* than about mechanical failure.

On 5 September 1970, Jochen Rindt, the German war orphan

who became Austria's hero on the race track, was killed on the Parabolica curve at Monza in Italy. He was posthumously awarded the World Championship. On the same day, Niki Lauda crashed in Formula Three, at Zolder, in what he now calls his 'anti-race'.[52] According to Lauda the connection between his own crash and Rindt's death was pure coincidence, although if any driver was ever Lauda's 'hero', it was Rindt. 'If I see his photos now, it makes me tingle. He had a good head. He looked like somebody who was somebody. He had real class, at least I felt he had.'[53] Prior to this F3 crash, Lauda had had two others of significance, one of them on the Nürburgring (1970). He says, 'There I was, in fifth place with nobody visible ahead of me and nobody behind either. In spite of that, I ended up off the track and I don't know to this day how it happened.'[54]

Three years later, in 1973, Lauda was driving a BRM, by all accounts a kart rather than a car, and on the Ring he was in fourth place after the first lap. At the Bergwerk, a second-gear right-hand bend, he noticed the car was understeering badly, and thought he had hit oil on the track. Immediately afterwards he changed gear coming into a fast left-right combination. 'I suddenly lost control over the car (we found out later that something had snapped on the rear suspension). I went into zig-zags – I was able to deal with the first few, then the car touched a kerb on the right, and it was promptly catapulted over the left of the track.'[55] The left front wheel slammed into a sloping rock, and the impact on the steering column broke Lauda's right wrist. 'That was the first thought that hit me – my hand's hurting.' The car tobogganed along the slope and Lauda was fortunate to escape more serious injury. As it was, he missed the Austrian Grand Prix and made his comeback at Monza. He now describes this as his second most serious crash (after the Ring '76). It was undoubtedly due to mechanical failure.

In 1974 Lauda was on the Nürburgring again, this time in a Ferrari. He had 'no problems' in practice, but just before the race it began to rain and the question of wet-weather tyres was raised. At the start Clay Regazzoni, Lauda's biggest rival for the Championship, got away from Niki, who had under-revved his engine and lost ground. 'All of a sudden I was only lying third. At that moment I should have been smart enough to ditch my battle plan of flying ahead [of Regazzoni] but I was not. I gritted my teeth and tried to pull it off by brute force. I at once tried to outbrake Jody Scheckter so as not to lose contact with Regazzoni.'[56] Lauda's car had a fresh right front tyre, which he had forgotten about and which affected the car's road-holding ability. At the braking point behind the control tower Lauda trod on the brake pedal and the Ferrari veered right, into Scheckter's blue Tyrrell, his right rear wheel hitting the Tyrrell's left front. The Ferrari was thrown up in the air and snapped sideways to the right, but missed further contact. Scheckter went on into the North Curve while the Ferrari spun and slammed through the catch fencing. Lauda was trapped for a moment inside the cockpit by wire mesh, but was unhurt.

In 1976 on the Ring, Lauda raced as defending World Champion. He was not popular in Germany because of his criticism of the Ring's safety facilities and because of his cautious style: banners around the track proclaimed, 'Lauda, the twenty-mile-an-hour driver, out!' It is probably true, although Lauda is defensive on the subject, that by now the Ring had become something of an *Angst* track for him. On the front row of the grid were Lauda and Hunt – his chief rival for the Championship – but at flag-fall it was Regazzoni who surged into the lead, followed by Hunt. Lauda's start was poor. The lead changed hands several times and at the end of the first lap most cars stopped for a tyre change because of the uncertain weather conditions. It had been raining at some points on the fourteen-mile track, and dry at others. Lauda was among those who changed tyres. After his pit stop, he passed Brett Lunger, Harald Ertl and Guy Edwards, who noticed that Lauda seemed to have trouble controlling the car ('he nearly lost it twice').

Halfway round the second lap, at the Bergwerk, the Ferrari was going flat out in fourth gear at about 140 m.p.h., when it suddenly turned sharp right, skidded across the track and slammed up the sloping bank into the crash barrier. (Lauda notes from existing films of the crash, which are not very clear, that prior to the sudden move to the right the car had touched the kerb in the apex of the left turn and that he had applied opposite lock to correct the tail-out.) The car came down backwards on to the road with its left side torn away, and its fuel ignited. Lauda was trapped in the blazing car while his rescuers fought to free him. Unfortunately, as it turned out, he was not unconscious, but struggled to remove his helmet, which had ridden up in the crash and jammed over his nose and mouth. (According to some reports, Niki's helmet was knocked off altogether by a pole. According to others it was knocked askew, and the straps were across his face. Had the helmet been torn off completely, it seems very likely that he would have been decapitated.) The flame-retarding balaclava, pulled awry, quickly turned black as Lauda cried, 'Get me out! Get me out!' and began losing consciousness. He was eventually air-lifted to Mannheim University Clinic, where it was discovered that in addition to hideous facial burns, his lungs were probably irreparably damaged from breathing in flame and fumes. He was given the Last Rites, but managed to remain alive by focusing his consciousness on the voices in the room, and particularly the name of 'Fittipaldi' whose doctor Grajales had come to see if he could help. His remarkable recovery was attributed to his athletic fitness before the crash, and to what we generally call 'will-power'. Arguably, one of the factors involved was his ability to concentrate and crystallize his attention which was part of his job and which he had perfected by hours of training both by himself and with Willi Dungl. Racing, as he observes, is all to do with 'the ability to concentrate entirely on what matters'.[57] And throughout his recovery programme, 'I have with me twenty-four hours a day Willi Dungl.'[58]

The cause of the accident was almost unanimously attributed to the Ferrari. The race organizers said that the car had left the track after going over a kerb, and that a rear wheel had come adrift. This theory was later abandoned in favour of a louder chorus in the British racing press about the rear suspension, which was alleged to have broken and caused the car to turn sharp right. At these and other allegations about the car, Enzo Ferrari was beside himself with rage.

Niki Lauda does not remember anything about the crash, or indeed, what preceded it. He told Harry Carpenter in a BBC interview shortly afterwards, 'I must have got a big bang on my head and so I lost the memory.' He told David Benson, 'I drove about 10 ks before the crash, but I can't recall them.'[59] The first thing that he remembers was the sound of the helicopter coming to air-lift him to hospital. But several things that Lauda said immediately after the crash, for example to the Ferrari team manager while they waited to be transferred from Adenau to Mannheim, indicate that the memory of what happened is not obliterated; perhaps Niki has 'forgotten' because of the intolerable unpleasantness of recollection.

The reader is left to consider these things; as F1 racing stands at the moment, there can only be sheer speculation, because despite the periodic intervention of psychiatrists like Berenice Krikler and

Freudian disciple Peter Fuller, sufficient attention has never been paid to driver psychology to warrant anything else. But perhaps the time has come to try to understand the phenomenon: perhaps the 50 per cent contribution that Enzo Ferrari believes is made by the driver to Formula One success has been somewhat neglected, compared with the obsessive attention paid by everyone to the cars. The retirement of James Hunt, proclaiming Grand Prix racing no longer depends on the drivers but only on the machines, brings that obsession into sharp focus. Yet James was often sick, and made his share of errors; Jackie Stewart had a stomach ulcer by the time he retired. The driver is a human being, not a computer, and he makes mistakes for reasons which we may easily understand if we devote our attention to them, instead of sloughing them off with references to pistons, turbo-charging and rear suspension (especially in the light of recent NASA research showing four out of five plane crashes are due to pilot error). In Montreal in 1982 Riccardo Paletti's Osellâ slammed into the back of the stationary Ferarri of Didier Peroni and burst into flames. Riccardo is presumed to have died on impact. The same season, in the Belgian GP at Zolder, Gilles Villeneuve died, and Pironi was seriously injured in practice at Hockenheim just when he looked well set at the top of the World Championship table. In May 1986, during testing at the Paul Ricard circuit, Elio de Angelis lost control of his Brabham BMW at a left-right bend and cartwheeled through the guard rails. Like Lauda, the young Italian was trapped in a burning car while rescuers tried to free him. De Angelis died of his injuries. Earlier, while I was researching this book, Ronnie Peterson died at Monza after a pile-up for which several drivers blamed Riccardo Patrese. Every effort was made to discover if Patrese had made a mistake, and if he had, to punish him for it. No effort was made to discover why.

4

The Slow Game – Golf

Let us suppose it takes between three and five hours to get round a golf course. Therefore a 72-hole odyssey involves between twelve and twenty hours of a golfer's time. How much of that time does he spend actually hitting the ball? Well, Nicklaus's swing, from takeaway to impact, takes 1.96 seconds. Palmer's, a wild, unpremeditated rush, took 1.36 seconds. Gary Player's, halfway between these two, takes 1.60 seconds. Let us suppose Player, on all of his strokes in a 72-hole tournament, takes this maximum length of time, and plays par golf. (In fact, all but his tee-shots would take considerably less because of the smaller arc they describe.) 72×1.60 sec. $= 115.20$ sec. Over four rounds that comes to 460.80 sec., or a little over seven and a half minutes, maximum, of actually hitting the ball. Even supposing the golfer is quite brisk about the course, taking a mere sixteen hours to complete the 72 holes, this leaves 15 hr 52½ min. during which he is not occupied with hitting the ball. Which means that 15 hr. 52½ min. were spent in another occupation. Thinking.

It should surprise no one, then, that however well a player may hit the ball, it is thinking that makes him or breaks him.

Golf is really a simple game, made religious and expensive (and difficult) in reverence of its simplicity. Golf balls, until the mid nineteenth century, used to be made of feathers, bound tightly, soaked in brine, and called 'featheries'. To put the feathery in flight is an act quite serious and important because man cannot fly, and is very much enamoured of things that can. Kite flying, archery, guided missiles, model planes, long jumping and high diving all testify to this abiding interest that man has, in launching either himself or his belongings into the air, and controlling the flight as carefully as possible. The golfer gets his ball aloft in order to fly it around an 18-hole golf course with as little interference as possible. The less hoiks he takes at it the better, because then the fiction of flying is preserved. If, at a hole that normally takes 5 strokes to reach, he has only taken 4, he is credited with a 'birdie'. He has flown. If he has taken even fewer swipes at the missile, he cards an 'eagle'. He has flown better. Or an 'albatross', which is better yet. And he is said to have 'shot' these birdies and eagles to get them in the hole, which demonstrates his control and supremacy.

The golf swing that would launch the ball as perfectly as possible, and keep it airborne as long and accurately as possible, is an icon that has long been worshipped. Ben Hogan is considered by many to have possessed this very swing. Long before Mission Control, Houston, Hogan's swing applied itself to the ball in such a way that hundreds of people would traipse after him across the golf courses of the western world, and huddle behind barriers in inclement weather, to see it. Nor was it Hogan the personality they were interested in. Tight-lipped and malicious looking, Hogan gave not a tinker's tiddle for the crowds, and never so much as acknowledged their low presence until the last putt was sunk. It wasn't Hogan they traipsed after, but Hogan's swing. A thing to worship.

A similarly wonderful mechanism belongs to the dynamic Spaniard Severiano Ballesteros. Not technically perfect – a flying right elbow is its distinctive feature – Seve's swing nevertheless fetches sighs from old pros. His big drive and 2-iron over the water at the 13th in the 1978 World Cup; driving the green on the 19th at the Belfry; his opening drive in the 1978 Masters that flew nearly 300 yards into the wind at Augusta – these are the stuff of stories in bars. Nor does it matter particularly where Seve's ball *lands*, for this is not generally thought to cloud the majesty of its launching. At the 17th at St Andrews in the 1978 Open – the loathed Road Hole – Seve drove fearlessly, wasted his ball, incurred a penalty, and drove fearlessly again. The hole won, of course: Seve finished with a 6. To his admirers, it didn't matter. Seve's swing is not to be analysed or criticized as part of an overall strategy. It is a thing to write home about. The image that golf writers have given him, of the intrepid matador, the free-swinging Spaniard who gives it a wallop, follows Seve about from tournament to tournament. As a matter of fact, he is hooked on it himself. Asked in the press tent if he can play defensively now, he replies with mock seriousness, 'I do not think so,' even when the situation warrants it, the course demands it, and his intelligence suggests it. And the thousands who follow him over the humps and hollows watch with some complicity themselves as Seve steps up to address the ball, because here is a creature they and the press have created. It is no longer Severiano, the Basque boy who shaves and wears pullovers, but a new being, Sever-your-arm-off, the possessor of a wild and wonderful mechanism for launching the ball. Sever-your-arm-off won the 1979 British Open, for example, in magnificent style. Royal Lytham's narrow fairways were no problem. He simply took an alternative route, down the rough and through the car park.

The obsession with launching has seriously affected the progress of golfers in general, but of British golfers in particular, because a nation inhibited by bad weather and baggy clothing is not remarkable for breeding free-swingers at anything, least of all at a small white warty ball. Swinging is something that is done properly across the Atlantic, where aggression and forthrightness have always been cultivated, and where men wear thin shirts and jog. So a remarkable thing has happened. British golfers have made an in-depth study of the mechanics of swinging to get themselves airborne, while American golfers, already airborne, have made an in-depth study of the mechanics of getting down again: on to the green, and especially, into the hole. Getting down is even more dangerous and difficult than getting up. Many regard the Masters as a putting contest: Lee Trevino observes that Ben Crenshaw won it in 1984 on his putter.

As Jim Dent, one of the long game's big boomers put it, 'If you can't putt, you can't win',[1] and when Tom Watson won the 1978 Byron Nelson Classic in Dallas, Gibby Gilbert commented, 'Tom is a fantastic putter. That's the name of the game out here. The rest of his game obviously is good too, but he is as good as anyone on the Tour with his putter.' Watson himself said, 'The key to my game was my putting. I had confidence in it and that was a great feeling.' Lee Trevino – SuperMex – actually changed his putting style after watching Ben Crenshaw. Said Lee, with obvious admiration, 'His arms just seem to hang down natural.' Arnold Palmer, whose cult following bordered on the fantastic, never mastered putting to his own satisfaction. 'No,' he told writer Tom Place, 'I never was a great putter no matter what the other guys say. I putted out of desperation.'[2] Putting frightens even the fearless.

Ballesteros will not play with a golf ball bearing the number '3' because he believes this will make him three-putt. After he has examined a putt from all sides, he will never walk back to the ball on the right-hand side. This is 'unlucky' for putting, he says.

Palmer thinks even Nicklaus is a bit of a 'desperation' putter, though Jack obviously does his best. Palmer says Jack has been 'the target of complaints by pros who feel that 4 or 5 or 6 holes back they're being held up while Jack stands over a putt for one or two eternities'.[3] Despite Jack practising his short game in his back yard, he admits that his putting is not as scientific as the rest of his game and deplores its competitive importance when compared with the 'real' game of golf – from tee to green. What is it about putting that Nicklaus doesn't like? Well, it gets on his nerves. 'It doesn't take much technique to roll a 1.68-inch ball along a smooth, level surface into, or in the immediate vicinity of, a 4½-inch hole. With no pressure on you, you could do it one-handed most of the time. But there is *always* pressure on the shorter putts, even when you're just playing around the course alone.'[4] Just like most human beings on a golf course, Jack gets nervous – '90 per cent of the rounds I play in major championships, I play with a bit of a shake' – and although this is not in itself a bad thing, it can cause problems in the putting department: 'I've never been a great putter in major championships. I've won most of my major championships through playing golf, not through putting. Maybe my stroke isn't sound enough, or my method sound enough, to overcome the bit of nervousness that I have, so if I start getting aggressive with my putter – except in the latter stages of a tournament – I'm afraid I'll three-putt too much. That's why I think I'm a great two-putter, or in other words a slightly defensive putter a lot of the time.'[5] Nicklaus is unusual in that he is brave enough to admit it. He says he lifts his head as well – an astonishing revelation.

His 1978 Open victory at St Andrews was a triumph in spite of his putting rather than because of it: on the second round he had fourteen reasonable birdie chances and missed the lot. As a matter of fact, Nicklaus was thrilled that he *had* won it from tee to green. Recent events he had been winning 'with my chipping and my putting, which is the way I never won tournaments before! I won this without a putter for most of the tournament,' observed Jack with a smile, as if to say: 'and that's how it should be done'. Nicklaus is a big man, and it has been suggested by Dr David Morley, psychiatrist and author of *Golf and the Mind*, that putting comes very hard to men who pride themselves on their physical power. Putting, a delicate act on a small scale, is humiliating for them to have to do in front of their peers. Palmer himself was always an immensely powerful driver of the ball, to whom putting came unnaturally. His familiar knock-kneed stance, combined with much perambulation about the hole and much hitching of trousers, was a sight not easily reconcilable with the image of a slugger who feared no course in the world. Palmer has tried various techniques to improve his putting. 'Locke is still a fantastic putter, even now,' said Palmer recently.[6] 'I'd like to putt as well as he does today. I'm serious. I don't think I would have any trouble winning.' He abandoned the reverse-overlap grip he had used – the one with the left forefinger stuck downwards towards the bottom of the shaft. He tried the less knock-kneed or semi-knock-kneed stance, and shifted his hands so that he had all ten fingers on the club, and the left forefinger curled around the shaft. Then he went back to the full knock-knee, and the reverse-overlap. More recently he has tried returning to his boyhood stance to relieve the tension in his shoulders, and then he adopted the cack-handed grip. 'The difference is phenomenal,' he said, after using the left-hand-below-right style in the 1977 (British) Open. Mark Hayes, the blue-eyed boy with the Oklahoma drawl, shocked everyone at that tournament with an inspired round of 63, and said, 'I putted very well, hitting every putt as I wanted. I've started putting cack-handed because I was missing both sides of the hole with the conventional grip. You're afraid to do it,' said Mark, 'because people will laugh at you, but it makes you keep your shoulders level.' Orville Moody won the US Open using the cross-handed grip. It is not new, but to the golfing *cognoscenti* it does look silly, and one of the ways of applying pressure to the sportsman in the middle, to increase the excitement of the experiment, is to make him feel silly.

Putting humiliates more than anything in golf, other than the air-shot. It renders a man ludicrous in his own eyes. Sam Snead was one of many great golfers who have been transformed by its ridiculous requirements. Sam tried putting croquet-style, between his legs. When this was outlawed by the rule-makers, he developed what Palmer calls a sloping 'side-saddle' technique: that is, 'he putts with the stance of a surveyor lining up on an ant-hill' and with a grip like that of 'a matron wiping away breadcrumbs with a napkin.'[7] In 1971 on the West Coast, a chap by the name of Kent Meyers turned up at the Pacific Coast Amateur Championship putting from behind his back with the shaft stuck between his legs. Many golfers believe that because putting mobilizes certain of the smaller muscle groups, it is susceptible to a kind of twitch, loosely associated in their minds with Parkinson's disease, which will attack them in middle age. This disease, which like so many strange afflictions thrives on human credulity, is spoken of in hushed tones. It is called 'the yips'. If you go into a club bar anywhere in the country, and start talking about the yips, your drinking companions will disperse pleasantly and quietly to the four corners of the room. (The long game has a similar 'disease': 'shanking', or socketing, is another expression guaranteed to clear a bar.) 'Yips', or 'twitch', is believed to be an affliction of the small muscles of the forearms and hands. Palmer: '. . . there are changes involved in the body as one ages that profoundly affect your putting. It's not "nerves". There is a change in muscular sensitivity – in "feel", so to speak.'[8]

Indeed. Why then did Bernhard Langer get it, reversing his hands on the putter to steady himself after conspicuous attacks in 1979? And why does Philip Jonas get it? Philip was 16 when at Troon he crashed out of the 1978 British Amateur Championship after an attack of yips in the third round. From tee to green in a class of his own, the South African prodigy missed more two-footers than he holed. In fact, when he reached the green everyone was turning away, not wishing to look at the young man's heart-breaking attempts to putt. Golf-writer Chris Plumridge explains, 'The yips is a disease of old golfers – over 40 as a general rule – who have had time to realize what missing a short putt can mean in terms of lost prestige and lost money.' There have been instances of such 'astasia' very seriously affecting a golfer's career. 'Ben Hogan was the greatest striker of the ball that ever existed, and although he was never a great putter he still won tournaments by the length of a street,' said Plumridge wistfully. 'But as he got older his putting became worse and worse, till in the end it was pitiful, really. He used to stand over the ball and freeze.' Like Nicklaus, Hogan was invariably tense and nervous – 'tight as a banjo-string', as he put it. 'By 1953,' said Hogan recently, 'My putting had gone to heck . . . I putted awful in the British Open. The caddie wouldn't even look at me when I putted. He'd turn his head and cover his eyes.'[9] Yet such was Hogan's mastery from tee to green that he shot 274 in the Masters and broke the record by 5 strokes. Asked what the reason was for his ten-month lay-off prior to the 1953

Masters, Hogan replied, 'I don't remember, and if I had any health problems I wouldn't tell you about 'em anyway. Everybody's got problems – they don't want to hear about mine.'

Of course, Hogan was badly injured in a road accident in 1949 which may eventually have contributed to his difficulties, but this is not the point. Consider the case of Ken Venturi.

Ken had a block in his mind about winning the Masters. In 1956 as an amateur, he stormed the field with rounds of 66, 69 and 75, and then fell to pieces with a final round of 80. It was not his whole game that was affected: the Augusta greens were fast and slippery and he died on his putter after good drives and chips. In 1958 at the same tournament, Venturi came home on the heels of Arnold Palmer, just short again. During the late 1950s Venturi had become recognized as one of a handful of leading Americans. In 1960 Palmer again beat him in the Masters, this time while poor Ken sat in the clubhouse nursing a 283. As author Michael Hobbs points out, perhaps this was the straw that broke the camel's back: 'In 1960 he stood second in the list of money winners. In 1961 he was 14th. Worse was to follow. In 1962 he was 66th, and then 94th, winning a derisory $3848 in 1963. His swing was gone. . . . For most golfers it is the putting stroke that seems to suffer the most. This happened, amongst others, to Walter Hagen, Bobby Jones, when he came back from retirement to play in the Masters, and Ben Hogan, who in later years seemed to sweat over the impossibility of taking back his putter.'[10]

Venturi's entire game had gone, his swing had gone, and of course his putting had gone. At the moment of impact his hands appeared to flinch in a reflex action, and this indecisiveness distorted a swing that had been fluent and natural into the flat crouching loop of an old man. Michael Hobbs comments – and the reader should note the reverential tone – 'The only cure can be to await the time when a minor miracle occurs and the true path of the golf swing is suddenly there again.' (As we shall see from later chapters, there is no need for such dreary fatalism about golf swings or anything else.) Meanwhile, Venturi also developed a stammer and facial twitches. The odd thing was, that this yipping, stammering, twitching 'old boy', who had to be accompanied by a doctor to the first tee and throughout the final round, won the US Open in 1964. Clearly, here was another vindication of the theory that the most important inches in golf are the ones between the ears. After four years of being old and palsied, Ken Venturi was young again, putting and winning. It was one of the most astonishing comebacks in the game. Yet golfers continue to make a connection in their minds between failing putters and middle age. 'There is no logical reason for that,' says Nicklaus perceptively, 'but putting is the least manly thing in golf, and therefore, when a player gets older and he does not win as much, he blames it on his putting. He does not want to admit that his power may be leaving him.'[11]

The argument that the yips are a 'muscular thing' mysteriously bound up with the male menopause or the onset of senility, and wholly controlled by the spinal column rather than the mind, is part of the golfing canon that has to do with denying fear. Most golfers, if we are to believe everything we hear in the press tent, are never afraid. Never nervous. And they certainly never make mistakes because of tension or pressure. Arnold Palmer's description of twitch includes the significant assurance, 'It's not nerves.' But Arnold, it is. One of the principal problems associated with putting is that one is obliged to do it at a crucial stage of the tournament. Often, at the very choke-point. A final putt – 'this one for the championship' – is a make-or-break affair, a sorter of men from boys, like match-point in tennis, when all but the most foolhardy feel their racket arm begin to seize up with tension. Thus putts – all putts – become associated with tension and fear. Very often, to make it all the more exasperating and the tension all the more unbearable, it is a short putt, which a child of five could manage without too much difficulty for an ice-cream cornet. The irony is, that the yips can almost certainly be cured once a golfer accepts responsibility *for what his muscles are doing*. As psychiatrist Dr Morley has suggested, the muscle spasm itself is often caused by ball hypnosis, which can be cured by looking at the club head, by visualization practice, and by learning to relax before addressing the ball (see pp. 234ff. for relaxation techniques). As Lee Trevino observes, the yips 'is all in the mind – a person with the yips needs mind control over the nerves to give him movement. He needs to be talked to constantly to make up his mind to make the stroke. A man with the yips is afraid he's going to miss the putt – what you have to do is to think the putt into the hole.'[12] Lee adds a word of warning: never ground your putter, because if you do, 'You find your hands fighting – the left hand says take it back and the other says don't move.'

Refusal to admit fear is what writer Dudley Doust calls 'the first law of competitive golf' – never showing 'a soft underbelly'.

Dudley Doust is one of the new breed of sports journalists who can do rather more than file match reports. His article for the *Sunday Times* after the US Open '78[13] was an analysis of golfing fibs and sops to the press. Andy North had just won the US title at Cherry Hills in Denver, Colorado. Up to the press stand came Andy, with a sheepish grin, not the first golfer to benefit from being the only man left sailing after everybody else had bailed out. Faced with a short putt – forty inches – for the gift of his first major championship, Andy had backed away, looked at it, crouched on his haunches, addressed it, backed away again, looked at it, measured, squinted, and putted for $45,000. The press waited on their marks for the True Story of Andy North. 'It really was an easy putt,' said he, as though discussing the time of day. 'If ever you have a putt to win an Open or a Masters or whatever, that's the one you'd want.' The press glowered. 'Uphill, perfectly straight, about three or four feet. All you've got to do is hit it solid.' Dudley Doust comments, 'What North was saying seemed incredible, almost annoying and certainly unfulfilling for those who were grilling him. Something near to hostility briefly swept the inquisitors. He wasn't *sharing* his fears.' The journalists persisted. 'Why did you back away twice from that putt?' 'Well,' said North, 'the wind was blowing very, very hard when we got to the hole.' He figured, why not wait for a little lull? Says Doust, 'That's not what his face said on the green, but North clearly was going to stick to his story.' Only a few minutes before, J.C. Snead had also kept his lip buttoned about the US Open Experiment. The reason why J.C. missed a putt on the final green was nothing to do with tension. It was the North wind again. Had he made the putt, he would have ended up in a play-off with North. Dudley continues his story: 'A day earlier, moreover, the great Nicklaus had faced a similar problem. Where was he to put the blame for a hideous sand-wedge shot that he fluffed into the water? Nicklaus thought and thought. He had suffered a lapse of concentration, he said at last. It had been brought about, he added, by a visit he paid to one of the plastic portable lavatories on the course.' Said Jack, 'I don't know how this will look in the newspapers, but after I went to the john out there my mind wasn't on the next shot.' The term 'guts' is used to mean 'courage', and golfers are understandably anxious to avoid discussing the effects of competition on their guts, lest it should reflect on their courage.

Golf is a game of pressure. One of its less communicable agonies is that it attacks the stomach. Digestive illnesses are a feature of all sports, but the press, which freely discusses war, sex and wife-battering, is still a little chary of the Sporting Stomach. Even though, as Chris Plumridge has pointed out, 'Some people say that waiting to drive off that first tee at Augusta is the finest laxative in the world.' This is Plumridge being frivolous, of course, but it is certainly not funny for a man to have his insides turned upside down while he is trying to concentrate on golf. It adds to the already painful and potentially humiliating predicament in which he finds himself. Bobby Jones, a golfing hero of golfing heroes, lost pounds in weight during the week of a major tournament. He was invariably sick between rounds and could never keep a meal down because of the tension. In 1930 he retired, at the age of 28. Perhaps his digestive system had had enough of competitive golf. Henry Cotton won the 1934 Open having built up a massive lead, only to come close to losing it all on the final round. A big crowd had gathered, certain that Cotton was about to become the first British winner since Arthur Havers in 1923, and Henry's start was delayed fiteen minutes whilst people shuffled about the tee. Those close enough noticed that the Cotton visage was the same colour as the grass, and afterwards Cotton confessed to having had terrible stomach cramp. Jim Simons, when he won the Memorial tournament in 1978, said, 'I'm what the guys on the Tour call a grinder, a very intense person. I couldn't find enough rest rooms out there today. It's a continual battle for all of us to fight nerves, but some won't admit it.'[14]

The reader who has followed all of the foregoing discussion will notice two things. The first is that with few exceptions, golfers are prepared to go to some lengths to convince the world that they were not nervous or frightened while they were playing. If they made a mistake, it was because of some technical fault, which they then go on to explain, such as a grip or swing aberration, or else it was because of something over which they had no control: the weather, or luck, or an opponent, or the greens, or an *involuntary* spasm of the muscles, called the 'yips' (compare 'yips' with the child burping who says, 'Pardon me for being rude; it was not me, it was my food.' The golfer is saying, 'It was not me, it was my muscles.') The second thing the reader will notice is that, in spite of all these explanations and protestations, it does appear from the golfer's *behaviour* that he is sometimes very frightened indeed.

Why should the golfer be afraid? Ostensibly there is nothing to fear on a golf course. It's just a track of land, with a few humps and hollows, where men can amuse themselves in the fresh air. On the face of it, the golfer who feels afraid in such circumstances is prudent to keep it to himself, so as not to look very ridiculous. But as we have seen in the opening chapters, the Sport Experiment is designed to appear harmless fun, and 'a game'. Powerful unwritten laws ensure that this fiction is maintained. Only after the sportsman has turned professional and committed himself, and agreed to be locked in the pressure-cooker of a major event, does he see the experiment from the inside, and then it is too late to do anything other than produce his skills as best he can. Certainly, once he is inside, things take on a different appearance. For a start, let us look at the golf course. What is it? Why is it laid out in such a way? Why does Capability Brown, or whoever designed it, lengthen it to counter long hitters, and place obstacles where they will cause split decisions and gnashings of teeth? Why did he devise ways to make the golfer think left when he should be thinking right, backwards when he should be thinking forwards? Consider this:

It has often been said that golf is a tremendous character builder, and never more so than when the ball is bunkered. When you step in that trap, you must believe in yourself and your method. It really is a test of the mind.[15]

Or this:

14. Long. 567 yrds. Par 5. The Beardies Kitchen and the infamous Hell Bunkers . . . as fearsome a test as any in golf.[16]

Or this:

Hazards on the golf course are a rich source of anxiety and tension. Bunkers precipitate anxiety in all but the most expert golfers, and water, with all its regressive implications, has a strange way of mobilizing tension. . . . All obstacles are designed to mobilize fear. . . .[17]

Or this:

For of all forms of exercise theoretically designed for recreation and relaxation, none can be so unerringly guaranteed to produce nervous exhaustion and despair leading to severe mental illness and in some cases petulance.[18]

Bunkers called 'Hell', for example, are intended to suggest a place where a man is afraid and exasperated. It is more than a physical place: it is a mental and emotional one. Bobby Jones said of the Road Hole at St Andrews, that it was 'one of the most terrifying experiences the game has to offer'.[19] It is not just a hole: it is a 'terrifying experience'. Like the great allegories of literature, the golf course is a journey (a 'course' is a journey) through a man's own mind. On this journey he will meet up with his own feelings, as he comes to the different parts of the course that are designed to trigger them off. Disappointment. Anguish. Exhilaration. Childhood memories. And especially fear. As he works his way around the course, so he makes this journey in his head. Naturally he has to swing the club and hit the ball. Naturally he has to hole putts, and the way in which he does these things is based on hours and hours of grooved technical perfection. But as he goes from tee to green in a championship, these skills change. They may desert him altogether, or they may eerily seem to produce themselves (called 'playing out of one's skin') so that the player can apparently do no wrong. As he progresses across the hills and hazards, with thousands of pairs of eyes glued to his every move, the professional golfer knows that they are not simply watching where he puts his hands on the club, how he swings, or even where the ball goes. He knows that they are watching the journey in his mind. They want to know what happens when he comes across this or that emotion. They want to see if he can beat his inner self; if he cannot do that, the bunkers will get him, or the Road Hole will get him, or he will 'take the gas' on the 18th green. And because the golfer has more time to consider this inner journey than other sportsmen, the chances are that only the psychologically strong and the mentally trained will reach their goal.

This is why so many people laughingly refer to golf as a game to drive you mad. Even psychiatrist Dr Morley admits that it occasionally seems not so much a game, as a conspiracy to reduce men's brains to mush. And this is why Arnold Palmer's father 'Deacon' (Milfred) reminds us that '90 per cent of golf is played from the shoulders up.'[20]

It is *this* game of golf, rather than the mere swinging of clubs and launching of projectiles, which the professional golfer has to play. And it is this game of golf for which a player must be coached and prepared if he (or she) is to succeed at competitive level. Hollis Stacy, the 1977 US Open winner and one of the many young challengers of Judy Rankin's earlier sovereignty, has the tendency to 'space out' and lose concentration – the golfing equivalent of Evonne Cawley's famous 'walkabouts' in tennis. Hollis sums up the feelings of many of her fellow-players, both male and female, when she says, 'You are your biggest opponent and you must *cope* with yourself. I often call the game "cope" not golf.'[21] This is the department in which British pros so often fail to matriculate. Girls trying to gain access through the US qualifying schools express this inadequacy at 'coping' much more openly than their male counterparts. Suzanne Parker, the Hertfordshire professional who had fared well enough in Australia, failed three qualifying schools, missing one by a single shot. She says, 'It's like Chinese torture at the school. Every stroke out there is pressure on your head.' She told golf-writer Liz Kahn, 'I really think I might have gone completely mad if I had stayed there. I don't think I know how I survived at all.' Young Christine Langford went to qualifying school thinking it would mean playing the game of golf she knew and suddenly found herself three-putting. She said, 'The tension just hit me.'

Lapses of concentration hit the men, too, of course. American Billy Casper, after a disappointing showing in the French Open in 1978, confessed that he was just about sick of all his missed chances; every round he loses concentration for a spell, and doesn't know how to cure it. Then there are the famous tempers of golf. Tommy Bolt threw clubs. Tom Weiskopf, whose swing has been worshipped as one of golf's holy mechanisms, throws the occasional fit. Weiskopf's temper has resulted in fines from the PGA, walk-offs in the middle of rounds, and a reputation for surliness which he is always half-expected to live up to, in spite of his own good intentions. Temper tantrums are a symptom, rather than the cause, of a golfer's difficulties, and it is very hard for a man who is agitated to pretend he is not: golf is quite capable of exposing what he is trying to conceal, even if he grits his teeth together. Howard Clark, the blond Yorkshireman, has also been criticized for outbursts of temper, as though the whole secret of success lay in containing his wrath. Peter Alliss, always one of his severest critics, gave Howard a talking to on holiday in Tobago. He told Clark not to keep losing his temper, and to 'keep looking forward and not dwell on the bad holes'. Clark focused his mind on this advice, and there followed a string of successes, beginning with the 1978 Portuguese Open. Only after this first victory did the real reason for Howard's temper tantrums come to light. He had been, to borrow Hogan's expression, 'tight as a banjo string', and there had been 'plenty of terrible moments which had me shaking and even feeling frightened,' he said. Which moments? 'Take the last round of the Portuguese. I stood on the 16th tee knowing I needed two pars and a birdie to win my first major professional tournament. I three-putted the 16th to drop a shot.' This was the point at which his mind clung on to Peter Alliss's advice to think forward instead of back. He said, 'Sound thinking in that moment of crisis was just as important as a sound swing.' And what was it that had bugged him at that 16th tee? Well, after his first victory Howard was greatly relieved because now, 'The fear of winning has been removed.'[22] Since then, despite a long slump after winning two titles in 1978, Clark has had another surge of success. He is still bothered by tension, and does mental exercises on the course to relax. One of these is to imagine he is 'carrying enormous weights in both hands as I walk down the fairway'.

The fear of winning – 'taking the gas' – is something that even the greatest golfers have to overcome. Crashing through this barrier at championship level is an experience known to most players as a thing to postpone, to worry over, to throw temper tantrums at, and to tremble in the face of. To find out what happens to a golfer's insides on the last round, or the last hole, you have to ask a player who has just won a big tournament. In the flush of victory he might just tell you. Fuzzy Zoeller (after winning the 1979 San Diego Open and before winning the Masters): 'I'm ready for it. In other years, with the position I'm in, I'd feel the shakes on the last hole.' Larry Nelson (after taking the 1979 Inverrary Classic): 'Looking back, I'm sure it was a lack of experience that kept me from winning. I never felt comfortable the last round. I was nervous in the wrong direction, in a negative way.' Bruce Lietzke (having won the Tucson Open): 'I still don't feel comfortable with a lead. I seem to play more aggressively when I'm a shot or two back.' Hale Irwin (after victory in the '79 US Open): 'The night before the final round was the longest of my whole life. . . . My stomach was growling like a wolf.' Irwin had just stumbled to double-bogey then bogey on the last two holes. As we shall see from the chapters on this particular anxiety, it has profoundly affected many great sporting careers. Very often famous victories are somebody else's famous 'chokes'.

5

Elbow, and the High-Strung Game – Tennis

If golf is the slow game, F1 racing the fast game, and cricket the brain game, tennis is the high-strung game. Of all experiments carried out on a sportsman's nerves, tennis is the most jet-lagged, the most sleepless, the most gruelling and most anxiety-producing between events. It pays well, and it demands everything. The year-long tour is the player's whole existence. He lives in hotel rooms, in planes and on courts with widely varying surfaces throughout the world, under inexaggerable pressure to produce good performances, his entire professional life. There are no holidays as such. No off-season. Any player who takes a vacation does so at his own risk; while he rests, others are amassing the computer points to squeeze him off the tournament entry lists. The money is staggering, and like a drug. Players rush from one end of the world to the other, half out of their minds from intensive competition and lack of sleep, to play far-flung venues they do not like, because life is short, a player's life is shorter, and any minute the bubble may burst. The players are greedy, often unscrupulously so. They sense that they are being bought, and they sell to the highest bidder. They know that the cardinal rule in pro tennis, irrespective of who they are or what they win, is not to act as a moral light-house for humanity, but to keep their heads, to stay glued together. They string their rackets at sixty pounds and their nerves at fifty-five – or at least they try. Before Wimbledon in 1978, *Daily Express* columnist James Lawton spoke to Björn Borg about his chances of equalling Fred Perry's record of three consecutive Wimbledon titles. Borg told him a few things to surprise anyone who thinks Wimbledon is all strawberries and cream. 'It is sad to see what the game can do to people. It is sad to see a great player like Nastase being brought down by the pressures of the game. You ask yourself, why do people have to take these pressures? Is it necessary to go out after so much money? In tennis at this level it is an easy thing to wreck your life.'[1]

Borg retired from the game in 1983. The man who 'wrecked his life', John McEnroe, has not found the pressures delightful either. In 1979 he told me: 'I can't see myself playing when I'm past thirty or so. I don't want to play tennis for the rest of my life.' During one of his subsequent bad patches he said, 'I am sure the reason I'm not playing well is that I've had too much tennis. The trouble is that the most difficult thing is to say "no". You make yourself a schedule and other people ask you to play, or you get a good deal and you keep adding to your plans.' By now he was complaining of 'mental lapses', cameramen, the Press and the crowds. The most magical player the circuit had seen for years was walking about with a sour-puss expression and nicknames like SuperBrat and The Mouth. He was beginning to crack. He told me at the Benson and Hedges tournament, 'they're out there booing and clapping and whatever, and they don't even know what's going on. I'm not doing anything to harm them, I'm just trying to do a job for myself. I'm out there trying to do the best I can. I'm only hurting myself anyway – why should they care? That's the way I look at it. They should understand what's going on before they make their decisions.'

McEnroe's fractious behaviour on court reminded a lot of people of Nastase. Was that a fair comparison? 'I don't think there's any comparison between me and Nasty: I mean, he deliberately set out to bother you, to try and excite everybody. I'm just trying to win the points, myself; I'm not trying to get everybody screaming. I just try to hit the ball where I can and if you get a weird call then sure, you ask about it. I do think line judges and officials are harder on me because I have a reputation that precedes me. So they're watching out for me more. That's partially my fault because it all happened the first time I was ever here. They didn't like my attitude then, and it's just built up. You get other guys questioning calls, but they don't notice that, because they don't expect it. But they're waiting for me to do it. That's the difference.'

Jim Connors, himself made to stand in the corner by angry officials and crowds in his bellicose youth, puts it like this: 'The public will never fully understand about sport celebrities. They see them only when they are competing and therefore under stress'.[2] And stress is what makes players behave strangely. The reader might interject, well why don't they quit? Or at least slow down? Nobody's forcing them to play. Nobody is forcing anybody to take part in any sport experiment. But as human beings we feel frequently compelled to do all sorts of things we are not visibly forced to do. As Borg said before he took the decision to retire, you can't quit, and you can't slow down, because 'you are on a sort of trip'. And the machinery goes round so fast it is very difficult to get off, especially if you happen to be at the top. Sponsors have bought a piece of you, and they want you to win. Friends and fans want you to win. And above all, *you* want you to win. So you stay on the machinery, and it continues round at a cracking pace. If you get sick, you fall off. Otherwise you cling on like a mad monkey, literally for all you're worth. The public pay to see whether you can do it. They are unaccountably interested in your behaviour under these circumstances.

Nastase (telling me about his sense of panic on court):

It's the tension of going in front of the people. It's like an actor: you're going in front of an audience. You make one mistake, or two, or three, and they're all there, and you get nervous, and you don't know what – you're getting confused!

Some time ago writer Peter Bodo was collecting material for a piece on players' superstitions. One player he consulted was Sashi Menon:

For a while, I was convinced that I had to walk around the outside of the court when I changed sides. I got out of that, luckily. . . . Tennis is 70 per cent mental. It is almost like a force-field you are fighting out there. There are no real visible barriers in the game. Two guys go out and hit the ball around, the rules are set, all that. But there are enormous barriers. It is a mental game, almost all mental.[3]

From what Sashi says, perhaps the players are 'almost all mental' too, Or if they aren't, some have come very close to the wire. Dominique Nastase:

Sometimes, something happens. He goes mad, I guess. I think there are times when he does not know what he is doing, when he does not know where he is.

Perhaps this is why Tracy Austin and Andrea Jaeger were burnt out in their teens, and why Martina Navratilova travels the circuit with a medical staff.

As a behavioural experiment, tennis is unrivalled in its efficiency. It takes the players to the limits of the human mind, and on into the twilight of half-understood psychological phenomena. Writers and psychologists have for a long time been telling us that winning may be very traumatic, and several have suggested how, under certain circumstances, we may seek to avoid it, so as to preserve our equilibrium. Walter S. Tevis's masterpiece on pool-shooters, *The Hustler*, is about this subject. Bert tells the Hustler, Fast Eddie Felson, 'You want to be a winner, you got to keep your head. And you got to remember that there's a loser somewhere in you, whining at you, and you got to learn to cut his water off.'[4] Abraham Maslow, the psychologist, calls this loser syndrome the Jonah complex. Others have pointed out that to fail is, in many ways, safe. We may use our negative thought-patterns, our 'erroneous zones', or our sense of 'fate' or 'luck', to do it.

Should these writers and psychologists wish to demonstrate the cogency of a failure principle in human motivation, with live human subjects, they would need to look no further than the sport experiment called tennis. Here is Virginia Wade, on 'hitting rock bottom' in 1970: 'My back only became strained when I was in a predicament. Obviously, it was because my muscles were tensed up and more injury-prone; even more, it provided me with a legitimate excuse for failure. Once I discovered that in myself, I didn't have to look far to find it happening all over the place – players getting cramp at match-point, or pulling a muscle when in a tight spot. In addition, I had the revelation that somewhere in my nether being there was a fear of winning.'[5] Yannick Noah had a similar revelation after he became the first Frenchman to win his native title for thirty-seven years. Deeply affected by the emotional upheaval of victory, Yannick seriously contemplated jumping in the Seine. He says, 'Having the No. 1 hung on me doesn't interest me at all . . . you end up thinking you're God. That's dangerous.'

Watching Wimbledon on TV as a child, I was always mystified by Jack Kramer talking about the players' '*airs*'. Unfortunately for my childhood understanding of Kramer's rather distinctive American accent, these 'airs' would usually occur at the turning-point of the match and were more crucial, on the final scoreboard, than any amount of cunning placements and put-aways. Airs, whatever they were, obviously determined the winner.

For years, I was baffled. Then suddenly, on Centre Court at Wimbledon 1976, it all came clear. Nastase lost the final on account of *errors*. Of Borg's six service breaks, five came on Ilie's mistakes, four of them quite definitely unforced. At 0–3 down in the first set, Borg took control of the match. This had been Nastase's dream final, the one he had always avowedly wanted to win. Yet here he was apparently doing everything in his power to avoid it. Normally a hell-raiser over doubtful calls, he conceded a faulted ace to Borg. Normally a spirit on his feet, he plodded. Normally voluble, he was passive and empty. And when it was all over, Nastase did the strangest thing of all. He leapt the net. Celebrating, we are to assume, something of his own. ('I was happy for him, that's all,' Ilie says.)

Critics have dismissed all this by pointing to Nastase's reputation as a sort of tennis weirdo, who ought to have been suspended – preferably from a bridge. But Nastase was no weirdo. Under pressure he was all too human. In danger of winning the title of his dreams, Ilie blew his chances. He showed openly a fear that most players prefer to keep to themselves, if indeed they are aware of it at all: that losing, vile though it may be, is at least a devil you know. Winning, especially winning your dream championship title, is not.

Björn Borg was less often accused of odd quirks of temperament. Fellow-players called him 'The Clone'. His pulse rate at rest is 38, which makes him the best place to store your ice-lolly if you don't have a freezer. But on the brink of victory in the Sweden–Czechoslovakia Davis Cup decider in Stockholm in 1975, Borg saw a devil he had never seen before. Serving for the match against Kodes, he volleyed and then lost control, smashing wildly over the base-line. After his faltering victory he confessed, 'I was never so scared in my life. I was shaking. I could hardly hold the racket.' Borg had dreamed of winning the Davis Cup for his country since he was 15.

Rod Laver, who had one of the game's soundest temperaments, remembers the time his mouth went dry three points from his Grand Slam in 1962. 'I couldn't hear anything and my body felt boneless,' he said. 'My whole game seemed to have fallen apart.'[6] Going through the motions he had grooved on the crushed-anthill courts back home, Laver served twice more, zombie-like, and Emerson drove over the base-line. Out. Laver was US and Grand Slam Champion. What had it felt like, going through the winning barrier to that dream title, the one he had always wanted? 'If you have never been through a few moments of torture like that you just cannot understand how it is.'[7]

Considering the prospect of this 'torture', it is hardly surprising that many deserving talents never actually win a major title. Their form is never there 'on the day'. They don't get 'the breaks'. Laver's first coach Charlie Hollis had been a good tournament player. 'I had the strokes to win everything in tennis but I didn't have it *in there*,' he would tell his freckled, pigeon-chested pupil, tapping his forehead. 'I'd blow my top.' Frank Gorman was another great shot-maker of Laver's youth, as Rod recalls: 'For every gifted player who makes the big-time, they reckon there are a dozen just as talented who don't make it. Frank was destined to be one of the also rans.'[8] Under pressure, he would make nervous errors. Perhaps, seeing these disappointed careers, young Rodney decided on his own game: go for broke. And in the implacable Harry Hopman he found a coach ruthless enough to teach it to him.

Not all would-be champions are so lucky (if one can call Hop's drill-sufferers lucky). Between themselves, the players have a name for people like Charlie Hollis and Frank Gorman. They call them, though maybe not to their faces, 'choke artists'. They are said to suffer from 'the elbow', or as the French call it, 'the little arm' – *petit bras*. That is to say, they tense up and cannot hit through the ball when the crisis comes. Give them a 5–3 lead in the final set and they become wooden and incompetent. They 'blow it' from apparently insurmountable positions. They hand the initiative to the desperado across the net, who by this time is going for his shots with maniacal abandon, having nothing to lose, and nothing to fear, other than that someone has rifled through the locker-room and snatched his fresh socks. And so the story goes of another 'come from behind' victory: the sportwriters' favourite 'resurrection from the grave'. Good copy. Heart-breaking tennis.

Yet there are very few champions around today on the tennis circuit who have not choked, who have not felt the evil eye of the winner's devil. Sometimes he stares them out for years before they can make a breakthrough. For years, Arthur Ashe was branded as a persistent runner-up. His mail would contain helpful postcards from fans. 'Look, Ashe, if you can't win, get out of the game, we can't afford to have any losers so visible,' said one from a black well-wisher.[9] Between his Forest Hills victory in 1968 and his WCT–Wimbledon double in 1975, the winning barrier, for Ashe, loomed like an electric fence. He would often come within an ace of a title, and then his serve would disappear, or his toss would go peculiar, or it would rain on his glasses, or the wind would upset his delivery. And in the last resort there was always his forehand volley to fall backwards on. The match-point problem returned to plague him, both in the 1978 Australian Open and in the Masters final against John McEnroe. Said Ashe, 'I am a victim of fate, that's all there is to it.' He retired in 1980 with a serious heart condition.

For years, Manuel Orantes would show up at major finals suitably dressed and with a racket in his left hand, only to go away disappointed. For a long time even his speciality clay court titles eluded him. Five times in 1974 he came second in important finals. In Paris he faced Borg, reached a commanding position, and then collapsed. Rome 1975, another near miss. As a youngster he had suffered from cramp. Later on it was a strained back that was the cause of the trouble. Poor Manolo would always smile through his disasters, as if he were in two minds about winning major finals anyhow. After all, they loved him in Barcelona, and welting the ball wasn't really his style. His female equivalent, Evonne Goolagong (-Cawley) won Wimbledon in 1971 from a trembling Margaret Court when that nervous lady double-faulted at match point. After the title was stripped from her the following year by Billie Jean King, Evonne confessed to feeling relieved. 'I didn't want any more,' she said,[10] and her performance at Forest Hills proved it.

Even if you survive the evil eye, and the 'torture' described by Rod Laver, there's no denying that it's tough at the top. An expectant public waits behind you, fully complacent you'll do it again, wanting to know why not if you don't. And waiting in front of you, with nothing to lose and everything to gain, are your opponents, the 'under-dogs'. Ripples of applause begin to break out on your errors. You're under pressure, and you're on your own. Chris Lloyd, during the 1973 crisis from which she was to emerge a consistent champion, was occasionally seen crying her eyes out in the locker-room. People kept rooting for her to lose. And despite her court-sense, her precision and her immaculate groundstrokes, Chris kept obliging. Especially in major finals. Rome. Paris. Wimbledon. In a way, it was the graceful thing to do.

Jim Connors did the graceful thing during 1975, and shocked tennis correspondents the world over by coming second in all the championships he could find, including Wimbledon and Forest Hills. To some, it seemed like sheer devilment on Connors' part.

Perhaps he was doing it to spite everybody for depriving him of his Grand Slam in 1974, when WTT bans prevented him from completing the circuit. Stroke for stroke, Connors could handle anybody, including King Kong and Björn Borg, his nearest challengers. So what exactly was he doing? Well, as Arthur Ashe observed in an interview at the time, 'If you analyse the Wimbledon final, it wasn't me winning the points, it was Connors losing them. He was making a lot of errors.'[11] Ashe noticed something else about Jimmy too: 'He's scared about something. I don't know what's happened, but he's not the same.'[12] An investigation by Frank Deford for *Sports Illustrated* prior to Connors' victory in the 1978 US Open revealed that at that time he had played in seven major finals and lost six, and that he had defaulted from almost twenty tournaments, 'often with the most transparent excuses of ill health at the eleventh hour. . . . What he does not say is what is apparent, that whereas he needs a physical excuse to get him off the hook, he is "not right" for psychological reasons.'[13] Deford suggests that 'Ashe had belled the cat' in that 1975 Wimbledon final. But 1975 was not the beginning of Connors' problems at all.

What actually happened to Connors in that disastrous year, the mere mention of which still sets him visibly bristling, really began in 1974. During 1974, which he looks back on as his finest season, Connors won Wimbledon and Forest Hills, and announced his engagement to Chris Evert. The wedding was planned for 8th November. Questioned before the US Open on his chances in the tournament he said, 'If I choke here it would be the first time. The only time I might choke will be on 8 November.' Everyone laughed. Connors did not choke the US Open, but he did choke the wedding – that was called off. He had also begun to have difficulty over sundry other tournament finals. In the 1974 US Clay Court Championships, Connors had some trouble polishing off Borg in the final, after blowing a 5–2 lead in the deciding set. At one point he had indicated he might not play in the final at all, though his reasoning was unclear. He had slightly jarred his wrist in his match with Orantes, and he was peeved about the disqualification of Nastase, but neither seemed sufficient excuse for withdrawal. He explained himself as follows: 'I said earlier in the day that I might not play because I didn't feel like it. But I'm a strange guy. Sometimes you want to find everything wrong and sometimes you want to find nothing wrong. I guess today I was just nervous and wanted to find things wrong.'

In the Canadian Open he had lost in the early rounds, from

'sheer fatigue'. Most significantly, he had declined to defend his title at the US Pro Championships in Boston, so as to enter for the Medi-Quik championships at South Orange, NJ. This was on grass, and Forest Hills, also on grass, was looming the following week: Connors wanted to prime his grass court game. However, in that tournament Connors advanced to the final, against Metreveli, and then withdrew. He was suffering, it was announced, from 'severe gastro-enteritis'. At the end of the year came the most conspicuous withdrawal of all: Connors cried off the Masters tournament, which would have pitted him against one of his chief rivals for the No. 1 spot, John Newcombe. The reason given was 'toothache'. Newcombe, a dentist's son, was sceptical, and also very angry.

Whether or not the unfortunate Jimbo was suffering from nervous dyspepsia during 1974 (as many of his fellow pros have done), the minor difficulties he had experienced about appearing in and clinching tournament finals were to turn, in 1975, into a nightmare.

It began on 1 January. Jimmy had stormed to the final of the Australian Open, there to be confronted by John Newcombe and an ominous-looking crowd. At set-all and 3–2 to 'Newk', Connors was down 0–15 but pulled back to 40–15 on three consecutive calls that nobody liked. In those days, crowds didn't want locks of Connors' hair; they wanted locks of his head. The Brash Basher responded by serving a deliberate double fault. Whereupon Newcombe, needing only a spark like this to start a forest fire, won the game, the set, the fourth set tie-break, and the match. Afterwards it was clear to the press that Connors felt blackmailed. Asked about the deliberate double fault he shot back, 'Just don't put me in that position again.' In some mysterious way, Connors had been cheated out of playing his game, just as he had been cheated out of his Grand Slam the year before. And his status was in question now, since he had scratched from the Masters, either because of toothache, stomach ache, or mounting pressure to prove himself No. 1 against Newcombe and Borg. Connors was evidently tired of No. 1 pressure and, perhaps too, he was bitter. He had won everything, but nobody liked him. The crowds were after his blood. He had even been cheated of a private romance by the pressures of publicity. By the end of 1974, Connors needed a break. In 1975, albeit unconsciously, he took one. And he was subsequently very angry with the press, with the public, and with himself at the suggestion that he had 'choked'.

Britain's Sue Barker reached a similarly harrowing crisis of confidence during the 1977 Centenary Wimbledon, after she slithered to defeat against Holland's Betty Stove 6–4 2–6 6–4 in the semis. She hadn't played her normal game, and now Virginia Wade was in the final: Sue's record for the season against Wade was three to nil. In fact, the only girls who had beaten her, Martina Navratilova and Chris Lloyd, were already out of the Championships. 'Everything was within my reach – Centenary year as well,' Sue said afterwards, 'and I blew it.' She had begun the season with three decisive victories over Wade, whom she now seriously rivalled for the British No. 1 slot. She had sealed a huge contract with the Indiana Loves to play Team Tennis, and she had been hailed as the great British hope to topple Chris Lloyd's boring supremacy. The Americans were impressed with the Paignton girl's Virginia Slims wins, her aggression, and her powerful forehand – one of the strongest in the women's game. The Wimbledon defeat, at the hands of Stove, was a surprise. 'It's my own fault,' Sue said. 'Tomorrow I'll be kicking myself.'

The next tournament she played was Forest Hills: her worst ever fiasco. She was beaten by her own astonishing errors to give the match to 14-year-old Tracy Austin. Then came illness. She pulled out of the Colgate International in Sydney in November – with a leg injury. Then, midway through a tournament in Tokyo, Sue collapsed. Her illness was reported as flu, and later acute anaemia. A year later, in an interview for *Tennis World* magazine, Sue reflected on her miserable form, her row with life-long coach Arthur Roberts, and her broken engagement. 'Looking back,' she said, 'my troubles all began at Wimbledon last year.'[14] This was the occasion when she reached the semi-final against Betty Stove; when, as she says, 'I was nervous and I blew it.' Sue retired in 1985 after losing badly to a 15-year-old schoolgirl. What might have been is anyone's guess.

Another player haunted by a match that he 'blew' was the founder of the Inner Game of tennis in America, author and coach Tim Gallwey. Arguably, the impetus behind that tennis revolution, and the two best-ever sellers in tennis book history (*The Inner Game of Tennis* and *Inner Tennis*) was a choke: 'In the last set, I had been ahead 5– 3, 40– 15 on my serve. I was nervous but optimistic. In the first match point I double-faulted. . . . In the second I missed the easiest put-away volley possible in front of a packed grandstand. For many years thereafter, I replayed that match point in countless dreams, and it is as vivid in my memory now as it was on that day twenty years ago. Why? What difference did it really make? It didn't occur to me to ask.'[15] Gallwey's quest for a solution to this mystery led to the development of the now famous school of 'yoga' or 'unconscious' tennis (page 136).

Players who have suffered the ignominy of choking on big matches tend to keep their own counsel: not surprisingly since they are made to feel like sporting lepers. Jim Connors, who knew well enough how much it hurt in 1975, lashed out at Czech Ivan Lendl, calling the young man 'chicken' when he avoided a semi-final confrontation with Borg by losing his last match in a New York round robin tournament. Lendl suffered other taunts of cowardice when he lost three successive US Open finals, and much other rudery for other finals greatly missed. He finally broke the evil spell in the French Open in 1984 when, having gone two sets to nil down in this one as well, he managed to allow a despondent McEnroe to outlose to him in five sets. Since then Lendl has gone from strength to supremacy, but he will never forget the 'chicken' label. He tends to speak to the Press in monosyllables and prefers the company of his seven German shepherd dogs to off-court chatter, shutting himself in at seven o'clock at night and going to bed at nine. He attributes his success to diet, fitness and Tony Roche, whom he describes as 'like a big brother to me'. The Aussie veteran is Ivan's version of the 'guru' so essential to top-class tennis.[16]

Perhaps the saddest choking champion in recent years, however, was discovered by the Commercial Union Grand Prix: indeed, without its structure and support his talent may have fallen by the wayside, along with all the Frank Gormans of the game.

In Mar del Plata in the early 1960s a wealthy *escribano*, concerned about his only son's solitary bike-riding over the pampas, hired a local barber to teach him tennis. On the face of the little boy, as the barber recalls, were 'the signs of deaf protest'. He was packed off to a tennis club, 'to make friends'. This was the main purpose of the venture. Not having much of a backhand at the time, the lad made a complete ass of himself at tennis, and determined to practise and practise so that he could at least hold his head up among the other kids. From this chastening beginning grew the player who has been runner-up and losing semi-finalist in more major championships than he cares to remember. His name is Guillermo Vilas. To the Argentinian press, who labelled him 'The Eternal Second', Vilas was a mixed blessing. They loved his tennis, and they cursed and ridiculed his chokes. 'I was trying to convince myself that in the finals of the big tournaments I lost to guys who were playing very well,' says Guillermo, 'but people kept saying, like they wrote in one magazine back home, that I was paralysed in the finals. All the people came around and said that. Even my mother said, "You are paralysed in the final." '

Ironically, in view of Vilas's introduction to the game, the people who beat him to major titles were usually his friends. Panatta in Rome, Orantes and Borg almost everywhere else. Before tournaments Guillermo practised with Borg, no doubt grooving returns instead of volleying to daylight. In a match the Swede simply picked his return and moved in. Friend or no friend: on the day Borg took no prisoners. Said Vilas, 'These beatings do not affect our friendship.' He is philosophical, writes film-scores and poetry, and, in spite of his middleweight boxer's build, is passive and gentle. Only once had he ever really let fly, and this was in the Masters in 1974 at Kooyong, and on grass, allegedly not his *forte*. For one week he rained down what Newcombe afterwards described as 'bloody bullets', sweeping aside Newcombe, Parun, his friend Borg, Ramirez and an admittedly reluctant Nastase in the final. One can only assume he'd had a quarrel, as he later confessed, 'For the longest time, I hate every stroke I had done in the Masters.'[17] In theory, victory should have helped, but going through the winning barrier did not help Vilas; not in 1974. In fact, it seemed to make him ill. He withdrew from the circuit, apparently with a suspected ulcer, and from what psychiatrist Arnold Beisser tells us of other athletes seriously disturbed by victory, perhaps he was lucky to escape so lightly.[18]

The renowned Criollos of the Argentine have a saying, 'unreliable as a Palomino'. This splendid horse, physically capable of anything, is notorious for what they call 'running out' and refusing the fence. Vilas was a Palomino. A variety of explanations were offered for his defeats. He had meddled with his service. His volleying was suspect. He hugged the baseline. He had a wrist injury, a thigh injury, an ulcer, and so on. The real reason was that, seeing a title looming up, Vilas got nervous.

Usually he would storm to the semi-final, or the final, in superb form. He dropped only nine games on his way to the Italian semi in 1974. Once there he led Borg by two sets to love, apparently had him whipped, and then collapsed. In Paris the same year he reached the third round and led friend Orantes 6– 3 6– 3, made a tie-break of the third set and then broke down. Rome 1975, he lost again to Orantes in the semi-final. Paris 1975, he dropped only one set on the way to the final and seemed to be on what the players call a 'blue streak'. In the title match he looked across the net, saw Borg, and decided against it. At Forest Hills 1975 he excelled himself. He powered his way to the semi-final in straight sets and appeared to be adding three more to his collection when he led 2– 0. Five times he reached match point, and everybody thought his opponent had had it. He hadn't. It was Orantes. And so the story continued in 1976. The WCT Final: 6– 1 in the first set and then runner-up to Borg. The Italian final: 6– 2, and then runner-up to Panatta. Forest Hills, semi-finalist (Connors). Wimbledon, quarter-finalist (Borg).

Even in victory he visibly tensed up. On his way to the Masters title at Kooyong he complained of yellow vision, and several times showed signs of doing his victory roll. En route to the Canadian title, he faltered so badly against Jauffret that a spectator accused him of 'tanking' (taking a dive in) the match.

Vilas agōnistēs. But there are few players on the pro circuits of tennis today who would be shocked or even surprised at Guillermo's anguish: more or less, they have felt it themselves. After his spectacular choke at Forest Hills in 1975 and yet another bombardment in the Argentinian press, Vilas was in despair. He went for help to the only person he could think of who might be able to influence his game: Ion Tiriac. Tiriac is a very hirsute and brooding Romanian of frightening appearance, who used to play ice-hockey and get into fights. He is cunningly intelligent, plays pro tennis, manages German Wimbledon *Wunderkind* Boris Becker and has been likened to a grizzly, a loan shark, and a triple agent of Marrakesh. He was not the sort of man readily associated with Vilas, who for all his beefy muscularity is withdrawn and literary and pulls his punches. Tiriac assessed his new ward – 'This guy not capable in life to kill a fly,' he told reporter Curry Kirkpatrick[19] – and set about toughening him up. Tiriac says of his overhaul of Vilas that he did not change a stroke, but this is not strictly accurate. For a start, he wanted Guillermo to play serve and volley tennis, which he declined to do. Next, he wanted a backhand slice introduced to his repertoire (which is founded on top spin), and an adjustment made to the service footwork. These Vilas did. Then he wanted his pupil to train as though preparing to carry trucks up cliffs. Vilas trained. Most of all, he wanted Guillermo to think more aggressively, to develop the tennis-player's 'killer instinct', and to put his opponents away without flinching. To his great credit Tiriac was prepared to share the responsibility for polishing off Vilas's opponents. In fact he considered he played most of Vilas's matches himself: he has the boxing trainer's habit of referring to his fighter as 'I'. He told *Sports Illustrated*, 'I don't give a hell if Borg beat me ten more times straight. . . . I am far away from capabilities in every part of game'[20] – referring, presumably, to Vilas's superiority in every part of game.

For a time, this cruel formula obviously worked. After yet another choke at the beginning of 1977, when he was annihilated by Roscoe Tanner in the title match of the Australian Open, Vilas began winning his finals. It became such a habit that at one point, admittedly without meeting Borg, he had won fifty-seven consecutive matches on clay, including nine tournaments. His winning streak, breaking Laver's previous record of thirty-one matches in a row, was unsurpassed in nine years of Open tennis. Most significantly, where he had faltered before in major finals, Vilas began hitting his straps. First, it was the 1977 French Open. Yielding one set in seven matches, he swept Brian Gottfried off the court 6–0 6–3 6–0. Gottfried was nervous and overawed by the occasion, but this in no way diminished Vilas's achievement. Guillermo said that passing through the invisible barrier at match point was like 'breaking a giant piece of glass' hanging over his head.

Feeling a little burnt out by the experience, Vilas lost tamely at Wimbledon to Billy Martin, but then came the US Open, the last to be played at Forest Hills. This was supposed to be Jim Connors' championship. Throughout the tournament he had been more than usually sassy, and warned everyone, 'This is my home. I'm movin' in here. I'm rollin'.' In the final the only place Jim rolled was on his backside, as he skied his umpteenth mishit forehand into the stands. Vilas, having stormed to the final, and perhaps sensing that here was a man with a problem he knew about, capitalized mercilessly on Connors' finalitis. After all, 'If Jimmy having trouble with forehand, I'm stupid not to play it.' The score, to Vilas, was 2–6 6–3 7–6 6–0, and afterwards Connors fought his way out of the stadium, in his angry way close to tears. His errant forehand had let him down too, against Borg in the Wimbledon final a couple of months earlier. For his part Vilas, 'The Eternal Second', had come through. Guillermo showed great courage in the final set, and at the end of 1978 in the Australian Open he took the third crown of the

Grand Slam Championships too, on the same Kooyong courts where he had won the 1974 Masters. 'When I came close to the end I got nervous,' he said, explaining the 6–4 6–4 3–6 6–3 scoreline over John Marks.

How much of his success was due to Tiriac, it is difficult to say. Tiriac is a sports guru, a witch-doctor of enormous charisma, and the influence of such characters on athletic performance is incalculable, both in the West and in the Communist bloc. Despite his influence, however, Vilas continued to falter. In 1978, at Wimbledon, Tom Okker put out the number four seed 6–3 6–4 6–2 in a third-round match the Argentinian will not want to remember. 'I was trying to the last ball, but I was not there in the match. I cannot explain what happened,' he said, his voice breaking with emotion. Okker, you understand, was at the time ranked 104th in the world, and the whole year had won only three matches before coming to Wimbledon. Vilas was not ready for this new wave of disappointment. When I spoke to him the following week he admitted that he had in fact been very nervous, and at the US Open in September the defending champion was taken to hospital suffering from a gastric disorder: he had evidently been plagued by dyspepsia and a suspected ulcer after his victory in Kooyong in 1974. It was referred to in the Press as 'a stomach virus infection'.[21] Gastric illness is a common symptom of success anxiety in other sports. In tennis it is a nightmare, as on the occasion of Connors' reported 'gastro-enteritis' in 1974.

Nevertheless, with all this 'running up' going on, and people being 'tortured' and suffering the evil eye and the burbling belly, the astute reader will point out that *somebody* is still winning the major titles. The trophies aren't all in hock. So who does it? We all know that success breeds success, and that (though there may be exceptions like Vilas) the more you go through the winning barrier, the less nervous you are generally likely to be. But how does the would-be champion first break through?

It seems there are several methods. The first, and most common, is to meet someone in the final, and if possible the semi-final, who is even more nervous than you are. Mexican Raul Ramirez in Rome 1975 officially beat Nastase in the semi and Orantes in the final. What actually happened was that Nastase, whom he had kept waiting for forty minutes before the match, was so nervous that he had to retire and be given a sedative, and Orantes, who had been having major title trouble, listened a few times to the

Mexican's seven service bounces, and decided to have one of his fiascos.

Many a new champion 'beats a retreat' in this way. Panatta in Rome 1976 was four points from defeat in his quarter-final round when his opponent, Harold Solomon, lost control and stormed off over a call. In the final, Adriano had another lucky break. He met the Palomino.

The first time Nastase really pounced was at Forest Hills in 1972. Arthur Ashe, stiff and scared, led two sets to one and 4–2 in the fourth. After his defeat, Ashe wept bitterly. His service had gone. Orantes finally broke through at Forest Hills three years later. In the semi, it was Vilas who choked. In the final it was Connors. Roscoe Tanner's first major triumph, the Australian Open 1977, he acquired by way of Vilas, and Guillermo, as we have seen, achieved the long-sought breakthrough in Paris 1977 at the expense of a very pale Brian Gottfried, unaccustomed to major finals. In the US Open 1977, Vilas was given every reasonable assistance in the final by Connors, whose forehand on that day the reader might well have been able to cope with. Boris Becker's Wimbledon *Blitzkrieg* campaign in 1985 met with surprised expressions from Messrs Leconte, Jarryd and Curren in the last three rounds, but little experienced opposition. And so forth.

The player who benefited more than any other from opponents' nervousness was the cool Swede, Björn Borg. Nastase assured me, 'I don't think Borg is very calm. He looks calmer, but when he gets close, he's getting nervous too, because I've played him and I know.' I asked Björn himself, a couple of years ago, about his famous 'ice-Borg' reputation. Did he really feel composed? A crafty smile played about his lips. 'Sure you get nervous,' said Borg. John Lloyd interjected, 'You don't bloody show it!' 'Sometimes,' Björn continued, 'at crucial points I feel it, but usually I don't get that nervous on the court while I'm playing, but a bit, er . . .' Apprehensive, say, just before the match? 'Sure, I feel nervous then. That's to say, well, not *nervous* exactly, but immediately when you start to hit the first ball, then everything's gone. Then you look forward to the match.' Borg's close-set blue eyes scanned the press room. 'I think most of the players, everyone, feels physical fear, but some feels more than others. Well, sometimes I feel it too you know. Emotions, I feel them like everybody else, but if you compare to others, maybe I don't feel as much as other players. Coming from Sweden, you know, it's a cold country.' Cold country or not, Borg has been seized with fear on a tennis court on two occasions. One was the Davis Cup decider in 1975 when he faltered serving for the match against Kodes. The other was Wimbledon 1979, as he was about to become the first man ever to take four consecutive singles titles. 'I have never been so nervous in my life,' said Björn. 'It was unbelievable. At 5–4 40–0 I could hardly hold my racket.' This was exactly what he said on the previous frightening occasion. After surviving his most historic Wimbledon match point, Björn sat down by the umpire's chair with his face covered, waving away photographers and shaking his head. The young man had a reputation to consider, and 'You don't bloody show it!' was a very handy reputation to have.

Borg himself may not have shown his feelings at match point, but he made his name at the expense of those who did. His first WCT breakthrough was at the Albert Hall, when Mark Cox held five match points and shrivelled. In Rome 1974, Björn had looked a dead man in his semi-final before the Vilas collapse. In his final, it was the turn of the Nasty One. 'How *good* had I been, and how *bad* Nastase?' Borg asks in his autobiography[22]. Well, Ilie didn't exactly sparkle. In Paris, more of the same. Orantes led in the final 6–2 7–6, and then the Butterfly Man fluttered off, winning only two more games. And Borg came by his WCT and Wimbledon titles in 1976 from a flinching Vilas and a cowed Nastase respectively.

The reader will no doubt recall other instances of new champions who beat a retreat like this: goodness knows, there are enough of them. And anyone with the courage to *take* his first championship deserves all the breaks he gets.

Of course, if a player can't find any nervous opponents, there are other methods. A percentage player (one who plays the safe shot rather than the glamorous one) may break through by *going* for broke for a change. Or there's the crafty trick Billie Jean King always used, of pretending a 5–3 lead is a 3–5 deficit, thus avoiding the evil eye. Or else there's the 'Concorde' method, destined to become very popular. This method requires that you go through the sound barrier by pointing your nose at the ball. If you point it at the crowd, or the line-judges, your attention is not sufficiently streamlined to withstand the 'Gs' (G is the unit of gravity force in acceleration). Ignore the roar of the crowd, which gets louder as you go along: pretend it's your engines. Obey all calls as though they were flight instructions. Point your nose, and you go through in one piece. This is all 'concentration' really means.

Other more thoroughgoing remedies for success anxiety are available to the athlete willing to admit to himself that this is a problem. There's always something a player can do once he makes up his mind to go through with it. The fact is that most players never do make up their minds, and under pressure, the cracks show. 'Nervous' for most of us simply means 'undecided'. Those who are decided get the titles. Those who are not get the evil eye.

6

Taking the Gas

'Success phobia' or 'success anxiety', as the condition is called by psychologists,[1] is not confined to tennis. The sports public associate winning with the fulfilment of dreams and with ultimate happiness; there is no reason for them to suppose otherwise, because sportsmen are always saying this is what it is like. To the public, winning is ecstasy by association. Yet to so many sportsmen who stand on the threshold of victory for the first time, winning is not ecstasy at all, but shattering, devastating and frightening. Sportsmen are trained to think of victory as the supreme goal, a reward for all their efforts. Few of them care to meddle with this philosophy. Why else would they train, compete, sweat bullets and break their hearts if not to win? So most of them, when they see the dark side of the moon, keep quiet. Nothing raises a sportsman's hackles quicker than to suggest that he may be nervous of victory. As 'choke artist' is the filthiest insult in tennis, so choking, or 'taking the gas', is a thing that golfers loath and abominate. Hale Irwin at Carnoustie in 1975 had a *mot juste* for the occasion: he said the last two days would decide 'who could swallow and who couldn't'. Choking may be the most miserable experience in sport: it is also the most despised. In this chapter we look at approaching victory through the eyes of some sportsmen outside tennis to find out what they *actually* see, rather than what they are supposed to see. Like the tennis players in the last chapter, some of them have had a nasty shock.

When Tony Jacklin won the British Open in 1969 at Royal Lytham and St Annes, the thing that surprised him most about holing that last putt was not the rapturous ovation, or the trophy or the prize money. It was the fear. Almost the first person he spoke to afterwards was Jack Nicklaus, as he recalls in his autobiography.[2] He said, 'God, Jack, I never knew anyone could be so scared, so frightened.' Nicklaus, as big and reassuring a symbol of winning as one could expect to find on a golf course, squashed Jacklin with an arm. 'Don't worry,' said the Bear. 'It happens to everyone in the big ones,' adding candidly, 'They say it even happened to Hogan.' Just prior to Jacklin's harrowing fall from grace, he had a dream, which he recounted to writer Dudley Doust. 'Everybody was chasing me, and I couldn't run. My legs turned to rubber. I turned around to fight, but I couldn't fight. Then I woke up.' Tony had just won the 1974 Scandinavian Open, and was about to embark on his long and miserable journey to the bottom.

When history repeated itself, and Jack Nicklaus made his second comeback at St Andrews in 1978 after three years without a major title, he sat in the press room very pleased, with a lager in front of him (he doesn't normally drink), and tried to explain what victory in the Open meant to a person who had been missing his chances for so long: 'You get unhappy with yourself many times when you can't really perform under the right situations and I've had several times this year when I've had chances to win and I've done *some dumb thing*. I know I'm not as strong as I used to be. I know that I can't overpower a golf course like I used to but I'm still plenty long enough, and when I've played as well as I have the last couple of years and finished *second* in the number of tournaments that I've *had* that I finished second in – yea, sure you wonder whether . . . you think gee! well, you know, am I ever gonna win again. Am I really slipping or is it a figment of my imagination – or somebody else's reality I guess!'

He said he felt very proud of himself 'for being able to do what I did, and *finish the way I finished*'. He attributed his success from tee to green to a slight strengthening of his left-hand grip (on the advice of Jack Grout) which made his swing feel more natural. But there is more to it than that. Nicklaus had not won a major title since the 1975 USPGA championships, when he finished two shots ahead of Sydney-born Bruce Crampton. In 1972 Crampton had finished runner-up to Jack in both the US Open and the Masters. He won no tournament that year, despite finishing well up. In 1973, Crampton became the first non-American dollar millionaire in golf, but even so, it happened again: beaten by Nicklaus to the

USPGA title. 1974 was a lucrative year too, but again Crampton could not close out a championship. Finally, in 1975, came the USPGA that Crampton was definitely going to win, Nicklaus or no Nicklaus. On the Friday, Bruce put all those near-misses behind him: he surged to a 63, 7 under par, breaking the course and tournament records and dispelling all those rumours of 'taking the gas' in previous championships. This time Crampton was all set.

The next day, something happened. Bruce Crampton went back to the clubhouse with an amazingly bad 75. Although this gave Nicklaus the lead and ultimately the championship, it was not an easy thing for Jack to look at, for who else could be casting this shadow over Crampton's mind? And what was this peculiar thing that kept happening to him? He was a super golfer: Player said he had one of the best putting strokes he had ever seen, and Nicklaus himself said Bruce had been 'a good player for a long, long time', without winning any major titles. Perhaps in the clutch, his driving let him down.

Not long after that, Bruce Crampton withdrew from the pressures of major championships, and retired from the circuit in 1977. He had never succeeded in holing out for a major title. These are the bald facts of a sad story.

As psychiatrist Arnold Beisser explains in *The Madness in Sports*, the prospect of victory may be very traumatic, because of the symbolism involved. Winning has very powerful psychological connotations, and we do not fully understand, in spite of Dr Beisser's optimism, how some of these may affect the sportsman about to win for the first time. In some cases, the prospect of victory may be so disturbing as to cause severe disorganization of the personality, as happened with the international tennis player referred to by Dr Beisser, who faltered at match point and suffered a nervous breakdown. Sometimes a sportsman who is disturbed by the prospect of victory nevertheless (by luck, crowd support or some other circumstance) goes on to win – with similar consequences. You may recall the Ipswich–Arsenal FA Cup final in which the winning goal was scored by Roger Osborne of Ipswich. Osborne's team-mates immediately jumped on top of him, in the usual way, and when they dispersed it became apparent that something was wrong with Roger Osborne. He collapsed on the field, complaining that he was unable to catch his breath, and was taken away, suffering from 'nervous exhaustion'. I asked Roger what happened, as he hadn't played since. 'It was partly the heat,' he said. 'I was totally exhausted and excited at the same time. I suppose it must have been a combination of the heat and the tremendous relief and excitement.'

Whether or not Nicklaus was disturbed by what happened to Crampton, his own performances in the major championships after that 1975 PGA all had one thing in common: a lapse of concentration that made the difference between winning and coming up short. His record was what golf-writers call 'heartbreaking'. In the Masters during this slump he finished tied for third, second, and seventh; in the US Open, tied for eleventh, tied for tenth, tied for sixth; in the British Open, tied for second, and second; in the PGA, tied for fourth, and third. In 1977 in three of the majors, Jack was tied for the lead at the seventy-first tee. 'If I had been as prepared as I should have been,' he said, 'I should have pushed one or two of those over.'[3] As it turned out, Tom Watson beat him in the Masters and the (British) Open, and he finished one stroke out of the Lanny Wadkins–Gene Littler play-off in the PGA.

Strange things were happening to the Golden Bear, too, in other events. Take 1976, for instance – the last round of the Crosby at Pebble Beach. One minute Nicklaus was in contention: the next he was strolling back in the clubhouse with an 83. In the 1978 Los Angeles Open on one of his favourite courses, the Riviera, he collapsed on the last few holes to give the title to Gil Morgan, who almost passed out at finding himself so honoured. At the fifteenth, Jack pulled a 5-iron wide and his ball came to rest 'against a little twig'. There followed a lot of swishing, a double-bogey, a very shocked Gil Morgan suddenly the LA Open champion, and a very disappointed Nicklaus collecting his forty-third near miss. Jack blamed the twig. He also said, 'You make a couple of bad swings when you're under pressure trying to finish properly, and all of a sudden the next swing becomes a little more difficult.' The reader may notice particularly the phrase 'trying to finish properly', because Nicklaus has used it several times before: when he won the British Open in 1978, for instance, he said he was proud to have 'finished the way I finished'. For his part, Morgan, the new LA champion (who was emboldened sufficiently by all this to win the World Series later in 1978), was candid about his feelings on the threshold of that victory. He said, 'I didn't see the scoreboard until I walked up on to the 18th tee and it was a nightmare. I was floored. I thought I had a maximum of a one-shot lead and here I was three ahead. It scared me and I didn't play the last hole the way I wanted.'[4] Nick Faldo recalls a similar incident, involving a leader-board and a bunker. 'If you're in the lead by a couple of strokes you don't necessarily want to see the leaderboard until after you've played your shot,' he told me. When he won the Colgate PGA at Royal Birkdale – his first important title – he did so with a most unusual storming finish, carding eagle, par, birdie, birdie on the final holes. How did he manage that? 'I didn't let myself think I'd won till I walked down the 17th. People might think that's stupid but I didn't. I thought to myself, you've got to concentrate. Because *anything* can happen. I could have just cruised home and finished 2 in front, but I made myself keep concentrating. On that final putt, I was hammering the last nail in. My coach, Ian Connolly, was very pleased I kept it up to the end.' I should think he was, because this is the place where chokes usually occur. There have been some very famous ones.

In the 1939 US Open, Sam Snead needed a 6 on the last hole to qualify for a play-off. He finished with an 8. He lost a play-off in 1947 at St Louis to Lew Worsham when he missed a 2½-foot putt. Just as Sam was shaping up for the job, Worsham interrupted, 'Hold it, Sam, I think it's me to putt first.' Out came the tape-measure: it wasn't, but it might just as well have been. In 1949 Sam blew it on the 17th, putting out of heavy rough instead of chipping. He has never won the US Open, to complete his Grand Slam, in some thirty years of trying. (In golf, unlike tennis, the Grand Slam can be accumulated over a number of years.)

Other Grand Slams have gone begging too. Dai Rees came very close, but could never win the British Open to complete his record. Palmer had the same problem with the USPGA. Everyone thought he was definitely about to do it in 1964. Or else 1968. Or maybe 1970. Anyone wishing to strike up a friendly conversation with Palmer these days should steer well clear of the PGA. Palmer also had a problem with the US Open in 1966. From well in front, he sank into a play-off with Billy Casper, and lost that. On the 19th Casper had said, 'I'm really going to have to go to get second, Arnie.' Palmer said, 'Don't worry, Bill, you'll get second.' Bill didn't get second. From being in contention to break Ben Hogan's US Open record of 276, Palmer had slithered to a play-off, and then sank out of sight.

Just as many major tennis titles are lost rather than won, so many a great victory in golf is somebody else's choke. In 1970 at St

Andrews, Jack Nicklaus, hoping for a major title at 'the home of golf' to end a long run of disappointments, sat in the scorers' caravan on the last day with his head in his hands. 'I've blown it', he said. 'There's no way Doug Sanders can miss that putt. Who wants to be second here? No one.' The putt in question was just over 3 feet, breaking from left to right. To get in that position, Sanders had done several unusual things. After a superb bunker shot to about 18 inches at the Road Hole, he had then holed his putt to give himself an excellent chance: to win he had only to play the comparatively simple par-4 18th in 4 shots under ideal conditions. Sanders drove well, and then elected to pitch. Who knows what happened next? Perhaps at impact some doubt entered his mind, or perhaps he had looked up, or simply overhit. Whatever it was, the ball sailed eleven or twelve yards past the hole, and now he was left with a downhill putt – 'two for the Open'. Sanders putted, but came up short. All the same, he now had 'this one for the Open'. Nicklaus sat in the caravan in despair. Jacklin was looking at the action on TV, but Jack couldn't bear to watch. The dust settled. Sanders addressed the putt, looked up, caught sight of a minuscule speck of crushed ant's thorax on the line, leaned over to remove it, straightened up, settled himself, putted – and missed. Which meant that he'd really done it now: all alone in a play-off, with a well-known Bear. (Two years later, Sanders did hole out to win the $100,000 Kemper Open.)

The following day, though it was by no means a formality, Jack Nicklaus won the British Open. It was the end of a lean spell for him; the end of the 'Fat Slob' era, when Arnie's Army used to follow him over the greens to shout abuse. Most of all, it was the end of being an overweight upstart with a crew-cut, who often won but was never liked. Nicklaus's victory at St Andrews in 1970 installed him in the hearts of the golfing public, perhaps because, in a very rare moment of self-disclosure, he had holed out, tossed his putter high in the air, and wept. Spectators wondered if this was the same man they had hated for so long.

Winning after a lean spell is one thing; winning your first major, as any pro golfer will admit, is something else. The best hyphenated word to describe it is 'hair-raising'. As in any sport experiment intended to play on the nerves, what you really need is somebody else to blow the lead; then all you have to do is to stand upright and wait for them to take your picture. On the threshold of your first major title, you are unlikely to be capable of much else. It is generally believed to be easier to 'come from behind', because then you are in no danger of winning until the very last moment. Every sport has its praying mantis: a player who waits quietly within striking distance to pick off the leaders as they fall apart. Tennis, as we have seen, had Björn Borg. Most of his early triumphs were at the expense of chokers and psychological weaklings who collapsed near the point of victory. In motor racing, if anyone faltered in the lead, there was always Niki Lauda waiting around to finish him off. Lauda does not sweat, not even on a nice day in Brazil. There is something sinister about this kind of champion. He is invariably cool, often clinical and always feared. Horse-racing has had a whole history of cool jockeys, who wait patiently in the pocket and get through on the inside when the leaders start to 'smoke'. Coolness enables them to lie far back in the pack, leaving the front runners to falter, as they often do. The reader will be able to think of many more examples: Steve Davis (at least until recently) in snooker, Sugar Ray Leonard in boxing, Ed Moses over hurdles and so on.

In golf, the implacable little figure waiting 5 strokes back for you to blow the lead has always been Gary Player. People called Palmer a 'charger', because with Arnold's come-from-behind victories there was always an element of risk, of raw emotion and brute strength. You always knew where he was: up a tree, behind a bush, in a ditch – and coming out fighting. Gary Player's wins from behind were not like that at all. Player just suddenly *appeared* at the last moment, as though from nowhere: cool, precise, calculating – and in front. Player is golf's equivalent of the quiet man with the chloroform rag. (He has an understudy as well, who despite the 'yips' has already demonstrated a certain robotic efficiency – the German Bernhard Langer.)

Gary's own initiation to winning major tournaments was a nerve-jangling affair, with a 6 on the last hole in the 1959 Open at Muirfield. Still, he had told Pat Matthews the night before, 'Pat, I'm 8 strokes behind, but I really feel I'm going to win this tournament tomorrow,'[5] and win it he did. He has been coming from 8 strokes behind, or thereabouts, ever since, and he has generally preferred to let other people breathe the gas on those final holes. In 1961, when Player won at Augusta for the first time, Arnold Palmer obliged. Having secured a 1-stroke lead as a result of Player's difficulties on 10, 13 and 15, Palmer required a 4 at the last to win and a 5 to tie. Arnold died on his putter with a 6. Player's victory in the US Open in 1965 came about after Kel Nagle, with whom he was tied, hit a spectator on the head with one of his shots, and got upset. As Gene Littler says, 'Some people have backed up to help Gary win, but he has shot some super scores. . . .'[6] Player's reputation as a praying mantis has led at least one journalist to joke that he might drop a couple of shots deliberately, so as to avoid being in the lead. In New Orleans a while ago, Gary was trying for his fourth successive victory, but was none too optimistic going into the last round, perhaps because he was out in front. He bet a television announcer $50 he wouldn't make it four in a row, and he won the $50.[7] In 1974 he won the British Open under the most extraordinary circumstances. He says, 'For three days I held the lead – a frightening and nerve-racking experience.'[8] He particularly didn't like to have somebody like Palmer in his heyday breathing down his neck. Leading Palmer always gave him 'a very uncomfortable feeling'.[9] Said Gary, 'I'd rather be a stroke behind him than a stroke ahead of him.'

Player's more recent victims have included Seve Ballesteros (Tournament of Champions, 1978) from 7 in the lead on the final afternoon; Andy Bean, who led by 5 early in the last round at Woodlands, in the Houston Open; and all the people who choked at the 1978 Masters: altogether there were sixteen of them on the last round, and Player picked them off one by one with great relish. Most nourishing were Tom Watson, Rod Funseth of California and Hubert Green.

Watson 3-putted the 14th from 7 feet, but birdied the 15th and 16th to move to 11-under. Then, needing only par to tie, he hooked his drive into the trees at the 18th and finished with a bogey 5.

The more cautious Rod Funseth rolled a sensational 20-foot putt downhill that lipped the cup on the 18th. 'I didn't expect to be in it,' said he, 'so I'm not disappointed at being second.' Hubert Green, who started 7 strokes ahead of Player, 3-putted the 16th down the hill, and came to the last hole needing a birdie to tie. He was about to get it, too, for his second shot took him to within 3 feet of the flag. Player, who had disappeared into the clubhouse on 11-under to watch a TV monitor, stared at the set. Green addressed his 3-foot putt, but was suddenly disturbed by the sound of a radio commentator saying he needed this one to tie. He stepped away. Player looked on, without batting an eyelid. Green readdressed the 3-footer, stiffened his arms, and putted. A loud moan went up from the galleries. Player, in the clubhouse, turned to one side and punched the air with great violence. He was the 1978 Masters champion.

Golf naturally favours men like Gary Player, and naturally militates against men like Lee Trevino. Trevino – 'SuperMex' – has always been vulnerable to championship tension. He reckons he blew the 1970 British Open – 'I should have won dat. In 'seventy. I 3-putted five greens on the last day.' He works his tension off by incessant chatter to dissociate himself from the seriousness of his surroundings. By fooling around, Lee pretends he is 'just one of the guys', rather than a lone golfer on a green sea. His fervent following in the galleries – 'Lee's Fleas' – identify very strongly with him as their buddy on the course. There have been difficult phases in this relationship between Lee and the Fleas, but generally speaking, as long as he can maintain his involvement with 'the guys', stepping up occasionally to hit the ball, Lee does OK. Safety in numbers. As Nastase did in tennis, Trevino tends to incense his opponents with inane chatter and jokes when they are trying to concentrate, which has the effect of psyching them out. Tony Jacklin was a notable victim. Usually it is assumed by the press and the public that sportsmen do this deliberately. Sometimes they do. But more often, their opponents know that the hypertense comedian in their-midst is really trying to talk his way through a danger area. For many athletes under extreme pressure near the winning barrier, it becomes very important to make contact with somebody – any-body – so that they do not have to withstand all the tension on their own. So Nastase complained, and clowned and gesticulated, and Trevino tells his life story to anyone within earshot.

Like most players, Trevino won his first major title when some-body else took the gas. Like most players he had choked himself: weak iron-shots had let him down on one occasion, and his flat, do-it-yourself swing had attracted much criticism. In 1968 Trevino won the US Open. The man he won it *from* was Bert Yancey, an ex-West Point cadet who had spent almost a year in hospital recovering from a nervous breakdown. Yancey was a clever man, a thinker and a theorist on the mechanics of the swing. If there was one person on the course likely to be even more nervous than Lee Trevino, Yancey was him. Tony Jacklin, a personal friend, once remarked to him, 'It breaks my heart to see someone as good as you keep screwing up his game.' On the last day of that US Open, Yancey screwed up his game. His lead disappeared as he began missing short putts (on the 3rd and 5th). From the 10th he teed off into some trees. He 3-putted the 13th. By the end of the day he had given Trevino 7 shots to finish a miserable 6 behind. Trevino, who had faltered till now, seized his first Big One. In one stride he had moved from being a 30-dollar-a-week assistant club pro to being SuperMex, the champion with the weird swing. Yancey suffered another breakdown in 1975. He says he was diagnosed as 'manic-depressive', and prescribed lithium, which has more or less put paid to his golf because it causes his hands to shake.

There are many more recent examples of taking the gas. In the Masters, Tom Kite and Hale Irwin spring to mind in 1984; in 1985 it was Mr Chen, known as 'Mr TC', who blew it. In the (British) Open the list is endless because every year new names are added. Greg Norman of Australia; poor Bobby Clampett; South Africa's Nick Price; Australia's Ian Baker-Finch – all of them threw away last round leads and only Norman, who has admitted to choking the US Open too, has eventually come back to win it. Britain's golfers seem especially prone to the big occasion bellyflop. Wentworth golf fans in September 1985 went home with their umbrellas at half mast after Britain's heroes bombed out of the Suntory World Matchplay Championship. Sandy Lyle, reigning Open Champion, had been five up against South African Denis Watson only to lose two and one. His partner Ian Woosnam raced out in front of Seve Ballesteros and was four ahead after nine holes and looking all set. He lost by the same margin as his Ryder Cup team mate. Seve, much relieved, said politely, 'I was not playing well and was struggling, but Ian did not take his chances and did not putt well'. Some would say, 'He did not putt at all'.

Choking, or taking the gas, does not necessarily imply fear of winning, although this is often the case, since winning brings with it the threat of the unknown, as well as unforeseen responsibilities to continue winning, to fight off challengers, and to assume the role of hero or champion. As great a player as Palmer once suspected himself of such a fear. Palmer, in the mid 1960s, went through a slump that lasted almost three years. He began to wonder, as he says, 'if I was afraid to win'.[10] He started playing conservatively – he was now 36 – and by the autumn of 1965 he was 'totally unsure' of his game. At the start of 1966 in the LA Open he reached the last round as leader and had 'a sudden sense of fear'. He noted that he had begun trying to protect his lead by playing cautiously and just in time reverted to his old style of 'going for broke'. This was the beginning of a recovery and a run of success, though he says, 'It wasn't easy. I had to place all kinds of little disciplines on myself to keep from falling prey to Man's Natural Fear.'[11]

More often the case, when a player chokes, is that winning so tests a sportsman's nervous equilibrium that the smallest doubt or discrepancy will set up a vibration. Like the disused bell in Scrooge's room, it starts to ring, and sets off every bell in the house, and then Marley's ghost comes clanking up the stairs. Later on, we shall look at some of the methods being used by sports psychologists in the USA and the Communist bloc to prevent the original bell from ringing. For the moment, let us consider the case of A Very Conspicuous Choke at Foxhills.

Peter Dawson, from Yorkshire, in 1977, at Foxhills, took the gas. Neil Coles was the lucky man standing by to catch the £8000 first prize that Dawson threw up in the air, but it wasn't losing the money that really hurt. Dawson, at one point 6 strokes clear of the field, strode to the 18th with two to spare. And Coles, his nearest challenger, remarked, 'Once Peter had got past the 17th, I felt he was home and dry.'[12] Silly Coles.

Dawson sliced his drive into a ditch, then hit some trees, then landed in the rough behind an advertising board. The only obstacle with which Dawson's ball didn't come in contact was tournament director Tony Gray, who declared an immovable obstruction. After several more agonizing swings of Dawson's golf club, the ball finally landed in the hole – for a 79. It upset Dawson very much indeed, and in 1978 he resolved to prove that 'What happened at Foxhills didn't mean I was a blower.'[13] He started his campaign by arriving in Portugal with the wrong woods. His wife had to fly out with the correct ones. All his travel arrangements got mixed up. He missed the cut in the Spanish Open, and started having blinding head-aches. His eyesight went peculiar: he wondered why. Then he remembered he'd left his glasses behind. Finally, 'in a terrible state', he scratched from the French Open and came home.

To his enormous credit, and with the help of fellow-pro Norman Wood, Dawson is still trying to make a recovery: in any case, choking is not Dawson's problem, or even golf's. Choking is sport's problem, and the sooner it is seen as such, the sooner individual sportsmen can be saved the agony of thinking they are in some way mentally handicapped.

As we shall see, many players who earn themselves a reputation for choking, or who seem to be the victims of inexorable forces on the threshold of victory, are Thoroughbreds, reared by their parents with a view to sports stardom, and instilled with this purpose from a very early age.

Familiarity with success anxiety – 'choking', 'taking the gas', 'blowing the lead' and 'the elbow' – may help to clear up some of sport's long-standing mysteries.

Take F1 racing, for example. Consider the plight of the world's most 'unlucky' driver, Ulsterman John Watson. John, himself a Thoroughbred, has spent most of his career with one foot on the winner's podium and the other on a banana skin. Or consider another of motor racing's mysteries: whatever happened to James Hunt?

According to Lauda,[14] a racer's mind occasionally deceives him during the race, especially when he is leading and his attention is not focused by the effort of manoeuvring to the front. Says Niki, 'You keep close count of the laps that are left and keep a sharp ear tuned for strange sounds – you even think you hear sounds that do not exist. Then the race seems to last weeks.' He told author Ronnie Mutch that since you have nothing else to do but listen to your engine and watch the instruments, 'you must be careful not to get nervous and make a mistake.'[15] Some of James Hunt's experiences of leading have been rather more unpleasant. In his book, *Against All Odds*, Hunt frankly admits that leading made him sick. Literally. He describes the condition as 'a sort of release in tension, as though my body was physically loosening up, and although I was never actually sick, I was dry-retching. Whenever *I get a clear lead and am driving to finish* [my italics] as opposed to racing, the same thing happens.'[16] James attributed this feeling of nausea to muscular release after the pressure of racing. Naturally, the last thing a sportsman would suspect is that sickness might be caused by the imminence of victory. But as we have seen already, this is often the case. Let's look at a few other examples.

In 1973, in the Washington Star tennis tournament, unknown pro Steve Siegel took a set from Arthur Ashe and held him to 4–all in the second. Suddenly, he looked at the scoreboard, made a few wild mistakes, and rushed off court to be sick behind the stands. In 1978 in the Alan King Classic, Italian Corrado Barazzutti unexpectedly reached the final against Harold Solomon and mid-way through the second set, turned white as a sheet. He bent over double with stomach pains, defaulted, and tore off to the locker room. In the 1978 French Open, Briton Buster Mottram, at set-all in his match with Christopher Roger-Vasselin, staggered over to a linesman's empty chair. Ashen-faced, he sat holding his stomach. He had done this before in an early-round Wimbledon match in 1976, and retired with nausea and dizziness: he did it again – twice – in the French Open in 1979. It is not unheard of for a player to throw up in his towel during an important tennis match. Poor Arthur Ashe has done so; Vilas has more than once withdrawn with nervous dyspepsia, and so has Nastase – he was given (quite wrongly, according to a doctor I consulted), benzedrine and on one occasion a sedative.[17] Golfers have always been plagued with stomach disorders during the heat of competition. Bobby Jones, who suffered from lapses of concentration when he was in the lead, admitted that collapsing from winning positions was his Achilles' heel. He was not helped in this awful affliction by recurrent digestive illness. A number of prominent golfers have suffered in this way. The Tour patois for someone with golfing stomach is 'a grinder'. In athletics, stomach-ache causes hearth-ache too. Alan Pascoe, then reigning champion, was knocked out in the first round of the 400 m hurdle event in the 1978 European championships in Prague. Throughout the year, Pascoe had been plagued by a stomach complaint in almost every race, and was making his last appearance in a major event. He said, 'It is the first time in my life that I have felt I have let down myself and other people.'[18] He failed to make the semi-finals even as one of the four fastest losers: it was a major shock to athletic pundits.

F1 racing is particularly harsh on the digestive system. Rupert Keegan went off in practice for the 1978 Grand Prix in South Africa and damaged a wheel. He had felt sick, with severe stomach cramps. The year before in Spain, Frenchman Jean-Pierre Jarier had to keep getting out of his car to be sick over the pit counter. James Hunt felt queasy while he was leading to the chequered flag in the 1976 French Grand Prix. He said, 'Something I had eaten had upset me and I was sick in the car with about twelve laps to go.'[19] In Argentina in 1977 he was sick because he forgot his salt tablets and drank saline solution. 'It really screwed up my stomach,' said James.[20] In Brazil, it was a 'Brazilian gremlin'.[21] In France 1977 he had apparently 'been ill all week' but suffered particularly from stomach cramps in the closing stages. In 1978 he was ill again in France, and in Spain, where he had lost the lead to Andretti, he was so weak that he had to be lifted from the car at the end of the race. The McLaren team tried various methods of dealing with the problem, none very satisfactory – perhaps because they were treating a symptom rather than the disease. They experimented with bottles of fruit juice rigged up in the cockpit, with tubes feeding into the driver's mouth so that whenever he felt sick, he could suck the tube. This certainly made a difference. James went into the pits on the Nürburgring covered with half a pint of orange juice. Keke Rosberg, who won the Championship in 1982, got this drink tube business down to a fine art. His was activated by an electric switch connected to the red light. No one was going to say of Keke that *he* was sick as a parrot.

But how could Hunt's sickness have had anything to do with success anxiety, when in 1976 he won the World Championship? Surely no one with 'winner's stomach' could have done such a thing. In all probability, no one with winner's stomach *could* have done it, had he known he was going to win. James never knew. At no point did he believe he was going to be World Champion until after the last race of the season. He got out of the car at the end of that decisive Grand Prix at Mount Fuji, ready to harangue team manager Teddy Mayer for not calling him in for a tyre change, and thus wrecking his chances. James had to take that decision himself, by which time he was in desperate trouble. And he was quite convinced he'd blown it. Even when they put him on the third place stand on the winners' rostrum (giving him the points he needed to finish ahead of Lauda) James was highly suspicious that there had been a mistake; he refused to believe he'd won the Championship until he saw it in writing. 'I wanted proof,' he says. After the critical tyre change in that decisive race, James had come out of the pits in a seething temper, convinced that all was lost. He charged past everything in sight, and he could not tell, from the rather confusing pit signals, whether he was running 5th, 6th or 3rd. Arguably, had he known his real position – and that he was charging right at the title – his digestive system might well have mutinied. As it was, James was unable to keep down the soft drink given to him at the post-race press conference.

Shortly before this, at Watkins Glen, he had suddenly found himself 'driving like an old grandmother'.[22] He pulled himself together in the nick of time. Kenny Roberts, the American 1978 World Champion motor-cyclist, rode to the title on the Nürburgring, clinching it, like Hunt, with a third, ahead of Barry Sheene. Afterwards, Roberts told reporters, 'I will never forget the last lap. I felt like an old lady making sure of getting over the finishing line.' He added, 'That was the most nervous race of my life.'[23]

As for the Championship itself, Hunt found it 'a heavy deal'. He hated the victory ceremony, the pomp, the circumstance, and everything that went with it. His mother freaked out in front of reporters, and James was pulled about and exhibited like a prize bull. 'Everybody is gunning for you if you are on top, and the massive invasion of privacy is worse than being at school. My personal freedom is something I had worked for so long, and it seemed that just as I was getting it, it was sort of removed. . . .'[24]

Before he won in 1976, Hunt said that he was anxious to take the World Championship, but that he wanted to do it quickly, so that he would not be too long at risk.[25] He has always been perfectly frank about his fear of death. 'It's not *how*, it's the fact that I'm afraid of,' he said in an interview for the TV documentary *Havoc*. The same man who plunged into the flames to haul out Ronnie Peterson in a vain attempt to save his life at Monza also suffers *Angst* spirals, not in the racing car, but when he is relaxing at home. He has become, as he puts it, 'highly chicken about everything'.[26] Under the circumstances, his fall from grace in 1977 and subsequent loss of winning form, despite his acknowledged speed on the track and pole positions throughout 1977, may be easier to understand. So indeed may the much-publicized punch-ups with officials and marshals on the circuit, and the major sulk in Japan at the presentation ceremony: it was the anniversary of his original 'coronation' at the same Grand Prix the previous year.

It is important for us to understand Hunt's predicament: he is typical of prominent sportsmen who have been blown to hell in the win tunnel. Going through the winning barrier for the first time was very important and memorable for Hunt, because it was so hard. Here he describes that breakthrough at Zandvoort in June 1975: 'It was run and won under the most extreme pressure from behind. Hitherto my most obvious weakness had been in leading races and running under pressure. I simply had no experience of doing it. If I sat down in a room and talked about it, I could analyse it, but taking it with you on the track is another thing. . . . Crossing the line first at Zandvoort improved my driving more than anything. . . .'[27]

James's 'unaccountable lapses' when leading and being sure of victory had always puzzled Bubbles Horsley, his team manager at Hesketh Racing. 'It was irritating to say the least,' said he. 'Argentine '75, eighteen laps left and in front of Fittipaldi – he just lost concentration and spun. He went out in the first lap of the '74

Argentina and spun. Led the 1975 Spanish Grand Prix and spun. He always admitted it,' Bubbles explained.[28] 'He couldn't say anything else, could he? Spun the bleeding car, hadn't he?' Perhaps followers of sport in general, and motor racing in particular, might pause for a moment to consider how hard it is *not* to spin the bleeding car when one is about to throw up inside a helmet at 180 m.p.h. Perhaps racers who win anything under these circumstances, let alone a World Championship, deserve more praise and respect than they have ever received.

But choking Grand Prix leads is not a habit confined to any one racer. Niki Lauda's 1974 season went down in Ferrari history as the Year of the Very Nearlies, and ended, as already described, with Lauda visiting a well-known sports guru. When Niki stood on the threshold of the 1975 title victory, a number of racers firmly believed he would falter where 'he cracked up last time' and said as much to journalist Keith Botsford.[29] In 1976, when Hunt won by the skin of his nose, it was partly because his chief rival Lauda had retired after one and a half laps in the rain in the final race, remembering his horrific accident after one and a half laps in the rain (on the Ring) some weeks previously. In 1982 Keke Rosberg, sucking his drink tube, closed out the Championship against the 'unluckiest man in racing' – Ulsterman John Watson. In the last race Watson slowed with 'tyre vibration' having fought his way up to 2nd place behind Michele Alboreto to finish just out of the points needed in the Championship table. Rosberg, for his part, drove a 'failsafe' race, needing only to finish in the first six. He said afterwards, 'I had a bad pain in my right foot half distance onwards, but that was nothing compared with the need to keep going. The last few laps were mentally very exhausting, the hardest laps I have ever driven. I just couldn't believe my emotions on the slow-down lap'. Even finishing in the first six was no cakewalk, yet this was Keke Rosberg, one of the most fearless and forceful racers of recent years. Compare his reaction on the home stretch with that of jockey Brian Taylor, about to win the Derby. Said Brian, 'We got to the furlong marker and my legs gave out completely because I began to believe I was going to win'.

F1 chief Bernie Ecclestone told me about the phenomenon of racers who can go superbly fast in unofficial practice or when it doesn't count, and yet end up on the back of the grid on race day. Tantalizing. There is exactly the same phenomenon in horse racing. Horse–jockey combinations that can go faster than the Lone

Ranger when it is too early, or too late, are called, in American stables at least, 'morning glories'. They are not very popular.[30]

A conspicuous case of gas-taking occurred in snooker in 1985. Poor Willie Thorne, leading 13–8 in the 1985 Coral UK Championship against Steve Davis, missed a blue and went to pot. Even Barry Hearn said Davis had never come from behind quite like that before. Again, in the Masters quarter-final, Thorne appeared to be replying to Davis's 61 with a match-winning clearance in the deciding frame when he got out of position on the blue and missed the pink. He said, 'I don't know how many times getting on the wrong side of the blue is going to cost me a match.' Unfortunately there is more to winning snooker championships than sheer talent – which Thorne possesses to a remarkable degree.

Even boxers can take the gas. American Bernard Taylor, a clear leader after five rounds of his much-publicised fight with WBA featherweight champion Barry McGuigan, sank onto his stool at the end of the eighth, patted his stomach and refused to go out again. He said, 'I couldn't get my breath, it was the heat'. Unbeaten in 34 previous fights and with all America watching on TV, Taylor wandered about for five minutes and then sank to his knees. He had failed in his other big fights, in the 1976 American Olympic trials and his previous world title challenge against Eusebio Pedroza. A lesser opponent than McGuigan would have made his latest fiasco more conspicuous, yet no one would deny Taylor's talent.

In team sports the responsibility for winning is dispersed over a wide area, although anxiety about the win-barrier may indeed be shared by a whole team. Many teams with outstanding seasons have faltered in the middle of championships or been unaccountably 'unlucky' in the crucial match. In American football, teams who regularly storm through the season and the play-offs and then flounder in the super Bowl are called 'bridesmaids'; the Minnesota Vikings are a notable example. The Vikes reached Super Bowl IV and were skunked by Kansas City 23–7. Ah well, they would do it next time. Super Bowl VIII came along. The Vikes' quarterback, Fran Tarkenton, has broken every record in the game, and Super Bowl VIII was no exception. Leading Minnesota to nineteen victories in 1973, he now completed eighteen of twenty-eight passes in the big game itself, only to see the Vikes crushed by Miami in their most humiliating defeat of the year. The following season, the Vikings met the 'losingest team in the NFL' at that time, Pittsburgh, in Super Bowl IX. Another disaster. They met the

Oakland Raiders in Super Bowl XI. Oakland had known some bad luck themselves: they too had been labelled bridesmaids, and their quarterback Ken Stabler remembers, 'Some of our guys got up so high that they vomited before the game.' They needn't have worried. The Vikings, having come all the way through their Division title and two play-offs, did it again. By now they were on the mature side of 30, a lot of them, and their defeats in the Big Ones had become boring to the press. The Vikes had a monkey on their backs.

In baseball, there was another famous case: the Dodgers. The old Brooklyn Dodgers of the 1950s narrowly lost pennant races and were labelled 'chokers'. Dick Young of the *Dail News* blamed the pitchers and after one particular game in 1948 let them have it. 'The tree that grows in Brooklyn is an apple tree and the apples are in the throats of the Dodgers,' he wrote: Adam's apples make for difficult swallowing. During the early 1950s the players became the subject of crushing abuse and obscene jokes about their manhood. They were said to 'choke up on the big ones', yet the Brooklyn Dodgers' personnel individually ranked with the very best in the game. More recently, the Dodgers, now the Los Angeles Dodgers, suffered a similar fate, crashing to defeat in the World Series at the hands of the Yankees at Dodger Stadium. Afterwards, pitcher Don Sutton sat crying in the locker-room. He had been playing for thirteen years, and at 33 he couldn't expect to have too many more shots at the famous brass rings. 'I've been here three times before, and I might never be here again. It's tough enough to repeat once, let alone twice. If anybody can, we can. I can't help but think how fortunate I am to have been here four times, and I'd be pressing my luck to think about another World Series. Just once I wanna win it all. Just once.'[31] Team-mate Davey Lopes said, 'There's a lot of people gonna label us chokers.'[32] He is probably right. Losing the big ones has never been viewed with great public sympathy, for sports spectators are very watchful in this matter of handling pressure, and often very cruel.

In England, in county cricket, both Essex and Somerset used to be pipped at the post in conspicuously important matches: up to 1979 they were the only teams never to have won anything, yet they had the talent, as later events were to show. Poor Essex in particular earned the soubriquet 'unlucky'. Were they 'unlucky', or did they choke? It is not difficult for the more nervous members of a team to communicate their panic to everyone else in the dressing-room, though nobody truly knows what happens on the threshold of victory, other than the sportsmen themselves. And they are not usually eager to discuss it, for fear of being misunderstood.

Cricketers are certainly capable of 'taking the gas', on the verge of important achievements. As we have seen, batsmen may suffer anguish as the coveted century looms on the scoreboard, and one at least has come perilously close to nervous breakdown. Trevor Bailey would never look at the scoreboard when he neared the magic three figures. Neither does Clive Radley. Mike Brearley continued as England skipper without a Test century to his name, and many batsmen become noticeably foolish as they approach their maiden first-class hundred or their first century in Tests. Even Somerset all-rounder Ian Botham, who stirred the hearts of cricketers everywhere during 1978 with his power and poise, ran out Bob Taylor in Christchurch, New Zealand, in his maiden passage to 100, after spending half an hour on 99. For once, 'Goldenballs' had done something wrong.

Older hands at getting 100s are sometimes beset with difficulty at other symbolic milestones: one J. B. Hobbs, Knight of the Realm, travelled the country for what seemed an eternity looking for his 126th century so as to pass Grace's record of 125 (he finally made it at Taunton). And one J.H. Edrich endured a similar hiatus before scoring his 100th first-class 100. After his umpteenth unsuccessful attempt in a Surrey v. Warwicks match at the Oval, Edrich told Alex Bannister, 'I wouldn't have believed it at this stage of my career, but I feel tense.'

Bowlers may suffer, too, as they approach personal milestones. 300 Test wickets, for example. At this fence, even the great Trueman refused. It happened, of all places, at Headingley. This is Fred's description of that black occasion: 'Eight wickets to go and three more matches to play – I felt nothing could stop me. The next was in front of my own people at Headingley and I would have given a lot to achieve the "impossible" in front of them. But it turned out to be a totally frustrating experience and, according to some experts, the worst Test match I ever played. But they don't know what was going on at the wicket. I blame Ted Dexter, the skipper, for what happened. He gave the impression he knew more about bowling than me. . . .'[33]

Fred's biographer John Arlott does not apportion blame, but recounts the disaster as follows: 'England were in a dominant position. At 187 the new ball became available and . . . Dexter took it, and gave it to Trueman and Flavell to finish off the innings, as Trueman at his best would certainly have done. Instead he sacrificed the match to his theory that Burge was an uncertain hooker. On a fast wicket he might have proved it: here he was discredited. He loosened up and took the new ball against Hawke who scored a single. Then came this incredible series of medium-paced long hops which rose in a simple arc and, in what must have seemed like a bowler's nightmare, Burge – always happier against pace than spin – hooked him with murderous ease.'[34]

Dexter eventually took Trueman off, but by then the damage had been done. Australia went on to amass 389 and Burge a match winning 160. The match, and as it turned out the rubber, had been decided. Arlott remembers an elder Yorkshire player shaking his head in sad disbelief. 'Trueman bowled bad,' he said: 'a Yorkshireman can offer no sterner condemnation.' Frederick was dropped for the following Test, and at the Oval he bowled 26 overs for 80 runs and no wicket before eventually, in a fit of pique or profound wrath, he at last took his 300th wicket, along with his 299th, 298th, and several others of lesser significance. No one in his right mind would ever have accused Fred of success phobia or success anxiety – no one at least who did not relish the thought of bodily mutilation. But the fact remains that of all the invisible barriers in sport, 300 Test wickets was the one that hurt the performance of Fred Trueman.

It is a sad reflection on all of us if we do not realize how hard it is for professional athletes to go through sport's psychological sound barriers. And an even sadder reflection if we do realize, and yet persist in criticizing those who perish in the attempt. Before steps can be taken to help success-anxious athletes or sportsmen who choke in *any* sport, it is important that choking be recognized as a real problem, both collectively, by the sports media and public, and individually, by the sportsmen themselves. Without this recognition sportsmen will continue to be criticized, and to criticize themselves, for falling victim to the pressures of high-level competition. Worse still, sportsmen will always be obliged, as they are now, to lie to themselves and to the press about their experiences on the threshold of winning. Until the public understand the nature of such experiences, they can never fully appreciate the extraordinary courage of athletes who win, or the anguish and fear and heartbreak of athletes who throw victory away.

7

The Mediums

Many sportsmen are admittedly attracted to spectator sport by the prize money, but there is something else too. As Australian fast bowler Dennis Lillee once remarked, 'There must be easier ways to earn a living.' Few sportsmen, however mercenary or mundane, stay in the pressure cooker of professional sport for the external rewards *alone* – for the trophies, the money, the adulation. Great though these may appear to the outsider, they in no way recompense the sportsman for the price he pays to sport – and he pays dearly, both with his body and his mind. Many athletes publicly festooned with goodies are hostile to this 'bargain', and despise for the rest of their lives the fans, the press, the sponsors and administrators for having had a hand in it.

Yet such is the fascination of sport that even the most hard-bitten and disillusioned professional rarely lets slip the chance of another spell in the high-pressure chambers of sport experiments, even though he may realize what it involves. Why? Why are there always subjects available for this sometimes callous public study of men under stress? Why do they come back for more? The answer is simply that sport, like war and other dire emergencies, calls forth qualities in a man of which he would be otherwise unaware, and which he greatly values. Sport enables him, by its very pressures, to transcend himself, to become more than he thought he could be, and even to become – according to some revelations – someone or something *else*.

Every once in a while, a sportsman suddenly produces a glittering display which comes as a shock, not only to the spectators, but to himself. A genuinely stunning performance. A *tour de force*. If he consciously tries to reproduce it, he cannot. It comes and it goes, like a mystical experience, and each time it happens, the sportsman feels himself to be truly alive, truly exhilarated. There is an odd, even chilling sense of having been possessed, or of having dreamt the whole thing, of having been in another world. Sport's 'peak experiences'[1] lure the athlete back again and again, in spite of all disappointment and injury, and whether or not he ever actually 'wins'. When a sportsman talks of loving his sport, he is invariably casting his mind back to some such other-worldly performance. Indeed, we could call it 'ecstasy', for it seems to happen outside the self. The great Nijinsky (the dancer Vaslav, not the horse) was once interviewed by a psychiatrist, Nandor Fodor, about his dancing.[2] Apparently Nijinsky's wife once remarked to the Russian, 'What a shame you can never see yourself dance,' to which he replied, 'I do! Always. I am outside. I make myself dance from the outside.' Interestingly, Nijinsky, who had studied yoga, was also a competent automatic writer: he could apparently act as a medium, that is to say, for another intelligence. Sportsmen, too, are 'mediums', waiting for their skill to take possession of them; waiting to act, as it were 'from outside'. As Nature took the pen from Wordsworth's hand and wrote, so it takes rackets, bats, balls and clubs from the hands of sportsmen – and plays. Said Arthur Ashe: 'I thought *I* was playing unconscious, but Borg beat me 6–4 7–6 tonight, and he is in what we call *the zone*. . . . He has no concept of what he is doing out there – he is just swinging away and the balls are dropping in.'[3]

Tennis players are the most forward in discussing their experiences as 'mediums'. 'Playing unconscious', and 'in the zone' are part of the Tour patois, as is the phrase, playing or being 'spacey', thought to have been coined originally by Chris Lloyd, and meaning on the court but out of this world. A 'no-brainer' is the summit of stroke-making. The two best-selling tennis books in history, *The Inner Game of Tennis*, and *Inner Tennis: Playing the Game*,[4] both by Tim Gallwey, are instructional programmes for playing tennis in this ecstatic way. Gallwey's influence on the sport in the US has been nothing short of staggering, if a little confusing to those trying to use the method for winning matches.

There are similar 'ecstatic' moments in golf: 'If you're on a high, even before you select the club, you can see the shot. It's *there*. And then you pick your club and reproduce it. It's almost scary. It *is* a bit scarey – or it was to me' (Golf writer Chris Plumridge).

Golfers call their own mediumship 'playing out of your skin' or 'playing like God's professional'. They freely admit that it is not something they can control, although many have tried. They talk of their 'visions' of perfect shots. Arnie Palmer: 'But something else happened that is harder to explain – and yet is vital to continued great play whenever trouble looms. That something was visual, not intellectual; I could literally *see* the shot that had to be made.'[5]

More of such golfing visions later. What about athletics?

Commentating on a 200-metre race, poor Ron Pickering, who is sometimes apt to get carried away, looked at the action replay and said, 'This is where Ainsley Bennett's legs didn't belong to him'. Who did they belong to? Donna Hartley? Harry Carpenter? Fortunately viewers knew what he meant: it has long been recognized that it is possible to get a 'high' from running. Usually this is attributed to hyper-ventilation or lactic acid levels in the blood-stream, but perhaps there is a psychic experience, as well as a physiological one: 'My thin shirt clung to me, and I felt like a skeleton flying down a wind tunnel. My times at the mile and two miles were so fast that I almost felt I was cheating, or had taken some unfair advantage. It was like getting a new body that no one else had heard about. My mind was so crystal clear I could have held a conversation.'[6]

Cricketers are always having weird experiences (apart from being interviewed by the author). David Bairstow, Yorkshire skipper and wicket-keeper: 'I remember stumping Mike Brearley off Dick Hutton at Lord's and I didn't really know I had the ball. I just felt it hit the gloves and appealed, and when he was given out I said to myself, "What on earth am I doing here?" '[7]

Colin Cowdrey remembered producing one of his best performances when he had been feeling under the weather and had no apparent control over the outcome: '. . . Suddenly, after two or three shots, the ball was bulleting off the middle of the bat and I was launched into as fine a piece of batting as I have ever been able to produce. . . . Occasionally it frightens me to have no control over it, particularly in more recent years when people [have] said, "You are the best player in England now. You should be 400 runs ahead of everyone else in the country and 15 runs clear of anyone in the averages." Sometimes, after a remark like that, I have tried to work for runs. The approach has lasted for three or four days. Playing cricket like that gives me no pleasure whatsoever.'[8]

There is a distinct difference between between batsmen who rely on conscious intelligence and those who bat largely by instinct. The former is sometimes referred to as a 'grafter'. The latter is said to have 'all the time in the world' to play his shots. Gary Sobers, Barry Richards and the on-form David Gower have belonged to this élite, for whom runs just seem to 'happen'. But when Viv Richards says, after his third double century in a season, 'It just comes natural', what exactly is the 'it' that 'just comes'?

Research in the Communist bloc[9] using highly sophisticated versions of the electroencephalograph (EEG) or electromyograph (EMG), and research in the USA on the physiology of the brain and spinal column (for example at the Langley-Porter Neuropsychiatric Institute) has produced clinical evidence for the existence of two distinct kinds of consciousness. One has to do with what we could call 'rational' and reflective thinking, logic, speech, sequential thought and analysis. The other is concerned with imagination, intuition, spontaneous creativity, the production of images, and association. These two faculties of the brain – let us call them 'B' and 'A' – have always been distinguished in philosophy and literature.

John Locke, and his followers in the eighteenth century, shunned 'A' – imagination and association – as a faculty inducing madness, and the Age of Reason held rationality, or 'B', to be the only worthwhile activity of the human mind. 'A' at this time was thought to be the province of lunatics and 'enthusiasts' as religious people who claimed to be inspired were called. The nineteenth-century Romantics took the opposite view. 'A', or imagination – 'the Associative Faculty' as Coleridge called it – was regarded with reverence and awe. The Romantics claimed quite fairly that 'A' was the fount of creativity; the images of poetry and art were all produced by 'A'. They pointed to the philosophical writings of Kant and Reid which said that there was more to human knowledge than could be apprehended by reason alone. By the light of mere 'B', the human race would never know where it was. So in the nineteenth century 'B' was flung out, and 'A' was the common pursuit. If you wrote, or painted, or acted, or did anything worthwhile, you did it under the influence of 'A'. The Victorians floundered unhappily between the two mental disciplines: 'B' was probably right, they thought, but it got in the way of anything one wanted to do. Constraints on spontaneity were a great worry to the Victorians, which is why Carlyle propounded his Theory of Antiselfconsciousness and John Stuart Mill, whose analytical training caused him to have a nervous breakdown, wrote sadly that 'self-consciousness' was 'that daemon of the men of genius of our time'. Thomas Hardy, who likewise loathed his 'B' but couldn't get rid of it, complained that 'thought is a disease of the flesh' and 'the ache of modernism'. Compare this with Mike Brearley's comment that '. . . unless you're a genius like Compton, you don't go out and bat without *thinking what you are going to do next* [my italics]. The number of times a player like me gets to that moment is very rare indeed. If I could trust my body, and let my body go, I would do better.'[10]

Baseball's Yogi Berra once remarked, 'Ya can't tink n' hit at da same time,' and there has always been a 'no-think' school of batters in baseball who would agree with him.

Compare Arthur Ashe's insight into why Britain's own Mark Cox never really fulfilled his potential on the tennis court: 'But Marcus is something like me in that he thinks too much. . . . If Cox got beat, he started analysing why. . . . I have the same kind of problem. My mind has gotten in my way all along.'[11]

Or consider Jackie Stewart's opinion as to where F1 racer Brett Lunger went wrong: 'He is a thinker, but maybe he thinks too much. Too calculating. He should put more effort into physically driving the car than trying to rationalize what he's doing.'[12] Matthew Arnold, Carlyle, Mill, Thomas Hardy – almost the whole Victorian age – felt the same sort of difficulty. So then along came Dr Freud with a revolutionary new theory about 'A' and 'B'. 'B' or rational intelligence, he said, was taken care of by the 'conscious mind', and 'A' – imagination, intuition, association – was the province of the 'unconscious'. These last two terms, 'conscious' and 'unconscious', we are now rather lumbered with, though Freud himself would have been the first to admit they are often unsuitable. Sportsmen tend to use them willy-nilly. A tennis player who comes off court and says he was 'playing unconscious' just means that he has been using his 'A'. When An Olympic skater complains that she is 'too conscious, too thinky', she doesn't mean she has been sitting on her behind on the ice reading Hegel's *Phenomenology*; merely that she has been using her 'B'. When she should have been using her 'A'.

Simple.

Many sportsmen, mercifully eschewing Freud, have their own words for 'A' and 'B' consciousness, which sum up the difference with refreshing clarity. They call 'A' concentration, focusing, or getting it together. 'B' they call being too thinky, or going to pieces or breaking up (or down). We could, according to sportsmen's descriptions of their experiences, think of 'A' and 'B' in terms of mental physics: fusion and fission; like this:

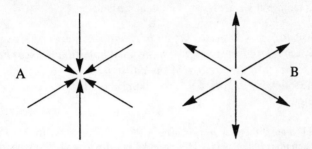

If a player says he is 'together' out there, or if he says 'I became very concentrated, and the shots just seemed to flow out of me' (as John Newcombe did after the 1973 Davis Cup final against Stan Smith), he is referring to the 'A' diagram. In tennis, 'he broke me and then ran through me' means he broke my serve and then won the match, but it also means what it says. To 'break him up' means to get him guessing. To 'fall apart' is to lose. When a sportsman comes apart in front of our eyes, it is invariably because he has fallen to pieces in his head. We say his concentration has gone, and if the meaning of 'concentration' is considered – it refers to condensing, compressing, coming together, fusing and crystallizing – the diagrams above make good sense. Association ('A', the Associative Faculty) and analysis ('B' or rational thought) have always implied joining together and breaking down into component parts, respectively.

So as to familiarize the reader with the 'A' and 'B' concepts and enable him to distinguish between them when sportsmen are talking, we might take a few examples. Let's start with an easy one, a few years ago, from Nastase:

Everyone keeps telling me I'm 31 and now I start to worry about my strokes. Now I'm thinking twice and three times before I hit each shot. Before I just used to play and everything came naturally.[13]

Translation: everyone keeps telling me I'm 31 and now I start using 'B'. Before I used 'A'. How about this:

With that, the club theorist moves off, leaving us to ponder his words. When he is well out of sight we try and adopt his suggestions and, of course, as soon as we do this we are done for – doubt enters our minds and we end up with the most appalling slice or half-shank. Yet another victory in the cause of science and analysis. What is needed to combat this obsession with science is a return to the natural way of doing things. Think what would happen if we analysed our eating methods. . . .[14]

Translation: With that, the club 'B' thinker moves off, leaving us to our 'B', and we end up with the most appalling slice or half-shank. Yet another victory in the cause of 'B'.

The following is Tony Jacklin, talking about his good buddy Bert Yancey:

He is a great theorist and lectures at PGA schools and universities on the mechanics of the swing. This great knowledge of what really happens during the stroke sometimes affects his game. He is always experimenting and working on new ideas, and gets bogged down by theory. On a practice day before the Crosby I remember him saying, 'Tony, what do you think of this?' I said, 'For God's sake, Bert, just go out there and play. It breaks my heart to see someone as good as you keep screwing up his game.'[15]

There is an unfortunate codicil to this, as we have seen, for Yancey became one of sport's many casualties to pressure and illness. Jacklin is pointing out to him here that 'B' is doing his game, and perhaps his head, an awful lot of harm. Compare the case of an 'A' player, who has used visualization to pull down major titles, Gary Player:

My concentration was so intense that at times it seemed as if I were in a trance. In fact, this was true throughout the entire tournament. For example, one time while on the practice tee, I was so deep in concentration that when Jack Nicklaus walked up I asked him how he'd done and was amazed when he replied that he hadn't even been out on the course yet.[16]

Translation: My 'A' was so intense I never knew Jack Nicklaus wasn't there.

In cricket, a fast bowler's success will depend very largely on his ability to keep his rhythm during his run-up and delivery, and stay in 'A'. If he starts thinking what he's doing, the rhythm disappears and no amount of 'B' will get it back in shape. Consequently, many

Even 'Beefy' succumbed
to the pressure
eventually

Ivan Lendl used to be called
chicken over major finals

John McEnroe demonstrating
the 'choke'

Nastase. Took a nose dive in his dream final

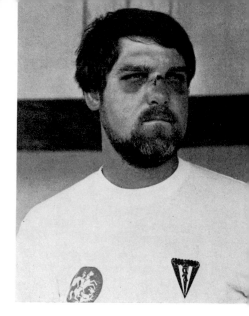

Mike Gatting saved from a worse catastrophe by wearing a helmet

Boycott. The scalp most prized

Viv Richards – a suitable case for
treatment. Here he exhibits
sporting stomach

1982 World champion Keke Rosberg had difficulty on the home stretch

Kirk Stevens – drugs in high pressure sport have claimed notable victims

A genius in his own right

Johnny Owen – an accident at work

Barry McGuigan and Bernard Taylor v. Bernard Taylor

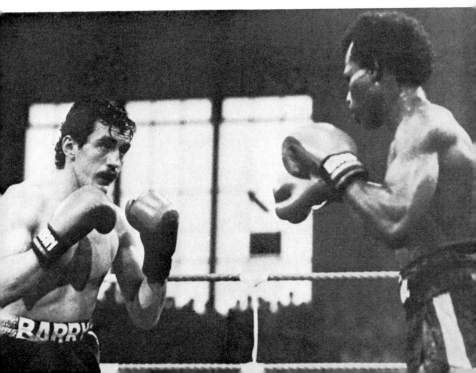

J.P.R., face stitched, rejoins needle match US football. A savage business

Pressure cooker, extra large

John Wile, shedding blood for West Bromwich Albion

Soccer violence. Part of the game?

Tony Jacklin. The face of despair

Doug Sanders. Unkindest putt of all

Bernhard Langer – a case of the yips

Seve Ballesteros uses self-hypnosis
especially for putting

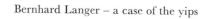

fast bowlers focus their minds on a particular spot as they begin their run-up and just think, as New Zealand's Richard Hadlee says, 'smooth': 'What I try to do is think aggression. Think smooth. When I know I've got the rhythm, I know also I'm going to be dangerous.'[17]

When Bob Willis was about to take wickets, his run-up became smooth as silk. 'Yes,' he told me, 'I wish it could always be like that.' Unfortunately, as soon as a bowler starts thinking about doing something special, he becomes conscious and rational again. Dennis Lillee described a high-speed photosonic camera test of fast bowlers in Australia: 'An interesting sidelight occurred when one of the bowlers, who had been regularly recorded at speeds around 145 Km/h. (90 m.p.h.), gave a pre-arranged signal to the cameramen that he was going to "let one fly". The ball was actually the slowest of the over.'[18]

Batsmen need to stay in 'A' too. The late Ken Barrington tells us how not to think when you're at the crease:

When you're playing well you don't think about *anything* and run-making comes naturally. When you're out of form you're conscious of needing to do things right, so you have to think first and act second. To make runs under those conditions is mighty difficult.[19]

Translation: when you're playing well you're in 'A'. When you're out of form, you're in 'B'.

Figure-skating champion Linda Fratianne's coach was concerned that she should become an artist, rather than 'remain a brilliant technician'. Linda says, 'Sometimes I get too thinky. I don't skate as free as I can.'[20] She has since turned pro and joined an ice skating revue.

South American cavalry schools teach the rider not to look at the jump or interfere with the horse's movements, because this makes the horse conscious ('B') that he is about to do something out of the ordinary. The great show-jumper and trainer Count Toptani describes how riders who have previously jumped in the old-fashioned hunting saddle are difficult to teach because they communicate their nervousness about the jump to their horses. 'My advice to such riders,' says the Count, 'is never look at the first jump, but always at the last.'[21] The horse is a highly intelligent creature, and if the rider gives it 'the feeling that it is doing anything unusual', the horse will rear or become skittish. Rider and horse are a very good analogy of the sportsman's 'B' and 'A'. Whenever 'B' starts to interfere with 'A', it will falter: 'Never punish it or call it to attention if it stumbles over the poles and knocks them down – this will only make it conscious that something unusual is being demanded of it. Let it carry on as before and you will see that the next jump it will hop over with a foot to spare.'

This is all very fine, the reader may think, but is there really any scientific basis for talking about 'A' and 'B'? If we put a sportsman in a laboratory and run a series of tests on his brain, is there any evidence of these two faculties? Even supposing they are there (which looks very speculative, with all this 'A' and 'B' mumbo-jumbo), is there, after all, anything he can do about them?

Indeed there is. On an electroencephalograph, an instrument for measuring and recording brainwave frequencies, different frequencies have been found to correspond to different states of mind. Pioneers in electro-neurology acquainted with the differing functions of the brain's left and right hemispheres have discovered that the higher frequencies – 14 Hz and upwards – correspond very closely with the mental activities of our 'B', or conscious, rational intelligence. The Mexican founder of brainwave training in the West, José Silva, calls this 'outer consciousness'. These higher frequencies are signified by the notation β, or beta, conveniently the Greek 'B'. The middle range frequencies – 8–13 Hz, or 7–14 according to Silva – are signified by the notation α, or alpha, the Greek 'A'. Alpha frequencies have occupied the minds of scientists in America and Russia since the turn of the century, because yogis and initiates in the oriental disciplines were found to generate alpha on the EEG, and to have apparent control over its generation. José Silva calls the alpha range 'inner consciousness'. It corresponds to our 'A'. (Lower levels, delta and theta, correspond to slumber and deep sleep, but may also register in certain states of trance and meditation.)

When we are wide awake, conscious of everything around us and conscious of ourselves, when we are thinking rationally and intelligently of a thousand everyday things and analysing and distinguishing between them, our brains are firing beta – 14 Hz and upwards. When we are in a meditative state, or a state of relaxed awareness, our brains are firing alpha. We produce alpha rhythms before we fall asleep and we produce them in the shallow levels of sleep when we are dreaming. Simply by closing our eyes and focusing inwards, we start to register alpha waves on the electro-encephalograph.

In alpha frequencies our faculty for producing images – imagination – is enhanced, taking over from the more rational and sequential habits of everyday thought. Leaving analysis and logic aside, we sink into an associative state in which we are not very conscious of judgement or reason, or conscious of ourselves. We become 'inspired'. Streams of ideas and images not logically related begin to flow through our minds. We are relaxed and yet aware. Brain-waves in the alpha range register a very high degree of synchrony. Interestingly, if our lives are threatened it is to this level that we go: the middle of the alpha range, or 10.5 Hz. This is the most synchronized of all the brain's wave-rhythms. (Synchrony or coming together may remind the reader of our diagram for 'A', with the arrows pointing inwards.)

Interesting, too, are discoveries in Russia and the Eastern bloc by pure scientists and parapsychologists (there are no 'psychologists' as such in Russia) that the alpha range is associated with the so-called para-normal faculties of mind – telepathy,[22] precognition, PK or psychokinesis, 'psi', 'higher intelligence' and the Bulgarian 'suggestology' of Dr Georgi Lozanov.[23] Only recently has the West begun to take an interest in the enormous (and even frightening) implications of this phenomenon, and to exploit it scientifically. Oriental philosophies have, since time immemorial, concerned themselves with little else: the lower frequencies of alpha, delta and theta are their milieu.

There are training programmes in the West, some using cybernetics theory and biofeedback equipment (see pages 244 ff.) and others of a more oriental slant (such as TM, or transcendental meditation, and the various techniques derived from yoga) which effectively teach the brain to produce 'A' – or α – at will. The most significant and straightforward of these so far is the Silva Mind Control method, the first programme of its kind specifically designed to teach alpha functioning, and used by the Chicago White Sox to improve baseball performance. Various spin-offs of Silva's method, using the same techniques but calling them something else, are now widespread, including Mind Dynamics and Alphagenics (which has spread as far as Australia). One spin-off is a US organization called 'Focus' based in Connecticut, which produced tapes for 'goal-oriented meditation', like the one entitled 'Inner Tennis', designed to help produce a relaxed and inspired performance. Tim Gallwey's enormously popular Inner Game method is itself based in the USA: Gallwey writes books, holds clinics and had a television series with which most of the pros are at least indirectly familiar. There are also many sports psychological programmes and methods which emphasize deep relaxation and image-production as an aid to performance (see pages 243 ff.).

Sports psychologists Vanek and Cratty refer to recent studies by Czech and Russian 'psychologists' of the intellectual processes of sportsmen prior to and during competition.[24] These studies suggest 'that during competition an athlete thinks in visual images, rather than in words; while following competition the athlete may be able to verbalize about his performance. Thus,' say Vanek and Cratty, 'it is suggested that two types of thought processes may be involved – one in which visual imagery is more pronounced, and a second in which word cues are chained together to describe the movement.' Similarly, 'Athletes and coaches often experience or observe the manner in which an overemphasis upon word cues during the performance of a movement may result in "intellectual paralysis" '.[25]

Although American Tim Gallwey has probably never heard of such research, it is interesting that his Inner Game method which took the US tennis world by storm in 1974 corresponds very closely indeed with the findings of Eastern bloc sports scientists. As a young man, not all too successful as a tennis player, Gallwey was greatly impressed by a book by the German philosopher Eugen Herrigel, *Zen in the Art of Archery*.[26] (Mike Brearley skipped through it one night in bed and was out the following day for a duck, but this in no way detracts from its importance as a seminal work in sports literature.) Herrigel's vivid little book describes the course of his apprenticeship in the 'Great Doctrine' of archery. The Japanese Zen masters hold that archery is not a sport as we in the West have hitherto understood that term, but a contest of the archer with himself. (The reader may recall from earlier chapters that the communists have arrived at the same conclusion about sport generally.)

Grasping the bow, nocking the arrow, raising the bow, drawing and remaining at the point of highest tension and loosing the shot form, to the Zen archer, a mystical sequence, a ceremony in which the archer acts as a medium for a higher intelligence. He himself does not loose the shot: he must wait at the moment of highest tension quite unselfconsciously, while it looses itself. 'It' shoots, as the master says, only for the archer who has learned to act as a selfless instrument.

This is not an easy thing for a Westerner to do because we are all taught that it cannot happen. 'If you want a job doing, do it yourself,' our grannies are always telling us. After months and years of trying, poor Herrigel despaired of ever being able to let 'it' shoot. The whole venture became a pain. One day he thought, I've had enough of this, and tried the trick of deliberately slipping his thumb. This got the shot off all right, so he very proudly demonstrated his new method to the master, and waited for his response. The master said not a word, turned his back on Herrigel and sat on a cushion – a sign of utter contempt. Eventually, Herrigel's dedication paid off, however. One day without being in the least aware of it, he learned to let 'it' shoot, and progressed to letting it shoot at targets, which the master could ace in the dark with the same serene accuracy as in broad daylight. Of course, Herrigel didn't 'win' anything, other than, perhaps, himself.

'Nature is a mysterious thing. It is just like me. Sometimes I wonder, when a big fist comes crashing by and at the last moment I just move my head the smallest bit and the punch comes so close I can feel the wind, but it misses me. How do I know at the last minute to move just enough? How do I know which way to move?'[27]

You can guess who this is. Fight doctor Ferdie Pacheco says of Ali that he was 'basically a *reactor*'. There is much in the martial arts that teaches 'reacting' in this way. The Kendo master learns to blend with his attacker until his attacker's move and his own are part of the same instantaneous pattern. 'Defence by telepathy' is possible at certain serene levels of the mind, and Ali's renowned coolness as a fighter (Pacheco called him 'scientific') may also have been, in a very real sense, inspired.

The discipline of 'mediumship' was practised by the ancient Zen swordsmen, the Samurai, on the path of chivalry (Bushido) 'in the most irrevocable way, at the risk of their lives'.[28] It is a feature of all the martial arts, of Aikido (the Japanese art of self-defence), and even of ancient oriental ceremonies such as O-char (the famous tea ritual). Sumo wrestlers and the Kendogi meditate before they fight. Like the Zen archers they seek to reach, as Herrigel says, 'a state which resembles the melting drowsiness on the verge of sleep', in which there is a 'rapturous certainty of being able to summon up energies in any direction'.[29]

Whether the 'higher intelligence' called forth in this meditative state is really outside the self, or located in the autonomic nervous system, the subconscious, or the unconscious, does not particularly matter for our purposes. Whichever is the case, the state of consciousness with which we are concerned is 'A' and not 'B', alpha and not beta on the electroencephalograph.

Tim Gallwey's 'Inner Game' tennis is founded on the assumption that a player has two selves. Self 1, the conscious, intellectual self, 'scolds and gives instructions'; Self 2, 'the unconscious, automatic self' or 'biocomputer', is extremely competent at tennis, given the chance to play. During the course of Gallwey's books, Self 1 becomes synonymous with the ego, and Self 2 with the body, but these are merely shorthand for the other things. Gallwey's method seeks to liberate Self 2 from Self 1's constant interference: to let the body play. The reader may have gathered already that Self 1, as Gallwey calls it, is our good friend 'B' or beta on the EEG, and that Self 2 is none other than the famous 'A' or alpha. With this in mind, we progress to higher things. Like playing 'unconscious': 'Perhaps a better way to describe the player who is "unconscious" is by saying that his mind is so concentrated, so focused, that it is *still*.' Playing unconscious is the province of Self 2, but Self 1 is such a know-all that it must interfere and give orders. A player whose volley goes into the net often shouts abuse at himself. This is his Self 1 shouting at his Self 2, blaming his body for the mistake. Self 2 becomes cowed, and makes a series of rotters. Left to itself, it could manage nicely. Gallwey points out that it is possible to programme Self 2 (the bio-computer) to carry out instructions. This is done by means of images. Show Self 2 a clear mental picture of what you want, and Self 2 will do it. Maybe not first time, but it will find a way. Self 1's rational interference merely slows down this natural process, and its tendency to make judgements and pronouncements on the body's performance just bungs up the biocomputer's innards.

Gallwey's emphasis on focusing on the ball, and his recommendations about visualizing clearly what the body is required to perform, are not unique to the Inner Game, but his insight into the mental physics of concentration, that it consists in crystallizing and focusing and condensing the mind's energy to a fine point, is vitally important. Gallwey takes as his focusing point an object – the ball – which centres the attention in the same way as a mantra in meditation (a mantra being a soothing Sanskrit word which is repeated in silent incantation to focus the mind). This act of focusing enables Self 2 to go about its business, and this is how unconscious tennis is possible.

Like Tim Gallwey, writer Michael Murphy has been very influential in linking sport with eastern philosophical precepts. At their Esalen Institute in California Murphy also teaches and brings out seminal books on sport and awareness (most recently *The Psychic Side of Sports*). In 1972 Murphy wrote *Golf in the Kingdom*, a remarkable tale of initiation into the mystical game of golf. Murphy's tutor in the story is Shivas Irons, an extraordinary self-employed pro at Burningbush golf club in the Kingdom of Fife. Irons is possessed of a pair of slightly crossed blue eyes that watch you from two directions at once. He has the Knowledge. He tells Murphy, 'Ye try too hard and ye think too much,'[31] and recommends not doing any of either. A driver goes by the name of a 'play club', to discourage unnatural effort, and the sweet spot on the club face is 'already joined' to the ball by auras and energy fields. According to Shivas, the golfer should relax and soak up the beauty of the course and the beauty of the game. 'Gowf is a place to practise fascination,' he says, not a place to curse and contrive sub-par rounds. He teaches Murphy awareness of 'the inner body' as he makes his swing, and to notice 'true gravity' by which all things are related. Shivas is John the Baptist to another figure in the book whom we never actually see, Seamus MacDuff. Seamus is the spirit of 'gowf' as it was played by the ancients. His 'baffin' spoon' is a magical club capable of a hole in one in pitch darkness on a brisk night. There is also, in this book, a good deal about visualization: 'And then a vivid image appeared in my mind's eye, of a turquoise ball travelling down the right side of the fairway with a tail hook towards the green. I took my stance and waggled the club carefully, aware that the image of the shot was incredibly vivid. Then I swung and the ball followed the path laid down in my mind.'[32]

Shivas Irons's teaching develops this visualization to a consummate art, until streamers of energy emanate from the golfer to the target. The conversion of Murphy takes place on the 13th, when Burningbush overcomes his struggling intelligence and he realizes the course is playing him, instead of the other way around.

he book is not wholly about transcendental golf and there is a
uarker side. Shivas Irons himself had a nervous breakdown prior to
his teaching career, and there is also a Dr 'Julian' Laing, a
psychiatrist-cum-GP who talks about the dividing self of the golfer
and the splitting of his personality. Shivas Irons believes the game
of golf 'rewards us' when the parts are fused together.

Visualization – emphasized by both Murphy and Gallwey – is
extremely important to all sports trianing methods seeking to
activate the 'A' or alpha consciousness. It has a long and well-
documented history in sports psychology.

Alternatively called ideomotor training, image-rehearsal, or
VMBR (for Visuo-Motor Behaviour Rehearsal), visualization has
to do with forming in the mind a clear picture of the task to be performed. If the picture is sufficiently clear, the brain registers it as an
instruction to be carried out. Images are better than words, it
seems, because they can over-ride intellectual difficulties. The
image must be stamped clearly and repeatedly, and in as much
detail as possible. This is the way in which the body receives its
instructions. A whole sequence of movements which the body is
required to perform can be inculcated in this way, provided the
instructions are given clearly and confidently. Programming must
be done without prevarication or ambivalence. It must be done
with 'thunk' (finality), or it will not work.

We do not know who invented this technique. It is certainly as
old as yoga; it was also part of the initiation training for the ancient
Egyptian priesthood (who called it 'precipitation from the ethers').
The Russians have documented experiments on telepaths in which
the brain's visual centres are activated.[33] The method is one of the
oldest tricks in sport. Many athletes who have never seen a sports
psychologist, who wouldn't know one if they stepped on him, and
who have never been anywhere near a lotus position or savasanna
(yoga relaxation technique) in a staring pattern, instinctively use
visualization. They visualize the shot they are about to make
because it seems the natural thing to do, and helps to focus their
attention. Many of the most successful sportsmen – the champions
– actually experience an involuntary 'vision' of the shot, which
suddenly flashes into their minds under pressure. Golf, for
instance, because of its slow tempo, is full of these experiences. A
pro golfer is often in the process of visualization, either by accident
or design. Nickalus calls it 'going to the movies',[34] and says he
never hits a shot without it, even in practice. Gary Player, remem-

bering Norman Vincent Peale's instructions (in *The Power of Positive Thinking*) to 'visualize winning', 'saw' his name on top of the 1965 US Open leaderboard. There it was: '1965 – Gary Player'. *He* saw it first. When Gary was 15 he broke his neck diving in a pile of compost. He spent most of the waking hours of his fifteenth year daydreaming – visualizing – long putts being holed and fairways being conquered. Most great sportsmen can recount some such childhood activity: Palmer as a kid spent a great deal of his time playing 'dream' chips and putts because his father didn't want young Arnie messing around on the club greens (he was allowed to use the rough). Arnold would visualize himself in major competitions – 'Here's AP on the 18th at Augusta.' 'And in my dreams,' says Palmer, 'I never lost.'[35] Billie Jean King did the same with tennis practice, and Björn Borg, when he was turned away from the local tennis club as a boy, went off and hit tennis balls against the garage door, imagining himself playing crucial points in Davis Cup matches. These children were undoubtedly programming themselves for success in sport.

Nick Faldo told me that as a youngster he would instinctively practise pressure shots, especially if there were a few club members watching, as a sort of dare. 'I used to try and hole wedge shots on the practice ground.' Now he practises visualizing his shots like this: 'The first thing you picture is your yardage, then the lie. Then you picture the pin, and the exact flight of the ball. *You almost hit the shot.* You do it automatically, even on the practice ground. You don't need to close your eyes: you're *there*. Of course, it's no good picturing what you're not technically capable of performing, but you do picture the ball going in the hole wherever possible. Especially on 4-foot putts! If you're under pressure, it's even more important. It plays an even bigger part if you're nervous.'

This was interesting, because Dale Hayes once told me visualization is 'impossible' when you're nervous: that's the disturbing thing about pressure shots. 'You stand up and you hit shots out of panic,' he said. Dale believed concentration is something you're born with, and that Player, Nicklaus and Watson possess it to an unusual degree. Nick Faldo remarked, 'All my life, I suppose I've practised concentration. One minute I'm sitting at the dinner table and people are talking, and the next minute, I'm just gone, thinking about golf. Palmer was like that: people might be talking to him and suddenly he'd be "gone".'

Palmer can remember all of the shots he has 'seen' in visions –

even as far back as college. There was one in particular, when he was off in the rough and screened from the green by several trees. And a bunker. The shot required to save him had to be low enough to go under the branches, straight enough to go between the trees, high enough to clear the rough, and hooked enough to get on to the green over the bunker. Impossible. 'Nobody knows,' as Palmer says, 'how to make a shot like that.' And yet, 'I could see, in my mind's eye, how that shot should look in flight. It never occurred to me that it couldn't be done; it never dawned on me that the ball would do anything different than I intended.'[36]

Tony Jacklin used to be able to 'see' shots too: 'I know when my game is right because after a few shots I can see the shape of the trajectory of the ball before I hit it. I see the fairway layout, the bunkers guarding the green, and can visualize in sharp focus exactly which path the ball should take. . . . This thing happens when I am relaxed. . . .'[37]

Of course, it doesn't have to happen by accident. The golfer can do it deliberately: giving his bio-computer a clear picture of what he wants it to do: visualizing the path of the club-head, the flight of the ball, and the exact target where the ball should land. The clearer the better. And the same applies to other sports. Even F1. Lauda: '. . . the driver will only be on top of his job if he regards a race as a sequence of situations and combinations of different and changeable factors. The more he has gone over the different possible situations in his mind's eye beforehand, the better he will react when the time comes.'[38]

Lauda, it will be remembered, was a pupil of Willi Dungl, who also trained the Austrian Olympic speed ski team. One of the most successful techniques employed for speed ski training (for example by the US Olympic sports psychologist Richard Suinn) is VMBR – visualization of the course ahead of time for fast reactions in the event.

One of the most straightforward programmes for activating alpha and functioning at that level of mind (which relies very much on visualization for programming the brain) was not designed specifically for sportsmen, although it has been used successfully to help baseball players. An experiment carried out with the Chicago White Sox, and widely publicized on NBC and CBS TV in America during the summer of 1975, was edited out of the British edition of *The Silva Mind Control Method* (copies of the deleted portion are in the author's possession, courtesy of SMC's

Philip Miele). Silva Mind Control, a programme devised by Mexican José Silva, uses alpha brainwave frequencies and relax visualization to achieve specific goals. One of its claims is that t.. graduate so enhances his alpha functioning that he is psychic by the end of the course. Calling to mind the advantages of psychic gifts for facing the bowling of Roberts or Thomson, I went along to a graduate course in London, to see if this method could indeed be used for sports training.

Two American psychiatrists, Clancy McKenzie and Lance Wright, describe the course as follows:

'What is Silva Mind Control?

'Silva Mind Control is a forty-hour course consisting of thirty hours of lecture and ten hours of mental exercises. The mental exercises not only teach persons how to relax the mind and body, as do other approaches such as biofeedback and Transcendental Meditation, but they go one step beyond. They teach persons how to function mentally when they are at the relaxed level.

'The entire course consists of techniques for using the mind in beneficial ways. After experiencing this ourselves and witnessing many others using it, we have no doubt about the superior ability of the mind to function when the person is using specific techniques in an alert relaxed state. It is similar to the state Sigmund Freud described in his paper on listening; like the state Brahms went into for creating his compositions, or the state Thomas Edison described for arriving at new ideas.'[39]

The student of SMC is taught dynamic, as opposed to passive, meditation, using focal points, countdowns and relaxed breathing. 'In deep meditation,' says Silva, 'you are acutely receptive to what you say to yourself.'[40] In this favourable state of mind, the brain is generating the synchronized alpha rhythms and is ready for programming, by means of visualization. It is also ready to scan for intuitive information not available to the conscious wide-awake mind. Many pro sportsmen have experimented with TM (transcendental meditation), including tennis players Arthur Ashe, Bob Lutz and Roscoe Tanner, and former American football star Joe Namath. The tennis players pointed out that although TM certainly made them more relaxed it didn't necessarily help them with their performance on the court. Silva Mind Control is rather more practical, as it is goal-orientated. One of its starting points is the use of positive thinking (both Billie Jean King and Gary Player used Norman Vincent Peale's formula to help produce their best performances) and Emile Coué's method of repeating beneficial statements such as, 'Day by day in every way, I am getting better and better.' But the Silva method places particular emphasis on the use of the 'mind's eye' as Lauda calls it, both to intuit solutions to problems, and to programme the achievement of practical goals. Sportsmen wishing to galvanize their minds for producing good performances under pressure could do worse than try Silva Mind Control. If nothing else it thoroughly acquaints them with the visualization training so widely used in sports psychology throughout the world, and it helps them to surmount the biggest obstacles to good performance: anxiety, tension and fear. 'Relaxed concentration,' as Mike Brearley says, 'is everyone's aim.'

A word of warning, though, about 'playing unconscious'. Many people who have followed Tim Gallwey's Inner Game method to the letter, and who use relaxation and image-training to enhance their performance in tennis and other sports, find that they acquire a new perspective, in which winning is no longer the eighth wonder of the world. They become interested in performance for its own sake, rather than simply for achieving firsts and collecting prize money. They may begin to think of sport as an opportunity to dis-cover themselves, rather than be discovered by others. *Others* of Gallwey's students, after playing unconscious, revert back to the old style of letting the ego play in matches, because they do not like being 'mediums'. They prefer to maintain control, even at the cost of ease and naturalness.

Conversely, winning is itself an ego-trip, however we may like to rationalize it into something else. Deep down, the player is always aware of this as he approaches the winning barrier, no matter what yogic preparations he may have swallowed in order to get there. If winning really doesn't matter, why is he competing? One is either genuinely disinterested, or one is not: there is no halfway house. It is not the business of 'A' consciousness to stuff our trophy cabinets, because 'A' is profoundly concerned with other things; however much 'A' may help performance for its own sake, it can-not be press-ganged into gratifying our ego needs for superstardom. Gallwey's *Inner Game of Tennis* is, on the whole, a very bright and honest book, but the discussion becomes immediately con-voluted and uncomfortable (not to say embarrassing, particularly in the passage about 'Dad was right!'[41]) towards the end, when Gallwey is trying to exploit his method to win matches. There are quite glaring contradictions in this latter part which raise the reader's latent scepticism. The fact is, sadly, that winning, in the Sport Experiment, cannot be tinkered with. As tennis pro Bob Lutz told Barry Tarshis, who had tried Gallwey's method with great eagerness in preparation for his book, *Tennis and the Mind*, 'When you're a point or two away from winning, it's very difficult to convince yourself that it's just another point. How do you get yourself to believe what is, *isn't?*'[42]

American football players have a saying, 'Keep the defence honest.' The Sport Experiment is designed to keep the defence honest. It is purpose-built to uncover hidden motives, whatever they may be. A player who has renounced the fruits of ego for the sake of playing unconscious cannot suddenly decide, three feet from the tape or the chequered flag, that he wants the fruits of ego after all. The Experiment is 100 per cent foolproof, and far too carefully tried and tested to allow discrepancies to come creeping in and spoil its findings. Under the kind of pressure that sport applies to the human mind, there is no room for devious self-trickery. A chimpanzee in a laboratory may turn his back on a bunch of grapes, and swing ever so casually round the cage to disguise his intentions, but in the end, grapes are grapes, and monkeys are monkeys. This is sport's Catch 22. As Yeats's old crane of Gort says,

> . . .'maybe I shall take a trout
> If but I do not seem to care.'

8

Split Mind

A funny thing happened to Ilie Nastase on his way to the net in the second set of his Centenary Wimbledon quarter-final clash with Borg. He couldn't, for the life of him, make up his mind whether to go in, or stay back. He had recovered his composure after the shock of being hoovered off the court 6–0 in the first set, and was beginning to find his rhythm on the volley to go up 4–1 in the second. Everyone was delighted, for Wimbledon spectators are an unusually forgiving audience and treasure the dreams of even the most recalcitrant and ageing of boy wonders. But suddenly the decisiveness vanished from his game. He was coming in, then he wasn't, then he was. He would try a volley; no, a half-volley; no, on second thoughts he'd stay back and see how the ball broke, wary of the Swedish topspin and what it could do to his game. All at once his rhythm disappeared and the Romanian genius began to look very ordinary indeed. With a green-stained behind from a previous 'get', and stumping back to his service position in what appeared to be four pairs of socks, Nastase lost heart, lost his 4–1 lead, lost his fourth-form altercation with umpire Jeremy Shales, and lost the match. His concentration had scattered like a flock of pigeons.

Borg progressed to the semi-final. The Blond Bombshell's next confrontation was with Vitas Gerulaitis, the New Yorker with the Rolls-Royce collection who tells me ability to handle pressure is 'something you're born with'. In mirrored sets the two young men fired everything they knew at each other. There was no margin for error, and neither seemed to need it: they went for the lines, and they got them. Their shots rattled off like ack-ack in an air-raid. No comparison could be made between this match and the Borg–Nastase fiasco of the previous round – or could it?

At 2-all in the final set, Borg momentarily lost the edge, went down 0–40, and stormed the net. When he got there, he couldn't make up his mind – volley or half-volley? The net decided the issue for him. Disgusted with himself, Borg had given the American his vital break. But now it was Gerulaitis's turn. With a point for a 4–2 lead Vitas hesitated for a millisecond about following his service to the net, and when he finally came in, found himself out of position for his volley. That split-second of indecision was enough, and Gerulaitis knew it. After the match he was miffed with himself. 'What hurt me was that I stayed back on that 40–30 point,' he said.

Experiments have shown that it can take upwards of 150 milliseconds for the central nervous system to process information about the flight of a tennis ball and predict where it will go, and an additional increment of time to select a response from memory and execute the stroke. The amount of time necessary depends on a number of variables – hand–eye co-ordination, visuo-motor training, court-sense, concentration and so on. But one factor commonly overlooked is the player's *repertoire*. If he has, say, three backhands (topspin, slice and flat), it takes appreciably longer to decide on the most suitable response, simply because the choice is greater. One of the most successful backhands of all time was on the end of the right arm of Ken Rosewall. Rosewall had, in his prime, one perfect backhand. Just one. The time necessary for choosing the shot on his backhand wing was in Ken's case that much smaller. Consequently his anticipation surpassed that of almost any opponent, and was once described as 'thought-reading'. 'That's right,' Gerulaitis told me emphatically. 'I've been working on my serve, trying to do more with it. That means you have a lot more to think about. You have more alternatives.' Vitas was annoyed with himself after a shock defeat by Tim Gullikson in the Benson and Hedges Championships at Wembley. 'In a way,' he said, 'if you have just one shot, one variation, it's almost better. Even if it's junk you just go right ahead and hit it.' Arthur Ashe made a similar point in his *Portrait in Motion* diary: 'It is interesting to note, for instance, that while both Muscles and I have backhands as our best shots, I have three different backhands and he has only one. . . . Muscles just hits every backhand the same – perfectly. He also never has to hurry a shot. I have no idea how he manages it, but 99 per cent of the time he is in perfect position to hit whatever you send back. This gives him an edge few people are aware of too. It gives him the time to disguise his shots; you seldom can tell what is coming.'[1]

To pursue Ashe's line of reasoning, then: under certain circumstances, too many backhands can spoil the shot. And if this is so, consider the plight of the player who has not only three backhands, but three of everything else as well, with unorthodox variations. What anguish would *he* endure as he skidded about the lawns of the All-England Club, one of the fastest surfaces in the world, trying to make up his mind? Well, there has been at least one postwar player with such a repertoire, and he was Romanian, never won Wimbledon, and threw 'inexplicable' tantrums under pressure. (Nastase's closest kin on court today would perhaps be Hana Mandlikova.)

I asked Nastase, who was continually working on his game and trying to make improvements, if he ever felt he knew too much already. 'I don't know,' said Ilie, his head on one side. 'Maybe I complicate myself too much. I want to win the point in the most difficult way, not in the easiest way. But that's always been my act. That's why I will throw a big tournament.' Nastase's tantrums, and his tendency to 'blow up' under pressure, were partly due to his extreme nervousness whenever he played. 'I'm nervous always. When I win or lose. I'm nervous the whole time, especially at the end when you have to win or lose.' He tried to calm himself down. 'I always do my best, I mean, I have to be – I have to move, I have to – I don't have no sleep before a match. Anyone can tell. They laugh at me: I have to move, I can't sit still.' What about Wimbledon? Nastase began to jabber. 'In a final like Wimbledon, you don't realize what you're doing. It's too much; the people, the ambiance. It's too much. For me. When I first play. I don't know. You don't feel – I mean, like, sometimes I don't feel like I was playing, you know, I was doing – just because I have to serve or go for his serve, but that was, you know, something I don't *feel*. . . .' Though nothing sure, yet much unhappily. He added that he didn't go for the lines. There was too much at stake. He said he didn't think anyone really went for the lines, which is not strictly true. The Australians were drilled to do just that; John McEnroe, a young man of great will-power who comes into frequent conflict over line-decisions, goes for such 'winners'; so does Connors, and so does Chris Lloyd, under certain circumstances. But Nastase did not, especially in decline. I wondered if this had anything to do with *his* many rows over close calls. 'I think line-judges get nervous, you know,' said Nastase, 'and they make sometimes mistakes because they are nervous.'

Anyone who doubts the horrors of a split-mind experience playing tennis should read Marty Riessen's account, in *Match Point*, of his defeat in a Denver tournament final in 1972. The match was an NBC TV spectacular, and for Riessen in particular a lot depended on it. 'I was facing Rod Laver in the final. Rod was generous enough to tell reporters afterwards that he had no idea how he was going to beat me when the match reached 4-all in the third set. Well, like an idiot, I showed him how. For some strange reason, I suddenly became unsure whether to serve to his backhand or forehand in the ninth game. Indecision at that stage was fatal. I lost my rhythm and promptly served three double faults. Inevitably I lost my nerve as a result and that was all the help Rocket needed. He ran out a 4–6 6–3 6–4 winner.'[2]

How can players guard against this sort of thing happening in a crucial match? One certain answer is correct coaching. A coach who is decisive and clear-minded himself, and who can cut a swathe through confusion and uncertainty in his pupil's mind, can work wonders. Jerry Teeguarden did as much for Virginia Wade and restored her confidence before her Wimbledon victory. Harry Hopman did it for the Australians. Hop had a very simple method of dealing with indecision, nerves and suchlike on the court. He would sit watching his protégés in their Davis Cup matches with imperturbable conviction, and say 'Go for the lines.' Whatever gruelling stage the match had reached, and however much pressure was on the sweating, tired, terrified player in question, Hopman would repeat, 'Go for the lines.' He knew of no half-measures himself, and saw no reason for tentativeness in others. The fact that the Aussies were more frightened of Hopman than anything else in tennis simplified matters for them to a marvellous extent. The Hopman Australians were decision-makers of the highest order.

One of them, Lew Hoad, now coaches in a similar tradition himself. His policy is: keep it natural, keep it simple. He thinks so many coaches confuse their players by offering too many corrective solutions in the interests of some 'ideal' orthodox stroke. The pupils become tentative, and eventually lose confidence in their own judgement. There is no need for such complexity, when a natural shot will do. The same applies to grips. There are not many one-grip players around, because it requires such great physical strength. But anyone who saw Hoad in his prime remembers with what decisive majesty he laid his shots about him. Lesser mortals must content themselves with a grip adjustment of some sort, but one notes that many of the best 'pressure' players have a minimal changeover. It gives them that fraction of a second advantage over a racket-fiddler.

Tennis players have evolved a fairly sophisticated phraseology for the psychological contest on the court, and all professional players know and use techniques for achieving psychological mastery of an opponent. In its more overt form, 'psyching' may involve dubious tactics for disrupting concentration, such as ball-bouncing, foot-stamping or shouting abuse across the net. Players who scorn overt psyching nevertheless regularly employ more subtle methods of breaking their opponents' concentration – of splitting their minds – such as disguising the weight of a serve or the direction of a shot on a crucial point, or stampeding into position to volley when the intention is to dink, or establishing sequences in order to disrupt them on a later point, and so on. The object is to unsettle the opponent's confidence in his judgement, to get him guessing, to grub at the roots of his game. A player who once becomes tentative is halfway beaten, though he had the best backhand in the world and the stamina of a camel. 'You shouldn't make your opponent feel one way or the other inside,' said little Eddie Dibbs. 'I'm fighting inside me all the time.' Ideally, an opponent should be psychologically reduced to this: 'I was playing so well against the Czechs in Bucharest. Now I have forgotten what to do. Sounds silly eh? But it's true. I don't know whether to come in or stay back. I've lost the feel for it.' This is Nastase again, this time talking to his biographer Richard Evans.[3] He said that now he was thinking twice and three times before he hit each shot. Before he just used to play and everything came naturally. This is the player of whom Ashe once remarked that fellow pros were so in awe of his genius that they would applaud his shots from the players' stand.

One of my objects in writing this book was to show that inner experiences of the kind Nastase is describing here are not the peculiar privilege of so-called 'problem athletes'.[4] They affect many sportsmen of the highest class in every sport, whose object is to apply pressure to the player's mind and body. Split mind is not Nastase's problem, or tennis's problem. Split mind is a condition induced in many outstanding athletes under the stress of competition, and quite deliberately induced.

The decision-making process in response to stimuli, on which the sportsman relies so heavily, has been the subject of much investigation. The physiologist Pavlov carried out a number of famous experiments with dogs (one of which, it must be said, threw itself in the river). According to Pavlov's findings, it is fairly simple to choose between two *different* stimuli, but when the stimuli became more and more similar, choosing became increasingly hard. If pressure was applied to a dog to make up its mind under these circumstances, it exhibited what Pavlov called an 'experimental neurosis' – it became angry, barked, snapped, trembled, and cowered on the floor. An experimenter by the name of Liddell, who followed up Pavlov's work, found that animals continually tested in this way became wild and vicious, even outside the laboratory. One dog in particular whenever it saw Liddell coming, would attack him or wet on his trousers.

What has this to do with sport? Let us suppose, for the sake of argument, that the two stimuli shown to the dog were cricket balls, one with the seam slightly to the left, and the other with the seam slightly to the right. The dog had to make up its mind which was which, so as to make the correct response. Gradually, the two stimuli were made more and more alike – both cricket balls' seams were moved towards the upright position – and the dog forced to pick which was which. It was under these cirumstances that Pavlov's dog would begin to show signs of emotional disturbance.

In cricket, as we have seen the job of exciting extraordinary tension and indecision in opposing players generally belongs to the bowler. The bowler's job, with his captain's assistance in the matter of field-placing, is to split the batsman's mind. This is the principal reason for the bowler's being on the field. Wickets fall, when they do fall, because he has been successful. More important, spectators have been able to study the batsman, and observe his reactions to each delivery. The romantic *Boy's Own* mythology in which cricket has always been shrouded should not be allowed to blind onlookers to this fundamental experiment on the batsman's nervous system: prolonged exposure to it has made more than one outstanding athlete mentally ill.

The MCC tour of Australasia in 1974/5 was memorable to the England batsmen for two reasons: Lillee and Thomson. Blindingly fast short-pitched bowling, of the type that fractured the ribs of John Edrich and is now the mainstay of cricket in the West Indies, was the order of the day. It was directed equitably at all MCC batsmen regardless of batting ability. English critics complained that the Australian umpires were far too lenient with the Aussie spearhead bowlers, but one of their most anguished victims at the crease, tail-ender Derek Underwood, disagreed. At least twice, says Deadly in his book, the umpires warned Lillee and Thomson for bowling bouncers at him. 'In a way they were a little harsh. . . . Perhaps I looked as if I couldn't defend myself, but cricket at Test level is a hard business. It was from that point that I knew I could look to play forward a little more against them for a few deliveries before they would dare slip in another one. That is giving me an advantage over the bowler. *No batsman should be able to make up his mind what stroke he is going to play before the ball is bowled* [my italics]. I'd hate to think a batsman could do that against me.'[5]

Underwood's objection here is professional: he is talking about his fellow-bowler's job. There has never been a great bowler, fast, medium or slow, who did not include in his repertoire techniques for 'getting the batsman guessing' or 'putting the question' to him. It is his principal method of demoralization and eventual wicket-taking. The fastest bowlers in the West Indies do not take wickets by pace alone. Like Lillee and Thomson here they would be severely hindered in their profession by the occasional prohibition of the bouncer – that Great Unknown of a ball – with which to break a batsman's rhythm and unsettle his judgement. On an even strip the batsman can go intrepidly on to the front foot, and has a reasonable chance of 'getting his eye in' – focusing steadfastly on the ball.

Sir Neville Cardus, the doyen of cricket-writing, once said of Hedley Verity's bowling, 'Maybe on good pitches his bowling didn't put the question to batsmen which they had to answer when faced with the curving, hovering flights of Rhodes or Blythe.'[6] Putting the question, by whatever aerodynamic art, is the bowler's brief. Derek Underwood relies on spin, a tight line and length and discreet variations of pace. He calls his quicker ball 'my Keith ball' (after Keith Miller). He also has a slower ball and a slower-still ball. Deadly says, 'My job then, as I see it, is to bowl a line and length, keeping everything in check and creating pressure for the batsman.'[7] More orthodox spinners frequently 'give the ball some air', tossing the ball up to lure the batsman into a cavalier stroke. Wilfred Rhodes, who believed he could bowl every ball that Verity ever bowled 'except the one they cut for four', used disguised pace, undercutting the ball on release. The batsman could not tell the flight from the fractionally altered position of Rhodes's hand. He was obliged to guess, and he often panicked.[8] Arthur Booth's apparently strenuous delivery was usually an optical illusion, too, inviting all sorts of premature swipes of the bat. Booth, when he was flighting the ball well, could feel the muscles aching at the base of his spine.[9]

All bowling, though physical in execution, is essentially a mental craft. The quick bowler may come stampeding in, but the ball has been carefully folded in the hand, its shiny half buffed, the delivery already loaded in its cerebral chamber. The batsman has to guess – and his reputation and his job depend on it – which ball will come. Thomson, especially with the new ball, sprays them about. Besides, he threatens a yorker, and you can't see his hand because of his slingshot action. What will it do? Mike Procter appeared to deliver off the wrong foot from a huge run. You couldn't always judge the moment the ball left his hand. He commanded the late in-dipper. Play forward or back? Mike Hendrick, like Trueman in his pomp, didn't know whether a particular delivery would swing in or out. The best fast-medium bowler in England couldn't read his own bowling: what chance did a batsman stand? Malcolm Marshall has skid as well as extra pace; whereas Joel Garner, from his great height, has bounce. Hook it or leave it? Split mind.

Many cricket writers, and a great many cricket watchers, believe that pace is the stuff of batsmen's nightmares; when a batsman loses his nerve, it is because of pace. But the problem is slightly more sinister than that. Dennis Lillee, who could shell-shock batsmen by sheer brute speed on and just outside the off stump, nevertheless made it his business to perfect the outswinger, and to change his speed up or down, keeping something in check, especially after his back injury. He also believed a great fast bowler should possess a slower ball: the 'knuckle' or 'baseball' delivery, the 'leggie' or leg-spinner's ball, a variation of the off-spinner (with the index finger digging in the seam), the half-ball grip, one-finger grip and the palm ball – these are all methods of achieving a slower delivery while still storming in off a long run. Lillee says the slower ball may not take many wickets, but 'it will keep the batsman on the lookout, and you will have effectively added one more thing to keep his mind busy when he is facing your bowling'.[10]

There are other things. Cut, for example. Snow's cutters were part of a repertoire that destroyed whole batting line-ups because they deviated fiercely after pitching. Or swing. Bowlers specializing in swing usually have a shock ball and a stock ball. Brian Statham's stock ball moved in. The other one left the batsman like a marooned punter. A seam bowler who can swing the ball late, with the seam remaining upright until the last moment, and whose action is more or less the same for both inswinger and outswinger, can cause a batsman to shake with fear. At Lord's in 1972, Bob Massie scuppered the England line-up, and there were jokes in the Australian dressing-room that the England players were being shown film of Massie's deliveries, incorrectly spliced.[11] By the time the England batsmen had learned to 'pick' Massie, he had done a lot of damage. In his first Test he took sixteen wickets with his vertical seam. He was openly accused of cheating, and pictures of lip-salve appeared in the press, with suggestions as to how it might be applied to the ball if a bowler had it in his pocket. Well, Len Hutton, whose mind was a storehouse of strokemaking the envy of his peers, lived in fear of the vertical seam hurtling towards him. He once wrote, 'Whatever defence I had, it was useless at these moments.'[12]

In a way, Hutton was worse off, as Nastase was, *because* of his enormous repertoire. There were more choices, their number tending to infinity. He knew too much. Not surprisingly he sometimes referred to a preference for 'resting' on the back foot: it gave him an extra shaving of time in which to make up his mind. Hutton returned from the 1954/5 tour of Australia in apparent triumph, to declare himself unfit for the 1955 Tests. The captaincy had bound him on a wheel of fire; he was never to endure it again, for Peter May took over. In Australia, the most noticeable alteration in Hutton's behaviour was a sudden arduous difficulty in decision-making. He could not choose his sentences at the press conference or even remember the name of Keith Miller. The pauses were so long that the England team manager, Geoffrey Howard, more than once glanced round to see if Hutton had fallen asleep.[13] His speeches were slow and fumbling. In the Tests he could not decide whether to go with his spin attack or with Tyson. At the crease on a turning wicket, he gave a convincing 'imitation of a great batsman in trouble', according to Cowdrey.[14] After the disastrous Brisbane

Test when he had mistakenly sent in Australia, he left the choice between Bedser and Tyson for the Sydney Test until the very last moment, forgetting even to tell Bedser he had been dropped.[15] He spoke to no one, as though in a trance; before the Third Test at Melbourne he was still in his room at breakfast time on the morning of the match, evidently in a state of nervous exhaustion. His players wondered if he would come out in time for the next Test of his nerves.

Hutton was a brilliant but cerebral batsman. His shots did not 'just come' like Viv Richards's. His strokes were nothing to do with chance inspiration or mediumship. Hutton took intellectual batting as far as it could possibly go, by careful, thoughtful, infinitely difficult decisions. 'There was no logical reason why he should ever get out again,' says Cowdrey.[16] Unfortunately bowlers, who may be thwarted by spontaneous batsmen with 'all the time in the world' in which to play their shots, tend to take their revenge on cerebral, thoughtful batsmen like Hutton. Bowlers spend most of their waking hours thinking up ways to overload such 'computers', sometimes with tragic consequences. The great Test batsmen of recent years who have been petrified in concentration at the crease – men like Ken Barrington and Geoff Boycott – have in common with Hutton a deliberateness, a lack of spontaneity, and a determination to eliminate risk by careful decisions. Barrington's 'inner battle' was a paralysis from which he could not escape by playing a carefree shot. Barrington didn't *have* any carefree shots. He was a back-foot player who thought of the pros and cons of each delivery.

In June 1967, at Headingley, Geoff Boycott made 246 not out and was dropped, as Barrington had been before him, for excruciatingly slow scoring. Brian Close, who sought him out in the tea interval and told him, 'See if you can open up and start playing your shots now, Geoff,' was nevertheless sympathetic. 'I honestly believe he tried to carry out those instructions, but he had got himself into a groove.'[17] The Nawab of Pataudi had sent his field back into defensive positions and Boycott was frozen at the crease, in a trance of thought. Close's frantic signals from the balcony were not noticed.

There are geniuses in sport as in other walks of life. They are the ones who suffer most under pressure to make decisions. Boycott, when he was dropped, said nothing, though his 246 runs cost him infinitely more than his time at the crease. He explained afterwards, 'I was never conscious of the time factor on the first day, but when you are in bad "nick" you never seem to get the half-volleys. And when you do play a shot the ball always seems to hit the fielders.'[18] Boycott could not, then or now, 'push the score along', because each delivery has him in thrall. It has nothing to do with selfishness, and everything to do with sport. There are ten thousand possibilities; he knows what they are and he must choose. As John Arlott tells me, Wally Hammond conducted his triumphant tour of Australia in 1928/9 on only three strokes, 'having eliminated all those that seemed to him to involve any possible risk'. Geoffrey himself, on the 1978/9 tour, tried to limit his scoring strokes to three, as Alex Bannister noticed in Perth.[19] A prodigious repertoire can become a liability when one's job is to choose, and choose quickly. Under these circumstances, 'equivocation,' as Hamlet says, 'will undo us'. An out-of-form batsman, according to Dennis Amiss, watches the pitch rather than the bowler because he expects every delivery to 'explode' at him.[20] He feels jaded and worn down with effort from considering alternatives. From considering balls *just* outside the off stump, which evoke an involuntary stab of the bat; from agonizing over 'dot' balls, so difficult to get away; or 'chin' balls which can be hooked, but upwards.

There is one other thing. English wickets are, shall we say, of *uncertain* bounce. A ball pitching on a spot the size of a sixpence may lift or deviate wildly, whatever the bowler's intentions. For a batsman, this means being reduced to a sort of 'spot the ball' competition, with no prizes. 'It could rise only to your waist, or leap at your head,' says Brearley, who told me he had not himself experienced split mind. There is even, at Lord's a mystical 'ridge', decisions about which so frightened Brian Close on one occasion (in 1963) that he charged down the strip to every delivery like a Scots Grey, and was roundly condemned afterwards for showing off. Barrington, apologizing in *Playing it Straight* for boring the reader with talk of nervous tension, said, 'I'm not the first cricketer to be brought to his knees by the strains and stresses of his profession.'[21]

Nor, unless cricket changes very radically from the game it is, will he be the last.

A comparable case is that of baseball. A major league pitcher has generally mastered four pitches, plus the time-honoured cliché that 'Speed is not enough'. America's renowned baseball author

Roger Kahn elaborates: 'But a fast ball moves if it is thrown hard enough. Depending on grip, one fast ball moves up and into a righthanded batter. Another moves up and away from him. A few men, like [ex-Dodger Clem] Labine, develop fast balls that sink. The fast ball intimidates. The curve – "public enemy number one", Chuck Dressen called it – aborts careers. A curve breaks sideways, or downward or at an intervening angle, depending on how it is thrown. Branch Rickey regarded the overhand curve as the best of breaking pitches [because it] breaks straight down, and, unlike flatter curve balls, an overhand curve is equally appalling to righthanded and lefthanded batters. The pure drop, hurtling in at the eyes and snapping to the knees, carried Carl Erskine and Sandy Koufa to strikeout records (fourteen and fifteen) in World Series separated by a decade.'[22]

Baseball pitchers – good ones – throw at speeds in excess of 90 m.p.h. on the catcher's mitt, and can make the ball swerve sharply in the air. The batter, with his three lives, winds up and prays he guesses right. There is 60 ft 6 in. between the pitcher's mound and home plate, and a lot can happen to a baseball between stimulus and response. Pitchers are clever and crafty. Ex-Dodger Preacher Roe perfected a spitter – illegal because of the difficulty of control – that even umpires could not catch him using, disguised as it was by an elaborate system of fake wipes and spits. 'So you see what I got. A wet one and three fake wet ones. Curve. Slider. Hummer. I'd show hitters the hummer and tell reporters that if it hit an old lady in the spectacles, it wouldn't bend the frame. But I could always, by going back to my old form, rear back and throw hard. Not often. Maybe ten times a game.... Well, now, pitchin', you know, is a shell game. You move the ball. You make the hitter guess. There's more than two pitches you can throw at any one time, so the more often he's guessing, the better off you are. The odds are he'll guess wrong. That was mostly how I won so many dang games. Thinkin' ahead of 'em. Foolin' 'em. Slider away. Curve away. Fast one on the hands. Curve on the hands. Curve away. There's a strike-out in there without one spitter, but maybe I faked it three times.'[23]

In a crisis, and there are many in baseball because of its alternating structure, a batter may miss the ball, not through incompetence, but through failure to make up his mind, and lose his side a pennant race. He may even be fully aware of the correct response, and yet watch the ball go by, apparently paralysed. On the baseball diamond, there are few illegal gestures, and profanity is accepted as part of the game, but there is one signal for which a pitcher may be sent off, as sportswriter Dudley Doust points out. This is to apply his open hand to his throat in a gesture of strangulation. It means 'you choked' – you couldn't perform because of the pressure. A batter who chokes needs no insult to compound his injury. He already has an ulcer worrying what to do.

In 1951 Dodger Gil Hodges, a fine, powerfully built athlete, hit forty homers, the second highest total in baseball. In 1952, in the World Series, Hodges made no hits in any of the seven games. He had been seized by a dilemma: he wanted to hit the ball, but also he wanted to get out of the way of it. As a psychiatrist tells us, 'If fight or flight are inappropriate . . . fright may then become increasingly prominent.'[24] For the rest of his career, Hodges fought down the mounting terror of this conflict, doing his best to bat, and making whatever technical adjustments were pointed out to him. At 44 he suffered a massive coronary. At 47 he suffered another, and died on a sidewalk in Florida.

Golf – the Slow Game – gives a player more time to think. He does not appear under siege as does the man with a bat in his hand. Everything moves along at a leisurely pace – or so it seems. At the start of a Masters tournament, though, somebody asked Dave Stockton which player in the field he most feared, and Stockton said, 'Me'. Golfers are familiar with 'me' watching over small decisions on the greens and telling them 'lag it up, now' or 'never up, never in'. They grow accustomed to 'me' interrupting swings with irrelevant considerations, and 'me' second-guessing their choice of clubs. However simple a two-foot putt may appear to onlookers, inside the player's head 'me' has already made suggestions about the difficulty of it, probably noting the direction of the grain from the shine, the speed it played yesterday, the position of the sweet spot, the position of the eyes, the arc of vision to the hole, and umpteen other nitty details parasitic on a single simple act. And that 'me' has already *changed* its professional advice several times on this particular hole, till the putter in the hands feels like a mace, or a banana. Too much time is as damaging to judgement as not enough.

Split mind can attack a golfer in a variety of ways: swing, for example. Tony Jacklin made an agonizing transition from the 'British' method, based on hitting against a firm, locked left side, to the 'American' method of sliding the hips and knees through the ball. During the months prior to the 1969 British Open, Jacklin was hitting the ball like it was Rocky Marciano. He now feels that his disappointing form was 'due to my falling between two stools of the game, the one I had been taught and the method I knew I must adopt'.[25] Years later, in 1978, he was to tell golf writer Liz Kahn of *Golf International:* 'I've been tossed between two shores for a hell of a long while' – referring to his choice between Britain and America – and added, 'With all the chopping and changing I feel I've been half doing it everywhere.'[26]

Choice of clubs, because the golfer has so much time to second-guess himself, can enervate all faith, especially on crisis holes. There is a theory that, as in cricket and tennis, the fewer choices you have under pressure, the less likely you are to go to pieces. According to Nicklaus, Bobby Locke, a superb chipper, did it all with a pitching wedge. 'Increasingly in recent years,' says Jack, 'I have come to rely on the sand wedge for a great variety of shots around the green. One reason for this one-club approach is that I can become more expert and confident in an hour's practice with one club than I could by giving, let us say, six clubs ten minutes' work apiece.' He adds, 'I still use other clubs down to the 5-iron for chipping, but I believe there'll come a day when I'll rely almost entirely on finessing the sand wedge and using just one other club – probably a 6-iron – when I need an unusually long roll.'[27]

Several psychologists have independently investigated indecision in golf.Dr Thomas Tutko, discussing 'the intrinsic challenge of the putt' as an example of sport's high-pressure situations, observes: 'Caught up in a welter of conflicting thoughts provoked by contradictory personal and socially conditioned needs, is it any wonder that your palms get sweaty and your vision begins to blur just a little?'[28] He goes on to talk about the physiological changes accompanying anxiety that can cause a player to lose co-ordination (and lose tournaments). Dr David Morley, author of *Golf and the Mind*, discusses the kinds of conflict that can arise over clubs, precision versus power, focusing on clubhead or ball, caution versus bravery, and putting.[29] Conflicting thoughts create tension; and tension, in golf as in all sports, is the giant-killer. The two psychologists do not go so far as to suggest that sport is designed to induce such conflict, and studiously avoid the sinister subject of sport's experimental nature. They make suggestions about relaxation exercises and correct attitudes on the tee, self-analysis, and so on.

Perhaps the most interesting comment on split mind in golf

comes from Dr Theo Hyslop, who in 1927 wrote *Mental Handicaps In Golf*. Dr Hyslop was an 'alienist' – the early equivalent of a psychiatrist – at 'Bethlem' mental hospital in London, and he was friendly with many eminent sportsmen of his day, including J. H. Taylor and W. G. Grace. He examines the psychological aspects of golf with surprising insight – for 1927 – and here he is talking about split mind: 'The "insanity of doubt" may in golfers attain to such a degree of severity as to warrant the diagnosis of "cerebral pruritis" or "mental itch". The conflicting emotions coincidental to doubts influence every stroke. The mental stance is affected by pros and cons until a mental "wiggle-waggle" manifests itself objectively by physical readjustments or grotesque flourishes. Some individuals think twice before doing a thing; others think oftener. As a rule, the oftener we think, the greater the hesitancy and doubt.'[30]

Dr Hyslop recommended, among other things, that 'it is better to know three clubs well than a dozen slightly'.[31] Mental wiggle-wagglers take note. He also talks about the need for what he calls 'automatism', and says that a golfer, like a musician, may ruin his performance by *thinking* about it (a theme developed in the previous chapter).

In Formula One racing, split mind is not just a hazard to winning. In racing, it can kill. The reader no doubt has seen a small animal, caught in car headlights on the road, transfixed between going forward and turning back.

There have been many investigations into the bombardment of the cerebral cortex, the so-called 'fight or flight' syndrome, and the speed at which the central nervous system can process data necessary to survival. Post-war studies of shellshock in fighter pilots suggest that some of those who perished actually froze at the controls of their aircraft. Consider the following cases.

On Friday 28 February, 1975, the 8.37 London underground train from Drayton Park to Moorgate reached its destination, accelerated along the platform, careered through tons of sand, demolished buffers and smashed into a brick wall in the over-run tunnel. Forty-one people were killed, including the driver, Leslie Newson. The post-mortem pathologist found no evidence in Newson of physical illness, drugs, drink, epileptic fit, heart attack or brain lesion to account for his failure to apply the electro-pneumatic brakes. The Westinghouse automatic airbrake on the driver's *left* and dead man's handle on his *right* were in working order at the time of the crash, but eye-witnesses stated at a public enquiry that the driver had appeared 'paralysed and frozen to his driving position' and that his eyes seemed to be 'staring straight ahead' as the train hurtled along the platform. A suicide motive seemed unlikely, in view of the driver's conscientiousness, his love of his job, and his 'normal' frame of mind on the morning of the crash. He had driven the train into that platform at Moorgate on 121 previous occasions without mishap.[32]

At Monza in 1970 during practice for the Italian Grand Prix, German-born Jochen Rindt, favoured to win the World Championship, drove his Lotus 72 into the 170 m.p.h. entry to the Curva Parabolica, slammed under the Armco barrier and smashed into a lamp stanchion. There followed speculation about mechanical failure, and a sheared half-shaft was suggested. Rindt, who had opened his jugular on the windshield, was made posthumous World Champion.

At Watkins Glen in 1974, Austrian Helmuth Koinigg, on the ninth lap of only his second Grand Prix, arrived at the curve where Mario Andretti and Jean-Pierre Beltoise had crashed in practice, and inexplicably went straight on. Eye-witnesses said there appeared to be no attempt at braking. Normally the driver would have been decelerating from a speed corresponding to peak revs in third gear for a second-gear corner. The Surtees tore through three layers of catch-fencing and hit a steel guardrail. Koinigg was beheaded.

We do not know, because dead men cannot tell us, how many of F1's fatal accidents may have been due to aprosexia (inability to maintain concentration) or aboulia (inability to make or act on decisions). Mechanical failure in the car, because a F1 car is infinitely complex, is blamed in all but the most obvious cases of driver error. But as we have seen racers must make decisions under phenomenal pressure, and at least one of them has referred to the difficulty of deciding where to focus his eyes in the exit of a curve. We do not know what happens to a racer's mind as he negotiates the hazards of a race-track at speeds approaching 200 m.p.h., and we do not know what happens under competitive pressure to his ability to make judgements involving centimetres and fractions of a second. But perhaps, if we are to have the experiment in front of us, it is high time we tried to find out. Jim Clark's 'most difficult task in life' was apparently 'making decisions'[33]. In other sports far less dangerous, investigations suggest that there is an overload point in the decision-making process at which mechanical coordination breaks down. In response to a request from the Training Committee of the Japanese Society for Physical Culture after the 1960 Rome Olympic Meeting, a hypnotherapist, Gosaku Naruse, questioned 125 Japanese Olympic athletes about 'stage fright' during competition. He found: 'For some, these conditions might serve as stimulation to do their best in the match; for others, however, it may produce undesirable effects. It may disturb the integration of concentration of motor components, resulting in a loss of control or disintegration of motor behaviour. . . . Stage fright on the athletic field, it seems, is the result of acute and intolerably strong psychological stresses in the face of competitive struggle. The situation appears so similar to that of a neurosis, particularly war neurosis, that it is possible to consider it in the light of principles of psychotherapy.'[35]

Two Canadian sports psychologists found from their investigations that gymnastic displays varied in their demands on the input, output and central processing systems of the gymnast. For example, a particular side-horse display surpassed one movement per second, 'indicating that the generally accepted limited capacity for making two decisions per second was being approached. Any major correction or adjustment that was required during the routine would probably result in a performance breakdown because the capacity for processing information was overloaded.'[36]

Psychological and physiological studies of stress which may have some bearing on this field are numerous and complex, and recent findings are inconclusive. Nonetheless, sport has inspired all manner of investigations into the biochemical effects of stress, reactive inhibition, the Yerkes–Dodson law, the fight or flight syndrome, galvanic skin response, ARF (Ascending Reticular Formation), introversion in athletes, extroversion in athletes, personality types and ego-strength, to say nothing of literature on sport as a conflict model. Discussion of conflict in motivation, central processing time, theories of neurone behaviour, synapses, arousal and the learning process are numerous, which should surprise no one, considering sport's experimental nature. Indeed, some studies give the impression that sportsmen are the very flesh and blood of behavioural and physiological research. I will not attempt, as so many of my predecessors have done, to lard this book with physiological data. I am not qualified to do so, and in any case it would defeat the whole purpose of this particular study, which takes as its starting point the humanity of all sportsmen, and their contribution to man's understanding of himself. In drawing attention to the phenomenon of split mind in sport, my aim is not to push back the frontiers of laboratory research at their expense but to invite some of sport's millions of critical observers to consider with compassion the anguish they may be watching, which we call a game.

9

The Violent Games

In all sports, even chess, there is an element of aggression. In some sports aggression becomes crucially important. It signifies the will to win against any odds, momentum, ultimate physical effort, 'killer-instinct' and the willingness of the athlete to sacrifice his own and his opponents' bodies in the cause of victory. This aggression is coaxed from the athlete by the coaching staff who 'psych him up', by the press who eulogize his efforts in war metaphors, and especially by the crowds, many of whom admire 'macho' in a violent age as a self-determining philosophy. Sometimes the pressure on the athlete to aggress – to show ruthless enthusiasm and 'fire' – is so extreme that he will risk incurring the penalties of the game and the law of the land to satisfy the clamour for aggressive behaviour. He may do this even in spite of personal misgivings, guilt feelings and confusion as to the ethics involved. And he will explain his actions by saying, 'Yes, but we won,' or 'Yes, but we needed the points.' His situation is always vulnerable: when, in his efforts to show macho, 'killer-instinct' and fire, he oversteps the very hazy distinction between aggression and brutality, a body of 'concerned' individuals and authorities will raise a hue and cry about his behaviour.

Those who criticize loudest understand least the psychological forces at work in the sport experiment, which is not a game but a most serious and meticulously devised test of human beings *in extremis*. Aggression is, of all emotions, the most dangerous and difficult to examine. The sport experiment enables man to examine it in great detail and, as far as is practicable, *in vacuo*. The more violent and war-like society becomes, the more it examines the mechanism of aggression in its arenas and stadiums. Many spectators attend sporting events specifically to see aggression given and received. Recent studies suggest that this is not necessarily because of catharsis, as was once believed, for there is little evidence that spectator aggression is 'purged' by aggressive acts on the field of play, and considerable evidence that aggressive play may incite spectators to further violence.[1] Besides, there is a much more simple and straightforward explanation. Spectators wish to see what happens to the aggressor, what he does, when he does it, and whether or not he succeeds. The prospect of his success – or punishment – is a compelling spectacle, with relevance everywhere in their lives. When one aggressor is pitted against another, the fascination lies in seeing which of the two wins, and how. This in itself is an exhilarating study. The ethics involved are complex, but ultimately boil down to the one governing ethic of all sport experimentation: the Need to Know. It is necessary to see what will happen; to see which force will win. 'Thus competition is a frequent source of frustration and frustration increases the likelihood of aggression. Social learning theorists have recognized this for some time, frequently using competitive situations to manipulate frustration in order to observe aggressive tendencies.'[2]

When President Kennedy was assassinated America grieved, but a full schedule of National Football League games took place on the Sunday following the Friday assassination, in spite of a handful of protests. Gridiron football is America's national sport. Apart from war, it is undoubtedly the most violent and brutal spectacle available to television. It celebrates man the Noble Savage three times a week on three stations, CBS, NBC and ABC, which recently shelled out $656 million, £328 million (the largest sum in television history) to cover the seasonal schedule of games. An estimated 100 million viewers saw Super Bowl XX in January 1986. 85 million watched Super Bowl XII in January 1978. Sponsors paid $325,000 a minute for advertising time. 74,500 spectators were in the Superdome, a $163 million megastructure covering thirteen acres of New Orleans, to see the action live. And the action is founded on legitimate violence: that is to say, violence within the scope of the rules. Individual players are occasionally singled out for criticism, but by and large brutality is accepted as part of the athlete's job. His job is to wipe the opposition off the face of the earth, by any means available which do not incur an 'infraction' or penalty.

The game is territorial. The field is a hundred yards from goal to goal, and the ball, a mere catalyst for the action, is moved *painstakingly* from one end to the other. Along the line of scrimmage – 'the pit', as it has sometimes been called – there is a collision between an irresistible offence and an immovable defence. This clash is of epic proportions, because the players on either side are the largest, fastest, heaviest, strongest, most terrifying and aggressive human beings in the United States of America. They get bigger, faster, heavier and more aggressive each year as the species perfects itself, and new ways are found, both chemical and financial, to increase their already considerable motivation. The players wear uniforms, not so much to protect their bodies, as to enable them to perform physical impossibilities. Enormous shoulder-pads, armoured forearms, hand-pads and hard-shell helmets give the players, already large, a colossal appearance. Their repertoire of blocks and tackles changes from year to year, as old methods are abandoned or outlawed and new ones found to replace them. The crackback, for example, which consists of driving full force at an opponent's knee at the line of scrimmage so as to displace some of his cartilage, was officially outlawed by the NFL in 1974, although the method dies hard. Raking, or rake-blocking, leg-whipping, clotheslining, face-to-numbers blocking, spearing, sticking or spiking, chop-blocking, butt-blocking, ear-holing and biting have all achieved great popularity at one time or another. So have the hayhook and the hammer, and a thing called 'piling on', the method by which a receiver, already down, is trampled, pile-driven, ruptured and punched by a 'pile' of opposing defensive players unable to stop their momentum. They are very heavy: 260 lb (18½ stone) is not unusual. Although there is considerable pressure on a player to 'bounce up' from these encounters, many secretly have trouble locating the sidelines. To 'ring somebody's chimes' is to deliver a staggering blow to his head.

The player's aggression, more than any other attribute, gets him noticed in college: he gets decals (merit badges) on his helmet, a favourable rating in scouting reports, and later, 'sack' bonuses in the pros. 'Pursuit' and 'second effort', very often euphemisms for late hits, are a sign of 'meanness', and a pro player who lacks the . prerequisite meanness for making his fair share of tackles is put on waivers and traded off. The player is required to 'hit'. There is nothing prissy about his training: training camp is colloquially 'hitting camp'. Coaches urge him to 'punish' the opposition, to 'kill', 'make 'em bleed' and 'whip some ass'. Some coaches are more discreet than others in their choice of vocabulary, but the player gets the message loud and clear, by means of class-rooms blackboards, playbooks, threats, cajolery, clippings on the wall, punishment drills (sometimes called 'shit drills'), insults to his virility and any other methods the coaching staff can find of driving it down the North West Passage of his intellect. Hitting is his job, and he is given chemicals: stimulants ('diet' pills like Dexedrine, Benzedrine, Eskatrol, for their amphetamine component), anabolic steroids (such as Gianabol) and analgesics (Xylocaine, Codeine, Novocaine, Cortisone) – so he can do it with reckless abandon.

The rules are designed to allow for sixty minutes of unremitting violence. According to a recent study by the Stanford Research Institute only 1.3 per cent of the sport's hideous injuries were the result of tackles made outside the rules. 98.7 per cent of injuries were the result of an athlete doing his job. *Sports Illustrated* in 1978 ran a series on 'Brutality – the crisis in pro football',[3] in which senior writer John Underwood researched the sport's startling injury statistics and their possible causes. He found that many of the most serious injuries – brain and spinal-cord damage, bruised kidneys, broken ribs and ruptured spleens – were caused by a player using his hard-shell helmet, a three-pound polycarbonate, styrene and leather hollow bowling ball (originally intended to protect his head) to spear and gouge an opponent's body. Others were the result of his using an opponent's faceguard (originally designed to protect his features) as a means of driving back his helmet and severing his neck. Three years ago, an estimated 40,000 interscholastic players were treated in emergency rooms for injuries to the head and neck. In November 1977 a Californian high school player, 17-year-old Gregory Cole, died of a subdural hematoma after making a head-on tackle. The same season Colorado line-backer Tom Perry collapsed in the locker-room after a similar collision and was taken to hospital with a cerebral haemorrhage. Doctors saved his life by drilling a 5/8 inch hole in his skull to evacuate blood clots. Dr Richard Schneider, head of neurosurgical research at the University of Michigan, has studied the case histories of 225 helmet injuries (including 66 deaths) and recommends the removal of the face-guard. The rules do not protect the player from injuries of this kind. Moves to introduce padded helmets have been met head-on by the authorities (as have similar moves in cricket, rugby and boxing) concerned not to mollycoddle the athlete with protective clothing. A recent spate of lawsuits against helmet manufacturers appears not to have altered the general attitude of the players to 'taking their licks' and 'paying the price'. This, too, is part of their job.

Eagle running back Dave Hampton was taken to hospital unconscious after being clotheslined (clubbed in the neck) by Cardinal Tim Kearney. When he recovered, he said, 'That's football.' His comment reflects the feelings of most of the players about being hit, and Oakland line-backer Phil Villapiano summed up the feelings of most of his peers about hitting. He said, 'When you play for Oakland, you play to win and you play tough. You are going to hit people and you are going to smash them if you are an Oakland Raider. . . .' Oakland's George Atkinson smashed Pittsburgh receiver Lynn Swann, who was carried off with severe concussion. There was no infraction called. Oakland's Jack Tatum, nicknamed 'Black Death' by his team-mates, smashed New England's Darryl Stingley, as the receiver reached high in the air to take a pass. 'He was in the air,' said Tatum, 'when I hit him. We almost hit head on. I knew it was a good shot. You hate to see anybody get hurt. . . . But I was just doing my job. I thought it was a good football play.'⁴ Stingley is still paralysed, perhaps permanently so. Team-mate Russ Francis found him lying glassy-eyed on the field saying, 'I'll be all right, I'll be all right.' He had two displaced vertebrae. The tackle was perfectly legal.

A typical season of injuries, according to *Sports Illustrated* writer Underwood, would include one million high-school players at approximately 20,000 schools, 70,000 college players at more than 900 schools, and one injury per man to every player in the pro ranks of the National Football League.

Few players escape the game without some permanent disability, or without pain-hangovers, usually by the age of 30 or before. And few players complain, because as Dave Hampton says, 'That's football.' But a handful of the more outspoken pros have written books on their experiences and one of these is *North Dallas Forty* by ex-Dallas Cowboy Peter Gent. The book is about 'the huddle' of 'battered, bruised and exhausted men, some already worrying about mistakes they would have to explain next Tuesday. Scared to death and angry', for whom it would be a miracle if they could even start plays in unison, 'let alone outthink, outmanoeuver, and outmuscle the men of similar talent across the line.'⁵ Gent's thinly veiled autobiography is about mutilated bodies shot full of novocaine so they can go out and re-injure their injuries, pre-game tension, nauseating locker-room lavatories, team prayers, amphetamines, and reactions speeded up by dope and fright to produce glistening plays in front of colossal audiences. Most of all, Gent's book is about fear: the athletes' fear that their personal thresholds for withstanding pressure on the field and emasculating pain and criticism afterwards, may not be quite high enough. Gent has something to say, too, about the White Mice Men discussed earlier in connection with the sport experiment: 'Looking up into the stands at the mass of grey dots that were faces, perched atop flashes of colors that expressed their egos, I suddenly realized how peculiar we must look. I thought of Al Capp schmoos paying six dollars a head to watch and scream while trained mice scurried around in panic.'⁶

So much for American football. The reader is asked to resist being pious because the originators of our aggressive sports never intended them to be good clean fun. Soccer, for example, seems to have evolved from a medieval game called 'Dane's Head', banned by Henry II, in which a skull, and later a cow's bladder, was kicked from town to town,⁷ and rugby and soccer went their separate ways, according to one of soccer's leading authorities, Sir Stanley Rous, not over handling but over hacking: 'The rugby followers claimed that the end of hacking would mean the end of "all the pluck and courage of the game". So far as university football was concerned they need not have worried for this remained an example of the philosophy "Don't worry about the ball. Let's go on with the game." Or, as it was more simply put to me, "Fouls have to be intentional. Gentlemen don't foul intentionally. So there are no fouls." Before the first match I refereed, the two captains, Howard Fabian and John Hazledean, told me, "We don't want you to referee as you do in professional games. We like to get on with the match without interruption." And I was indeed to see the Oxford goalkeeper with an ear half torn off shouting, "Don't mind me. Get on with the game." '⁸

David Irvine, *Guardian* correspondent and author of *The Joy of Rugby*, feels that calling rugby 'the man's game' does it some injustice, because the risks are greater in rock-climbing and skiing. Mr Irvine is anxious to defend the sport against carping critics of its aggressiveness, and goes to some lengths to point out its 'amity and goodwill' and the 'spirit' that distinguishes rugby from rumbles. 'It has never been easy to persuade those outside the game that there is a clear distinction between "rough" and "dirty" play but players generally recognize the different categories and those who cross the line of demarcation do so consciously and in full awareness of the penalties. Rugby would wither rapidly were "The Spirit" not observed.'[9] By a cruel irony, Mr Irvine's book was reviewed in *The Times* on 24 October 1978 next to another piece, on Rugby League, which bore the heading 'Allegations of biting denied by Australian Manager'. It referred to accusations made by the British manager, Harry Womersley that the Australians bite, and counter-allegations by the Australian manager Peter Moore that not only did his players not bite, but that the British players were guilty of kicking and stiff-arm tackles. Perhaps Mr Irvine is better able to understand the suspicions of 'those outside the game' regarding its aggressive requirements than he lets on, because he admits that the game is in many ways 'a ready-made vehicle for violence'.[10] He talks later about the increasing competitiveness of televised rugby, allowing that 'Many retired internationals have said that had these pressures [to win at all costs] applied when they were actively engaged in the game, they would not have cooperated and some still playing have felt disquiet at the way their involvement is developing.'[11] He adds, 'Already players are under too much pressure – often too much pressure to win.'

With all due respect to the idealistic Mr Irvine, J.P.R. Williams, arguably the greatest full-back the game ever produced, has said of rugby, 'It has come as close to warfare as sport can get,' because, 'At times there is so much tension and pressure that people tend to do things they might not otherwise do.' J.P.R. had just come out of an Ireland–Wales international in which he himself had incensed the Irish crowd with a late tackle that wiped out Mike Gibson. The tackle, said J.P.R., was 'an instinctive reaction. I couldn't stop myself.' Of course he couldn't. Violence is to rugby as jam is to doughnuts. Consider the game's etymology. A 'maul', according to Chambers dictionary, is defined as follows: '*Maul*; a war-club or mace, a heavy wooden hammer. In rugby a scrimmage; (in goal) a struggle for the ball when carried across the goal-line but not yet touched down. v.t. to beat with a maul or heavy stick; to handle roughly,batter, maltreat; to split with a maul – U.S. v.i. to thrust forward in a close mass (mall). *Mall*: a maul, large wooden beetle or hammer.'

And so on. A 'ruck' (which is slang for 'fight' but which is also a noun meaning 'heap' and a verb meaning 'squat') inevitably requires that several pairs of feet pass over the top of a player on the ground, and with some alacrity. This is hard to do in a mincing fashion. 'You can't provide an international front row,' admits the judicious Iain MacKenzie in his *Sunday Times* article on the dangers of violent tackles, 'by tiptoeing through the tulips.'[12] Former captain and coach John Dawes recently described a tour of New Zealand as 'a hundred-day war'.

The mid-nineteenth-century game of rugby was very rough indeed. In 1846 rules had to be devised to restrain players from throttling and strangling, from hacking (at least with the heel), and from wearing projecting nails, gutta percha and iron plates on their boots, the better to hack with. The 'maul-in-goal' was an excuse for a wrestling match in which spectators frequently became involved, and in the early days of twenty-a-side, the emphasis was on keeping the ball in the scrum for as long as possible, and gaining ground by pummelling. 'It was not unusual,' says Irvine in *The Joy of Rugby*, 'for the ball to be trapped deep within a heaving mass of humanity for upwards of ten minutes.'[13] Yet Mr Irvine remains steadfastly optimistic about the modern game. Television viewers of the 1975 Brisbane Test between England and Australia in which they noticed a few brawls, might not share his optimism. Or of the 1967 incident in Cardiff involving Brian Price. Or of the 1978 tour of Australia by the Welsh, which ended in brawls, thuggery and recriminations. From the joy of that particular piece of rugby, prop Graham Price returned home with his jaw broken in two places. Wallabies prop Steve Finnane, accused of 'jobbing' Pricey, retaliated, 'If they want to kick we will punch. That's it.' Price was scarcely recognizable when he arrived back from Sydney with his head swathed in bandages. Nor was he the only one: Alun Donovan was in a wheelchair with torn knee ligaments, Gareth Evans had a depressed fracture of the cheekbone, and Gerald Davies was still recovering from concussion. The joy of rugby may have momentarily escaped their attention as they hobbled home.

Things could only get worse. In response to mounting player violence England's Rugby Union finally slapped an automatic ban on sent-off brawlers, which was rescinded in 1985 through 'lack of support from other Unions'. The same year the Welsh Rugby Union instituted a similar ban in its own crackdown on thuggery. Said Welsh RU Secretary Ray Williams, 'The gloves are off'.[14] The decision followed a series of 'incidents'. Referee George Crawford had walked out of Newport's club match at Bristol in September in exasperation at conduct on the field. There had been numerous other punch-ups and sendings-off, involving Pontypool's John Perkins in a club match at Pontypridd in November 1983, England's Steve Bainbridge in a Gosforth club match, Welshman Richard Moriarty playing for Swansea at Llanelli, and Ian Stephens, David Bishop, Allan Martin, Mike Watkins and Ian Eidman in an assortment of other set-tos.

But first prize for recent Rugby Rumbles should really go to New Zealand's Kurt Sorensen and Britain's Jeff Grayshon, whose struggles were interrupted by police at Elland Road in the November 1985 final Rugby League Test between Great Britain and New Zealand. The game continued around the central mêlée, and Britain's hooker Dave Watkinson left the field looking like something out of *Texas Chainsaw Massacre*.

Various critics of the modern game, who remember it being played 'for fun', have suggested that the 'increasing level of brutality' in rugby will turn away its new-found masses of spectators. I doubt it. The fascination of brute force, controlled and unleashed by degrees, has never been lost on spectators. They do not normally 'mass' anywhere unless there is something intriguing going on. Performances of powerful athletes under pressure are interesting, and they are important. Society examines the sportsman because he is its visible representative; his skills symbolize all human endeavour. In seeking to understand the sportsman's reactions under stress, we seek to understand our own. Our violent sports are our means of exploring our violent selves. Let us not suppose that spectators come innocently to watch big men running up and down, while they themselves quietly eat their sandwiches.

As in the case of Scotland's World Cup bids in soccer, insufficient aggression in a crucial rugby game can have disastrous consequences. Forward superiority may win ball (possession) but unless the backs can capitalize by lungeing through enemy territory for tries, the only points on the board are likely to be from kicking. Similarly, the backs rely on the might of the pack asserting itself in the rucks and mauls to gain possession. The key to producing optimum aggression – sufficient to win, but not enough to draw penalties for brutality – is hard to find, especially with several thousand pairs of eyeballs focused on one's behaviour.

'The might of the All Blacks' and 'the attacking tradition of the Lions' are rugby clichés. I asked J.P.R. Williams, a man believed by many to be made of iron, if a formidable reputation was something teams needed to cultivate. John said it was. 'If your opponents are afraid of you, you do have a better chance.' Another factor, especially now that the game is watched by large numbers of spectators, is the need for a result (see pages 16–18). 'The pressures are greater on an increasing number of sides to win at all costs. The game is much bigger now, and the media have been largely responsible for this, through their intensive coverage.' These two needs – to assert authority over opponents by cultivating a 'tough' reputation, and to win – have produced brutality of a kind that shocks the players themselves, some of whom have expressed despair at the way the game is developing.

Violence, once set in motion on the field by a contact sport, is like a swinging pendulum. A team that feels unduly knocked about by a particular set of opponents eventually retaliates, perhaps not in the next moment, or even the next match, but eventually, even if the players are models of self-control.

Much has been said about the 'unwritten laws' of the game. One unwritten law not usually mentioned is that, as a player, you do not allow yourself or your team-mates to be publicly brutalized by an opposing team in the course of play. You are duty-bound to level the score; if you don't your reputation for toughness and pride is immediately compromised. Rugby is an uncompromising game, a fierce and formidable game, in which there are frequent physical collisions. No one likes to be made a fool of in front of thousands of people and no one likes to see his team-mates physically humiliated either. Under these circumstances, and in the excitement of competition, many normally friendly and civilized players have lashed out. We may not like to hear of these instincts; we may not like to have them spelled out to us. But if we place two groups of physically powerful men in an arena in order to yell at them, and observe their behaviour, we should not be too surprised if what we are eventually shown is the spectacle of men hitting one another.

One of the problems, as in all aggressive sports, is the question of degree. The line between robustness and brutality is a delicate one.

'The England Selectors helped us off the mark. They sent a team which included seven new caps to Cardiff! We all knew about Rossborough, the Coventry full back. He was rather "delicate" under the high ball, so we let him have it. We practised it hard beforehand, Barry and I kicking, Arthur Lewis smashing in on the catcher, and John Dawes lurking in a support position to pick up the pieces.'[15]

Who is this talking? Erwin Rommel? General MacArthur? No, it's the world's most capped scum half, the pleasant and personable Gareth Edwards. Gareth deplores the brutality creeping into the game, and believes it is up to the referees to draw the delicate line between aggression and violence.[16] In a game like competitive rugby, this is difficult, and not because the players themselves are a bunch of hoodlums.

In 1978 there were two extremely serious cases of brutality, both involving teams who had ordinarily played 'good, clean, attacking rugby football'. Llanelli is one of the homes of the game, and boasts one of the finest teams ever to play it. One Saturday in November they played Richmond, and former England lock Chris Ralston emerged from a ruck covered in blood from a head wound. A temporal artery had been severed, and Ralston needed thirty-two stitches. The referee did not see what happened; neither, it seems, did anyone else. Ralston and his Richmond team-mates believe he was raked (with boot studs) by one of the Llanelli forwards. Charlie Thomas was singled out, and retorted 'I am not one of rugby's nasties. Aggressive yes, dirty no, and never nasty.'[17] To this day, despite extensive investigations, the matter remains unresolved. Only two things are certain: one is that Ralston could easily have died, and the other is that the 'accident' happened in a ruck – where, to borrow Gareth Edwards's expression, the 'law of the jungle' operates.[18]

The second incident concerned the 1978 All Blacks, who were on a 'diplomatic' mission to Britain, having been handpicked from players unlikely to get into trouble, as previous teams had done. They had been kept on a very tight rein throughout their tour by the New Zealand management. No one was allowed outside the team hotel in the evenings without his regulation blue socks on, and 'no swearing'. The All Blacks had been unexpectedly successful, beaten only by Munster, the first All Blacks ever to achieve a clean sweep of all four unions. At the end of their tour the New Zealanders went to Bridgend to play captain J. P. R. Williams's famous Welshmen. There had been one or two rough encounters on the tour, but nothing to mar the All Blacks' overall good reputation as 'ambassadors of the game'. Four minutes into the Bridgend fixture, J.P.R., as he lay face upwards in a ruck looking into the All Blacks' metal boot studs, was stamped on, several times it seemed, by reserve prop John Ashworth. Ashworth said afterwards that there was a lot of mud about and that he couldn't tell if John's head was his head, or the ball. J.P.R. left the field looking like the victim of a stampede, and had his face sewn up by his father, a surgeon like himself. He had lost so much blood through a large hole in his cheek that he secretly believed he might die. With plastic sealer over the stiches, he went back and finished the game, because he had made a vow to himself that he would 'never be kicked off the field'. J.P.R. is understandably bitter about the incident: he had been nowhere near the ball, the referee had done nothing, and the New Zealand management would accept no responsibility. Indeed, they were strangely angry that they had been accused at all, since they thought they had been 'bloody tolerant' (as coach Jack Gleeson put it) throughout the tour, and had never retaliated for cheap shots taken at them. John Ashworth, for his part, rushed on to the field to replace injured prop Brad Johnstone in the All Blacks–Barbarians game at Cardiff the following weekend. Thrusting his arms high in the air, Ashworth seemed to be acknowledging the applause from some little auditorium inside his head.

Why has this happened to rugby, a game visibly awesome and exhilarating which used to be played 'for fun'? The incidents are piling up: a player blinded in one eye in Lyons; fifty-seven Scottish players sent off by November of the 1978 season; twenty-three Wigan players sent off in three seasons; forty-two suspended in France in a single week; disturbing medical statistics on the game from Guy's Hospital and researchers in South Africa; a coroner in Sheffield pleading for the game to be made safer after a 35-year-old police inspector died of injuries received in a ruck. The answer is that rugby is now a major international spectator sport, reaching across several continents into Russia, New Zealand, Australia, South Africa, France, Britain and elsewhere. Results have become crucially important; thousands of spectators wish to see what happens, and, though they may have certain allegiances, they do not care particularly whom it happens *to*.

The reader who has difficulty believing that rugby is *designed* to induce its players to be violent, or that American football brutality is the natural outcome of the game itself, may like to consider a more straightforward example of the violent sport experiment. Boxing.

Alan Minter's trainer, Bobby Neill, almost died after a brain operation some years ago, following a title fight. Soon after the death of Minter's opponent for the European title, Italian middleweight Angelo Jacopucci, despite brain surgery in July 1978, Neill told Alan Hubbard of the *Observer*[19] that he thought Jacopucci had weakened himself in a desperate attempt to get his weight down for the fight. He also said that although, all those years before, he had sat up in his hospital bed and defended his right to box to abolitionist Baroness Summerskill, it was true that boxing is philosophically indefensible. 'How can you defend two men attempting to batter each other insensible? It is simply that boxing fulfils a social need as an aggressive outlet for participant and spectator. It is the old gladiatorial syndrome.'

The boxer's job is to injure, maim, and render his opponent unconscious. Indeed, if the opponent dies from his injuries, it simply means that the fighter who hit him was very good at landing punches where they were likely to do the most damage. The first of the two operations on Jacopucci's brain was to disperse a blood clot on the right side of the head. This was where Minter's final punch, a left hook, had caught him and put him on the canvas for the full ten-second count. The European title fight with Minter may well have aggravated an injury received in an earlier title fight in 1976 when the Italian was punched in the head by fellow-Italian Germano Valsecchi. At all events, Jacopucci's death certificate bore the explanatory statement, 'an accident at work'.[20] Alan Minter, for his part, knew that his job was to knock his man out, because he would have been unlikely to get a points decision from the Italian judges. Consequently there was extreme pressure on Minter to win by a knockout, and knockouts are generally caused by blows to the head.

'I used to wake up all hours with it on my mind,' Minter said.[21] He was asked, before his next fight (with French–Maltese Gratien Tonna) if Jacopucci's death would inhibit him in the ring. Minter replied that it wouldn't, partly because the Italian had seemed all right immediately after the fight. 'If my last image was of him lying stretched out on the floor, dying in front of me, I'm sure that would really have done me over.'[22] Minter's next opponent helped him out of any inhibitions he may have had when they met in Wembley Arena. Tonna's brawling style and continual butting ('nuttin' yer', as Alan explained later) would have tried the patience of most fighters, and Minter gradually lost his temper. In the sixth Tonna quit. He said he was 'fed up with the referee', referring to an incident at the end of the third in which Minter had landed a reflex right to his jaw on the break. Tonna's decision caused one journalist to remark, 'In the measurement of human courage there can be no absolutes, but the man who described Gratien Tonna last week as "an absolute wanker" found instant forgiveness in the hearts of many.'[23] Yet Tonna had cuts over both eyes, and Minter had told reporters, 'He took a lot of stick.'[24]

A number of commentators have remarked on the extreme cruelty of boxing. One calls the sport 'legalized murder'.[25] Another study, painstakingly researched by interviews with sixty-eight boxers and former boxers,[26] shows how the boxer is trained to aggress: 'The boxer's persistent display of aggression is an aspect of status. Thus his aggression becomes impersonal, although competition is intense. Thus two boxers may be friends outside the ring, but each will try to knock the other out in a bout, and after the bout they may be as friendly as competition permits. Furthermore, the injury done to an opponent, such as maiming or killing, is quickly rationalized away by an effective trainer or manager in order to prevent an excess of intense guilt, which can ruin a fighter.'[27]

The boxer is obliged to keep his private fears and misgivings to himself, lest they interfere with his job. As Leon Spinks came down the aisle towards the ropes, his lips moved. He was saying, 'Yea, though I walk through the valley of the shadow of death I will fear no evil. . . .' In an interview with Dudley Doust before he lost his heavyweight title, Leon said, 'I got to fight to do my job but I can't wait to get out of the ring. I don't enjoy hitting nobody.'[28] Like most of his fellow black fighters Spinks learned to box in order to survive. As a child he was skinny and 'frailed up'. His mother encouraged him to learn how to 'throw and catch' in order to defend himself, not least from his own father. 'When I was about eight, my daddy hung me up by my shirt on a nail on the wall. Then he gave me a whupping with an electric extension cord.' Ali was his boyhood hero. The first thing Spinks did after beating the Greatest was to weasel his way into Ali's dressing-room and offer condolences. Indeed,he rose and led the applause when Ali stepped up for his press conference, and put his arm round the deposed champ's shoulder, saying he 'owed' Ali a return fight. Few of us are ever in a position to punch our heroes for fifteen rounds, a peculiar privilege the boxer enjoys. He also enjoys a permanent relationship with pain. Since 1970, according to Ali's Fight Doctor, Ferdi Pacheco (now disgraced, so far as Ali's retinue is concerned, because of his too-revealing book), Ali has had novocaine shot into his fists. The champ has bursitis, an arthritic condition brought about by hours of punching the heavy bag, and the hands needed anaesthetizing before every fight.

Once a boxer steps into the ring, he is under extraordinary pressure. 'The boxers are thus placed in a situation fraught with tension, physical punishment, and eventual fatigue. They may be harassed by the spectators. . . . Some defeated boxers, as a result of physical fatigue and self-recrimination, lapse into a condition resembling combat exhaustion or anxiety. They react by uncontrollable crying spells, tantrums, and random belligerency.'[29] Hence the recent medical concern.

A fighter's job is to withstand the pressure better than his opponent. Any attempt to circumvent this pressure – to sabotage the experiment – is viewed with scorn.When, at the end of the fifth round of his British heavyweight title fight with John Gardner, Liverpool's Billy Aird decided to quit, he had to wrestle himself free of his protesting cornermen to catch the referee's eye. Aird is self-managed, otherwise this little scene would never have taken place. In his dressing-room afterwards, Aird knew what he had done: he said simply, 'That's it. There's nothing left for me. I'm finished.' In the fifth round of another European title fight, Spanish lightweight Antonio Guinaldo raised his hand and walked over to his corner. He had been floored by Scot Jim Watt, was bruised and battered, had double vision, and felt he was about to vomit. His London agent afterwards described his surrender as 'a terrible thing to do'. There followed an inquest by boxing officials who considered withholding his purse or a token part of it, and the reaction of the crowd was so hostile that even the victorious Watt said he had been frightened. 'I don't blame Guinaldo if he was scared,' said the World Lightweight champion, 'but my job was to keep him that way.'[30] Roberto Duran, after his walk-out against Sugar Ray

Leonard in the WBC Welterweight Championship in 1980, was roundly condemned, fined and publicly humiliated in Panama. His honour was not restored until he won the WBA light middleweight title three years later.

Rather than succumb like Duran, Aird or Guinaldo and risk the psychological and social consequences, many fighters try to punch their way out of trouble when they realize they are already seriously hurt. They undertake fights even though they know they are likely to aggravate serious injuries, in order to prove 'they aren't really hurt', or that 'so-and-so didn't really do any damage'. Jacopucci got into the ring against Minter knowing that he had already suffered from vomiting and severe headaches as a result of his previous injuries. Joe Frazier, prior to the Thriller in Manila in which he and Ali almost annihilated one another, was a troubled man. Joe wanted his title back, and especially he wanted to prove that Ali had not really hurt him in their previous encounter; that rumours that he was a sick man, almost blind in his right eye, were false. Former British Featherweight champion Vernon Sollas was anxious for the British Board of Control to revoke their decision not to let him back in the ring – after a fit in his European title fight.

In view of the seriousness of injuries sustained in the ring, the British Medical Association in 1982 passed a resolution recommending a ban on the sport. There followed a detailed medical inquiry and a report, published in February 1984, on 'the problem of preventable injuries' in boxing, in which investigators emphasized the gravity of ocular and brain damage to fighters, and pointed out that boxing is unique in that *these* sports injuries do not happen by accident, but quite intentionally. A medical officer I spoke to viewed with concern a recent television series in which Henry Cooper encouraged young boys to take up boxing and knock one another's brains about.

The boxer is not afraid of pain, but he is very much afraid of appearing afraid. In the state of emergency that exists in the ring, the psychological threat always takes precedence over the physical threat. A boxer who is knocked down for the count makes every effort, in his concussed confusion, to get up. From the psychological fight there can be no escape, for to sidestep this pressure is ignominious. Consequently boxing has always had its psych-doctors and gurus, without whom a fighter cannot survive. His cornermen are working on his mind after every round, whatever else they may be doing with the gauze and gumshields. Ben Finkle – 'Evil Eye' Finkle – who was immortalized as Fleegle in Al Capp's *Li'l Abner* – could lay a triple-whammy on even the strongest physical specimen with his hex stare from the ringside, and was often paid to do so in big fights. But boxers who know how to fight the psych war themselves have been rare indeed. In recent years the sport has produced only one, a genius in his own right.

'I'm not saying they are not good boxers. Most of them – people like Doug Jones and Ernie Terrell – can fight almost as good as I can. I'm just saying you never heard of them. And the reason for that is because they cannot throw the jive. Cassius Clay is a boxer who can throw the jive better than anybody you will probably ever meet anywhere. And right there is why I will meet Sonny Liston for the heavyweight championship of the world next week in Miami Beach. And jive is the reason also why they took my picture looking at $1 million in cold cash. That's how much money my fists and my mouth will have earned by the time my fight with Liston is over. Think about that.'

This was Muhammad Ali throwing the jive at *Sports Illustrated* in February 1964. Since then, in all his long career, he shut up only once. Before his extraordinary defeat by little Leon Spinks, Ali maintained a vow of silence. He did it to prove that the talk wasn't necessary, and for two months his lips were sealed. When, after two months of jive-lessness, word came from Ali's Hilton Hotel suite that he was about to give a press conference, reporters climbed over one another to get to the front row. Ali said, 'I thought about it. I made my point. I proved I'm free. I proved that if I don't want to talk, I don't have to talk. I can get along without it.' There was a last-minute show of strength against 'Goofy' Spinks, a last-minute insertion of ridiculous false teeth and a few gags about 'this duck' whom Ali was going to roll over, but nothing to compare with the long psychological campaigns against his other challengers.

Ferdie Pacheco, who has watched Ali's career at close quarters, reminds us in his book[31] that there is an 'indefinable something called "punching power" which has nothing to do with bulky muscles'. Ali defied many of the conventions of fighting. As a 'fresh kid' his genius was apparent to anyone willing to watch, though he ignored the idea of attacking his opponent's body, held his hands by his hips, and pulled back from a punch to the point of over-balancing. Nor was he ever a devastating 'big puncher'; his prime weapon was the jab. Ali had no KO punch as such, yet over went

Sonny Liston, to a little overhand right that Pacheco had never seen knock anybody down even in the gym, and over went Foreman, whose thunderous body punches were 'rope-a-doped' in Zaire. All the while Ali would be talking, winking, grimacing, and calling into question his opponent's common sense about stepping into the ring with him in the first place. 'Now Ali is into his thing: he is leading the crowds in their Ali yell,he is mugging for the press, he is looking over at George's corner and making faces, and talking, talking, talking in George's face. Foreman is a beaten fighter as the fifth starts.'[32]

Norton and Foreman – who could well have finished Ali's career with sheer physical force – had been gradually demoralized by talk. So had the Rubenesque ghetto-kid Joe Frazier – 'ugggly' and bourgeois, according to Ali's outrageous propaganda. But Spinks – 'this duck' – had escaped almost scot free from such an ego-drubbing, perhaps through his lack of status.

Indeed, Spinks was so light and inconsiderable a challenger that bookmakers in Vegas refused to touch the fight, and some considered it a 'palooka'. Many spectators, and some journalists of several years' standing in the sport, were taken aback by the shock result. Ali was called 'an old man' at 36 and some speculated that he must have 'tanked' the fight. Ali did not tank the fight. He was a little out of condition and not very highly motivated, but above all, his 'strategy was wrong' as he afterwards admitted in a TV interview with Harry Carpenter. 'The first four rounds my strategy was bad,' said Ali, hushing his children. He had tried to rope-a-dope Spinks, he explained, but 'He didn't tire. I figured at this pace he'd go but he didn't go. I couldn't catch up. Next time I'll just have to come out on mah toes.' He said Spinks didn't hurt him, but that 'he was a lotta energy. He just kept coming'.

Spinks didn't tire, and just kept coming, because there was no psychological gum on his boots, no mental pounds laid on him at the weigh-in, no ego-jabs coming at his head. Leon Spinks was free to fight, and fight he did, with meathooks. Not that winning did him a lot of good: he has since, in the words of his champion brother Michael, 'dug a lot of holes for himself'.

The abolitionist lobby has occasionally rendered itself ridiculous by naïvety; still, its spokesmen point to the sport's fatalities: fifteen in Great Britain in the past thirty-four years, twelve since the war; to the death of Scottish welterweight Steve Watt after his fight with Rocky Kelly in 1986, to the death of

Trinidad heavyweight Ulric Regis in March 1969 by cerebral haemorrhage (after being out-pointed by Bugner); to the six deaths in the first seven months of 1978; to three fatalities in World title fights since 1980 – South Korean Duk-Koo Kim, Mexican Kiki Bejines and the enormously popular Welshman Johnny Owen. And they say this is a waste of athletes' lives. But boxing has survived innumerable campaigns against it. The experiment goes on, because it is necessary: because millions of people wish to see what it discloses. Ali, Bruno and Barry McGuigan apart, it goes without saying that these millions do not particularly care about the subjects in the ring. Most fighters, who earnestly hope for loyalty lose esteem very quickly when their careers are over. They fail to understand that their audiences revere not individuals, but their aggression. Many of them make several 'comebacks' in spite of slurring speech and pain hangovers, because they cannot live without the excitement and admiration they knew in the ring. 60 per cent become 'punchy', five per cent severely so.[33] Ali visited top neurologists after he retired, to find out the reason for his slurring speech. Like the subjects of other brutal sport experiments, fighters are notoriously abused by interested businessmen, managers and promoters who see them as a means of making a fast buck and abandon them to 'charity' afterwards, as Joe Erskine and Randolph Turpin were abandoned. In the context of the experiment as a whole, this exploitation scarcely matters.

Even more dangerous than boxing, in terms of fatal head injuries and post-concussion care,[34] is soccer. Soccer is ostensibly not an aggressive game, but anyone who watches the ball-manoeuvring skills of professional soccer players is fully aware of the difference between these moves and those of schoolboys in yards. The professional player has a directive in his mind. He is not playing with the ball for the fun of it: chimpanzees can do that, and with some expertise. What distinguishes the professional player is his ability to attack, to defend, to build momentum and prevent momentum from being established, to score, to strike and to win. These are aggressive skills, skills that rivet the attention of the sport's emotional spectators, and determine the vicarious satisfaction they get. After a World Cup fiasco in which Scotland went 1–3 down to Peru in 1978, their (then) manager Ally MacLeod said, 'The link between defence and attack seemed to go and we were under pressure.'[35] He thought they played well for the first fifteen minutes but then something went wrong: 'Our fiery temperaments were not there. We just did not get stuck in or play with enough force. We were a sloppy side.' One journalist, Mike Aitken of the *Scotsman*, thought 'They tackled like choirboys.'[36] For the game against Iran, MacLeod, long may he rue the day, had omitted Graeme Souness and gone with his three little 'buzz-bombs', Macari, Gemmill and Hartford. 'I thought the three wee men would buzz, but they didn't.'

The Scotland side played without aggression, and they lost. After their miserable 1–1 draw with Iran, demented, spitting fans rushed the bus, calling the players bastards, questioning their manhood, and warning them, 'Wait till you get home!' One player arrived home sooner than any of the others, and that was the normally fiery and brilliant winger Willie Johnston. He had been put on the plane in disgrace after taking two tablets containing fencamfamin. (Since then Scotland have reached the 1986 World Cup finals in Mexico only to go out in the first group.)

In October 1970 a California State legislative sub-committee on drug abuse and alcoholism held a hearing in Los Angeles on the misuse of drugs in sport. One of those invited to testify was the director of the Institute for the Study of Sport and Society, Jack Scott. Scott told the committee: 'Drug abuse is only one of the many symptoms that show that something is terribly wrong with the role sport is playing in society today, and if you are serious about doing something to correct this problem, you will have to look at the root causes and not focus just on this one symptom.'[37]

Generally speaking, professional sportsmen who take drugs do so because they feel extraordinary pressure to produce superlative performances. The greater the pressure, the more sportsmen will resort to drugs. This is a fact rather than a prediction, and German drug-detecting computers, urine tests, blood tests and the most stringent of rules will be necessary now to reclaim the professional athlete from his preoccupation with becoming a superman, because, quite simply, that is what he is expected to be. At the same 1978 World Cup, Brazilian fans, dissatisfied with their team's performance, burnt an effigy of Claudio Coutinho, the manager, in a Mar del Plata street. His predecessor, Mario Zagalo, had his house stoned. The Brazilians support soccer in their millions, as a religion to redeem them from national poverty and hopelessness. Losing managers, and losing players, may live, in years to come, in fear of their lives.

Under pressure to produce aggression, the athlete's ability to do so frequently breaks down. His performance becomes sloppy, or intermittently brutal. He cannot monitor his aggressiveness: he is not an engine or a hydraulic drill. He does his best, but usually he produces either too little force or too much. This is particularly conspicuous in crucial games and at crucial moments in those games. At the urging of Liverpool's Kop, a player may turn himself into a ball of fire. Phil Thompson often has. In the replay of the 1978 English League Cup Final at Old Trafford,he brought down John O'Hare of Nottingham Forest with a 'professional foul' – tackling him from behind on the edge of the penalty box – and caused a furore by saying as much on television. Thompson was on the receiving end of somebody else's momentum and excitement in Liverpool's 1–0 defeat at Arsenal in December 1978. On *that* occasion, Thompson limped away saying, 'I don't know what got into Sammy Nelson. I was on the ground. First he kicked the ball straight at me for no reason and then he jumped on the side of my knee while I was still lying there. I won't say he did it deliberately, but . . . It's not as if I go round the grounds of England aiming kicks at other players.' He added, 'I can't see how anybody should have had anything in for me.'[38] There can be no doubt that Phil Thompson believed he was doing his job by tripping O'Hare (who was about to score) with his 'professional foul', because he sees everywhere the consequences of not producing ruthless enthusiasm and competitive zeal of this sort. After all, opponents expect collisions in the interest of three points. After a head-crashing incident with Brian Talbot, then of Ipswich, West Bromwich Albion's John Wile was extremely angry at being substituted when he had blood squirting out of his head. His manager Ron Atkinson said, 'I thought he had shed enough blood for West Brom,' but Wile was peeved at not being able to shed some more. Brian Talbot, the man he had collided with, was involved in another misfortune in an Ipswich–Manchester City 'Match of the Day' seen by millions of TV viewers in November 1978. In the final moments of that match, City's Brian Kidd gave new meaning to the word 'striker' when he made a violent off-the-ball lunge at Talbot. City manager Tony Book commented that he didn't expect his senior professionals 'to react to explosive situations as Brian did'. Brian himself was sorry and surprised at what he'd done. 'I am not a vindictive person,' he said, and apologized, 'if on the spur of the moment I became excitable and reacted the wrong way. . .'.[39]

Tommy Taylor of West Ham in his fiery enthusiasm for the points at Upton Park accidentally kicked Chelsea goal-keeper John Phillips in the head. West Ham supporters on the North Bank chanted, 'Nice one, Tommy, let's have another one,' as Phillips was carried off unconscious, with blood streaming from his skull. In their efforts to satisfy the crowd, the players altogether produced thirty-six fouls, twenty-two of them coming from West Ham. Taylor said, of the head-kicking incident, 'I felt sick for him because as soon as I hit him, I realized it was bad,' adding, 'I apologized to their manager and he said not to worry, it was an accident. The main thing is we got the points.'⁴⁰ West Ham won 3–1.

It is easy to be pious. It is easy for armchair critics not exposed to the wrath of the braying, dart-throwing supporters who go through the turnstiles looking for an aggressive win and have to be restrained from surging on to the field themselves. The fan wars have a special significance for the players. These have already resulted in the splitting of a city – Manchester – and several deaths, including a young fan who was pushed under a train by rival supporters after a Millwall–West Ham game and a 15-year-old schoolboy. At the Molineux ground, Wolverhampton, sixty-seven arrests were made at the Wolves match with Manchester United, and machine-sharpened metal discs were hurled about, bearing the inscription, 'I hope it cut your fucking head off you Wolves bastard.' Millwall fans have a long and shameful history of running amok dating back to 1934. Four times the ground has been closed after crowd violence and attacks on the referee and players. In 1980 a linesman was hit by concrete during a tie with Shrewsbury. In 1982 primitive scenes of savagery followed Millwall's defeat at Slough. In November 1985, five policemen were injured in riots at a Millwall v. Leeds game. Players have themselves been attacked. In January 1984, former Millwall man Paul Roberts was set upon by fans during a League game with Brentford. In October reserve player Robert Isaac was slashed with a knife during riots in the Old Kent Road after a Chelsea Milk Cup tie. In 1985, 300 fans went on the rampage in March with pickaxes and sledgehammers, laying siege to a pub in Bristol. At a Luton FA Cup tie a knife was thrown at the Luton goalkeeper and hundreds of fans rioted and fought pitched battles with police. Occasionally these Millwall shindigs are orchestrated with leaflets advertising forthcoming 'orgies of violence'. The players are not saints: they seek to impress their peers and earn their respect by whatever values they perceive to operate. (Thirteen players were sent off in League matches one black day in December 1985 – a League record.)

Nor is pandering to bloodthirsty fans peculiar to British soccer, as many of its harshest critics believe. In Canada and America, ice-hockey has been the subject of much recent litigation because of its frequently erupting brawls. *Sports Illustrated* talked to the new National Hockey League chief, John Ziegler, about the sport's various problems and the interview went as follows:

SI: 'The NHL has taken steps to cut down the violence. Can't more be done?'

Ziegler: 'Hockey has gotten a bum rap on this. It's a violent sport, there's no denying it. You can't put men skating 20 m.p.h., where part of their purpose is to run into one another, and you can't fire a hard rubber puck at more than 100 m.p.h. and say there isn't violence. But people get confused. There's some unfortunate use of sticks in hockey and if that's your definition of violence, then yes, that's out. That's *bad* violence.'

SI: 'But what about the fighting? Doesn't that turn fans off?'

Robert Eagleson (executive director of the NHL Players Association): 'No, a lot of them like that aspect of it – I don't know why.'[41]

Ice-hockey and soccer bear comparison, not only in their unusual level of spectator violence, but also in their frequent failure to produce a result. Ice-hockey is the only sport in the USA, according to the *International Herald Tribune*, 'where a fan pays his money and almost a fifth of the time, sees nothing decided.'[42]

Modern soccer players are accused of 'bringing the game into disrepute'. Sir Stanley Rous, in his *Football Worlds*, talked about the decline in standards and the 'public display of bad temper and bad sportsmanship'[43] since the thirties, yet he described with obvious admiration the 'rugged destroyers' and crushing tacklers of his youth,[44] many of whom used the now frowned-upon shoulder-charge. There was at least one incident in which a player's leg was broken by a fierce tackle and his team-mates took the offender out of the game by way of retaliation: Hungary *v*. Italy in 1933 – the first International to be broadcast, for Mussolini's benefit in Rome. On that occasion, referee Rous had to 'fetch the bucket and sponge and attend to him myself: neither teams' trainer would do it'.[45] George Orwell, commenting on a series of soccer games between several British clubs and the Moscow Dynamo in

1945, wrote: 'Sport is an unfailing cause of ill-will, and if such a
visit as this has had any effect at all on Anglo-Soviet relations, it
could only be to make them slightly worse than before. . . . Serious
sport has nothing to do with fair play. It is bound up with hatred,
jealousy, boastfulness, disregard of all rules, and sadistic pleasure
in witnessing violence: in other words, it is war minus the
shooting.'[46]

In the light of this, perhaps the charge against modern players of
'bringing the game into disrepute' is a calumny. Perhaps the charge
of 'bringing the players into disrepute' ought instead to be laid at
the door of their supporters. Or at the door of sport itself.

Violence in sport has inspired an international bomb-burst of
literature castigating athletes for foul play or warning them of the
legal consequences of their behaviour. One notable recent example
was *Sport and the Law* by Edward Grayson. The book was written, extraordinarily enough, at the centenary of a criminal court
ruling that a foul tackle could result in prosecution for criminal
assault – as though this were the occasion of some historic triumph
over naughty jocks. It claimed to contradict 'the idea that the great
God sport transcends the country's laws',[47] and 'to remind all
aggressive-minded players and their belligerently-minded friends
in the Press Box . . . of the potential and *ultimate* consequence of
violent and *unlawful* conduct on sporting fields'.[48] Mr Grayson
cites various examples of prosecution for injuries received during
the course of play between 1878 and 1978, and warns, 'Tackle
fairly and there is no problem. Tackle foully but accidentally . . .
and there would be no legal liability; but tackle foully or hit below
the belt with deliberation and/or recklessness and there is no doubt
what the consequences would and should be: a criminal prosecution and a claim for damages.'[49] The book contained two
forewords. One by Dick Jeeps, recently retired Chairman of the
Sports Council, urged that 'sport can no longer exist in a vacuum'.
The reader will readily agree; perhaps this is why sport is becoming
increasingly violent. The other foreword was by former Solicitor-
General the Rt Hon. Sir Michael Havers MP: 'Anyone who
engages in competitive sport accepts that there must be rules and
referees and umpires to enforce them. If the rule book is torn up or
vicious fouls go unpunished then the sporting element is destroyed
and the fun for both the player and the spectator is lost.'

As Arthur Miller wrote in his anger at the murder of Robert
Kennedy, 'There is violence because we have daily honoured
violence.'[50]

10

The Thoroughbreds

Some are born to sport, some achieve sport and some have sport thrust upon them. We are all familiar with the 'nature versus nurture' controversy. Test-tube babies, cloning, and genetic engineering discoveries, for example in horse-breeding, have inspired the argument that athletic ability is inherited; psychological and sociometric studies have inspired the argument that it is not. The sportsman is a very lonely human being. On his own he makes split-second decisions of the utmost complexity in response to pressure situations he has never seen before. Even as a member of a team, his decisions are conspicuously his own, and irrevocably right or wrong. Under these circumstances, forty-six chromosomes do not a champion make; for however much of their strength, agility and aptitudes his parents may have transmitted to him, he will not win simply because his parents won before him, or fail because they failed. Jimmy Connors and Chris Lloyd were the tennis children of teaching pros rather than champion stock. Briton Buster Mottram, far less successful than they, was a thoroughbred in the truest sense, for his father Tony represented Great Britain in fifty-eight Davis Cup rubbers and his mother Joy *née* Gannon was 1954 German Open champion and a Wightman Cup player of renown. Yet Buster never won a major championship, while Connors and Evert-Lloyd have carried all before them.

More feasible than any 'star-studded' theory of sports success is the argument that parents with an aptitude for sport, and especially those whose own ambitions have been frustrated, transmit their dreams to their children. On the evidence of later performances these children are often unconsciously preparing to 'do their own thing' about such precepts at the first conspicuous opportunity.

A warning concerning youngsters pressured into sport was sounded at the 1986 international conference in Birmingham entitled 'The Growing Child in Competitive Sport'. The conference had been called by leading coaches and authorities wishing to draw attention to the effects of stress on children under competitive pressure, and it was suggested that young athletes are often caught 'between the ambitious parent and the unscrupulous coach'. One speaker, Dr Glyn Roberts, referred to a child waiting to bat in little-league baseball. 'He had a heart beat of 204'.

Many who have sport thrust upon them openly rebel, or register their independence more covertly. Even those who genuinely love what they have learned find it necessary to make a stand, so that their talent shall not be taken for granted. They can't help it; they aren't horses. Often, there is a mysterious 'slump'. Not that these children fail deliberately; few thoroughbreds are consciously disrespectful of winning. Rather, they become the victims of 'fate', of hostile forces outside their control, of ill luck, or ill health. Sometimes there is a freak injury, or an impasse with authorities makes competition impossible. In any case, a crisis of some kind awaits them all, if only because each one eventually must decide whether to go on winning for his parents, or try to win for himself. As Chris Lloyd says of her own nadir a few years ago, 'This was the first time I'd ever really been out on my own, with nobody in the stands rooting for me to win. All the while I was growing up, I never really won for myself – it was always for my mother or my father.'[1] One day,' says Chris, 'I had to win for myself; it was an entirely different thing.' Like many of her fellow thoroughbreds, Chris was not particularly entranced at first by her parents' choice of *raison d'être*. She told author Grace Lichtenstein, 'I had no feeling for the game. I just did it because my dad brought me over to the courts. It was his idea. I didn't *dislike* it, I mean, it was something to do. When you're 8 or 9 you don't really have many hobbies.'[2] Many such youngsters, after prodigious junior careers which raise expectations, find they cannot make the transition of responsibility to winning for themselves. They collapse at their most vulnerable point, just before victory, or just after it: sport's litmus test is quite thorough in examining motives and difficulties. And sadly, when disaster strikes sport's pro-bred children, the public unleashes the nastiness it saves up for family prospects and poodles on parade. Buster Mottram's numerous withdrawals from Wimbledon with nausea and throat complaints were criticized just as fiercely as his outbursts against authority. Buster was often seen staggering to the side of the court clutching his stomach, or retching pitifully during major championships. In the French Open in 1978 he was hauled before the tournament committee for 'unduly delaying' his match with Christopher Roger-Vasselin in this way. He was accused of squandering his obvious talent, and his later success in Davis Cup was a gleam of light in an otherwise stormy career. So long as Mottram could not stomach major championships, the press could not stomach Master Mottram. One journalist sent to probe his personality described him as an 'adult schoolboy' with 'carpet-beater feet, hogsback hair and naked ears like open car doors'.

Jimmy Connors continues, too, an 'adult schoolboy', both in appearance and behaviour. Sports psychologists researching the problem of 'success phobia' have found that 'The majority of athletes who have exhibited this phobia have been forced to compete since their very early years.'[3] Unfortunately parents who, with the best intentions, train their children for sports experiments often have no way of knowing just how good they will have to be. A discursive glance at the careers of our prominent sports thoroughbreds indicates that few have escaped crises of the most frightening kind over this question of winning. Like Mottram, Jimmy Connors riles easily. Two subjects in particular set his hackles bristling. One is the suggestion that he may have 'choked' a match, and the other concerns his reputation as the Oedipus Rex of tennis or, unkindest cut of all, the Oedipus Wrecked. During a WCT Challenge Cup final in the opulent Ceasar's Palace Hotel, Connors leapt out of his chair at changeover and assailed Nastase with a torrent of abuse on various topics, starting with his 'fucking backhand'. Nastase, normally pliant in rows with friends, retaliated, 'Why don't you get your bloody mother down here? You know you can't win anything without her.' In many versions this charge has been laid at Connors' door throughout his career and his on-off marriage with Patti. Fellow-players point to the nervous tic in his shoulder, the shirt-pulling, toe-dragging and occasional obsessions at changeover with 'towel-origami' and doing everything in fours, as signs of tension. Connors denies it all. But he, too, has suffered agonies over the pressures of victory and bitterly resents references to his nightmare year of 1975. That year he unaccountably lost all his major finals, in front of his mother. The previous summer he had said of her, 'I still think maybe she knows the most about my game.' Gloria Thompson Connors had groomed son Jimbo for stardom. Both she and her mother Bertha ('Two Mom', as she was called) had been teaching pros, and Jimmy was home-coached till the age of 16, when they handed him over to the Panchos, Gonzales and 'Segoo'. As Connors remembers, 'My mom said that if I had to go, the one she would give me to would be Segura.' Well, in 1975 she might as well have given him to the garbage disposal man. In two sets of the Wimbledon final Jim had amassed a total of 39 points, despite having his grandmother's letter stuffed down his sock.

Connors is a prodigiously powerful and fearless hitter of the ball. His game is founded on aggression, on cross-court winners from impossible 'gets' and volleys punched from no-man's-land by torturous effort to take the chalk. 'My mom gave me my game,' he says, ' and she taught me one way, that lines were made to be hit.' He goes for broke and commits himself more than any other player in his class (except perhaps John McEnroe), and his emotions are always visibly at risk, despite a small repertoire of comic gestures – the finger-wag, the expanded chest, the strut. Watching Connors, spectators are brought close to a realization of what sport experiments are about, for he is, of all sportsmen, the perfect medium for pressure. Spectators cannot see pressure, but they can see Connors wrestling with it, like a spirit invoked at a seance. They watch with avid and sometimes cruel curiosity. Nastase was a 'sensitive' too, but whereas Nastase frequently succumbed to the pressures invoked, Connors does not. It is a measure of his personal courage. Meanwhile his mother sits in the players' stand, invariably shouting, cupping hand to mouth, punching air, and hitting through the ball in vicarious concentration. In the realm of tennis mothers, she is Gloriana. 'Yes sir, we fought it,' she says of Jim's training. 'But if no one would play with Jimmy, *he had me*. I played him every day – every good day – of the year, every year.'[4] And 'Glo' was a mean opponent for the young man to hit with. 'I told him to try to knock the ball down my throat, and he learned to do this because he found out that if I had the chance I would knock it down his. Yes sir.' There are other examples of faltering children groomed for the courts: Stephen Warboys in the early 1970s who promised so much and retired to coaching; Kate Brasher who won many junior titles and yet gave up full-time tennis to attend London University – tennis's thoroughbreds are an endearing species.

Cricket's thoroughbreds are numerous and prominent. Colin Cowdrey's father had his own sporting ambitions frustrated – by *his* father. 'You're not going to be quite good enough,' said grandfather Cowdrey, and put him to work in a bank. Father Cowdrey in turn galvanized his son into become a batsman of great seriousness (what Colin calls 'the carefree showpiece' always eluded him), and Colin Cowdrey in turn sired Kent captain Chris, who has played for England, and Graham, an excellent prospect who was in the Kent team in 1985. On a more serious note, Colin himself shared the thoroughbred's tendency to succumb to illness and injury at competition time. Colin was often troubled by ill health before crucial matches and all his professional life he admits that, at the back of his mind, was a 'deep-down desire to pull out'[5] by being sick or injured. In 1955 he was openly accused of dodging the column for the vital Oval Test against South Africa.

Fred Trueman's career was sometimes hampered, too, by what he calls 'mysterious' injuries. Fred's grandfather Albert was offered modest 'terms' by Yorkshire CCC which he declined, but Fred's father Alan Thomas Trueman had high hopes of a Yorkshire cap for young Fred, and would hold evening inquests on the boy's performances. Fred's dad played for Stainton every Saturday and his son 'tagged along'. 'To be truthful,' says Fred, 'I only played so much because of my father. I really wasn't so enthusiastic about the game as a lad but I didn't dare say so to him.'[6] Fred's ambition at that stage was 'to become a bricklayer'. In later life Fred was hardly ever injured, yet he suffered from what he called 'stitch', from a mysterious pain under his heel, and an equally mysterious 'back illness' which cleared up when he drank lemon juice.

Some of golf's thoroughbreds have had mixed feelings about their careers when competitive pressures they had never sought began to bear down on them. This was particularly true of Dale Hayes, now a club pro. 'My father and both brothers are pros,' Dale told me. 'I reached a crisis in America. I wasn't happy; I was lonely. Those thoughts went through my mind. I thought, What am I doing over here? I'm not enjoying myself. I'm 25 or 26 years old and I'm not having any fun, and I'm playing golf, and I'm not near my friends. I'm playing badly, and it's costing me money.' Tom Weiskopf, whose big trouble with officialdom began in 1974, remembers how he was introduced to golf. 'My folks used to cart me out to the club, but I hated it,' he says. His father, also called Tom, never lost a college golf match and his mother Eva won eight straight Ohio Amateur tournaments. 'They could have been professionals, but they were born in the wrong period of time.'[7] Like tennis pro Marty Riessen, Tom won a college scholarship: Tom's was baseball, Riessen's basketball. Like Riessen Tom was pressed by his father towards a different sport that his father preferred, but that he didn't really like. In Tom's case this was golf; in Riessen's, tennis. Both Weiskopf and Riessen acquired a taste for their new vocations, but both of them later became involved in protracted rows with officials and incidents during the course of play. Like Connors, Mottram and innumerable other thoroughbreds, their careers have been querulous. Weiskopf is currently nursing a stomach ulcer.

Tom Watson was introduced to golf by his father Ray. At age 16, after some extra tuition from pro Stan Thirsk, Watson junior was playing with Arnold Palmer, if you please, in an exhibition match at his home club. Young Watson was 'pretty nervous'. Years later, at Winged Foot in 1974, Tom had a third-round lead and was about to win the US Open. Suddenly there was a crash. It was Tom coming into the clubhouse with a 79. In 1975 at Medinah, he led the US Open again. Nothing could stop him this time, other than carding two last rounds of 78 and 77. Tom carded 78 and 77. Even after his major victory at Carnoustie in 1975 (when at least half a dozen challengers faltered) Tom remained extremely sensitive about the subject of 'choking'. It raised his hackles, as it raised fellow-thoroughbred Jim Connors'. It was a bum rap.

1976 was a quiet year, 1977 a very noisy one, in which Watson locked horns with Jack Nicklaus. It started at the Masters in Augusta. Things had really come to a head for Watson. He couldn't go into the press room without some wiseacre asking, 'What's it like to choke?' 'Can you describe choking?' or 'How do you explain your recent collapses coming down the stretch at Sawgrass or Harbour Town?' Journalists who think sport is a game can be very insensitive in such matters, and Watson handled these outrages against his feelings as best he could. Sometimes he must have wanted to cry, or scream. On the last day at Augusta, Nicklaus birdied seven of his first fifteen holes. Nobody really expected Watson to follow that, what with his reputation as a choker and all. He saw a small lead disappearing, as here came the Bear at the 13th, closing the gap on him to a single stroke with a 3-iron second shot and two putts for a birdie. As Jack left the green he turned and waved back, quite ingenuously, apparently in the direction of Watson, who was waiting to play his second. Watson turned this gesture over in his mind. Who the hell does this blond SOB think he is, waving at me to top that. Who the hell do these people think they are writing me off at the 13th. Who the hell do those journalists think they are calling me a choker. I'll show them.

And he did. At Turnberry he had Jack's number, staying with the Bear until he did 'some dumb thing' to take his second British Open. He has since won three more, a US Open and another Masters. Even so, Watson, when he has no focusing point for his concentration, continues to choke. In 1978 he was one of the people who blew it at Augusta to give Player the Masters he so richly deserved, and at St Andrews he was frankly unwell. Going into the final round he was tied for the lead with Peter Oosterhuis and was favoured to win the title. He went out and shot 76, and hurried away without discussing the fact that he was heavily sedated that afternoon.[8] A month later he went into the last round of the USPGA at Oakmont with a 5-stroke lead. He had dominated the first three days. On the last day he shot 73, to go into a three-way play-off with Jerry Pate and John Mahaffey – the eventual winner. At Wentworth Tom was trailing Ray Floyd for 27 holes of matchplay and staged a charge at the end which almost hauled him in. I asked Tom if it was easier to be aggressive and go for your shots when you were behind. Watson said yes it was. 'When I was behind, I didn't have to feel any pressure, because I was in the jungle. All the pressure was on Ray.' On the 28th, Floyd 'lost a little confidence', and Watson started to feel the pressure, because 'I was in with a chance there' when Floyd faltered. Outside the press tent I asked Tom as tactfully as I could about the bum rap. It seems most people choked, so what could you do? 'All you can do is try to play better golf, try to maintain your confidence,' he said, smiling bleakly. At the '79 Masters he 'fell out of the plane' with Ed Sneed.

Another Watson, by the name John, has earned a reputation as Formula One racing's most 'unlucky' driver. John was encouraged to compete by his father, who had raced a 500 c.c. car after the war. Some of the unaccountable difficulties that beset thoroughbreds in other sports have unremittingly plagued the Ulsterman's career. His former boss at Brabham, Bernie Ecclestone, has an explanation for this phenomenon. 'Napoleon,' Mr Ecclestone says, 'would ask of any prospective general, "Yes, I know he's good, but is he *lucky*?"' Watson, you understand, *isn't*. There is a particular law of physics that says if you drop a piece of toast it will always land butter side downwards, and Sod's Law has governed John's entire career. If there is the merest duct or tube leading from one part of Watson's car to another part, the lining will undoubtedly fall in his fuel, and wherever possible, set fire to his engine. While others' tyres last, John's will 'go off' (a portmanteau term for anything untoward happening to tyres). Turning into the pit lane the car will shed a wheel and crash at fifteen miles an hour, or croak for fuel in sight of the chequered flag.

Throughout his extraordinary disappointments, the motor racing press had remained loyal to Watson; of all the talents in F1, John's is among the easiest to recognize, because as Ecclestone puts it, 'He can really go fast.' Poor Wattie was apparently the victim of some fatal dodge on the part of the car which ruined his chances, often at the last moment. Curious about mysteries of this kind, I went along and talked to Bernie Ecclestone. What kind of racing stable was this that had produced Watson a supply of heart-breaking vehicles? 'In all walks of life there are winners and losers,' he said. 'John's – unlucky. Sometimes, you see unlucky drivers with lots of talent, who can really go fast, and you take them on because you think they might improve. They don't. Winners are winners and losers are losers.' Watson subsequently switched to McLaren where his fortunes were again rather mixed. From failing even to make the grid in Monaco in 1980 he rose to lead the World Championship table in 1982 after wins in Belgium and Detroit, racing like God's chauffeur and overtaking three cars separately under braking in one lap. He told me, 'There was a harmony between myself and the car – a fantastic feeling you could never reproduce.' Yet despite all this superb driving and a car he described as 'quite sensational', he nevertheless contrived to finish joint second in the Championship – a bitter blow. That year he told me, 'I haven't had the success I should have had and I've been labelled "unlucky". But "luck" and "deserving" are just labels. I believe you earn success. There's no such thing as a "lucky" racing driver.' The following year he was sacked by McLaren and more recently reinstated to replace injured Niki Lauda. Yet the World Championship has continued to elude him. He told me once in a telephone interview, 'I try to rationalize what happened . . . .' no doubt meaning that he reasons out his misfortunes after they occur. Unfortunately 'rationalize' also means something else. Here is a psychiatrist, Dr David Morley, talking about sportsmen who rationalize on the golf course: 'This brings to mind another defense mechanism known as "rationalization" or, in non-technical language, "making excuses". This is very common. ... The rationalizer blames his misjudged putt on the fact that the grass on the green was cut too short or too long. He always sees himself as the victim of inexorable forces beyond his control; he can never recognize himself as being at fault. ...'[9]

There is a feeling amongst racers that when you have won once, winning becomes easier. As Jackie Stewart says, you have 'the key'. For some reason, this didn't apply to Watson. John won the Austrian Grand Prix in 1976. He didn't expect to; in fact he had made a sort of negative bet. He told sponsor Roger Penske that if he won a Grand Prix in 1976, he would shave off the beard he had had since he was 17. I wondered why he did that. 'I'd really wanted to shave it off,' said John, 'and that was a dignified way of doing it.' But winning the Austrian Grand Prix didn't provide John with any 'key', as racers generally expect it to. He went on being very unlucky with his cars, and the following season at the same event, when he really fancied his chances, he had a most disappointing race, setting fastest lap only when his chance had gone, and feeling unwell with his allergy. Why didn't Austria change John's luck? Well, Wattie believes that nowadays Grand Prix racing is 10 per cent driver, 90 per cent car. He believes the driver is more or less a 'chauffeur', who sits in the car and faces the front. Interestingly, he finds *leading* a Grand Prix fairly easy: sheer speed has hardly ever been a problem. He has often been on the front row and set fastest lap. Like other racers, John can sometimes go very fast in a lost cause, and he says people have asked him, 'Now, why can't you always race like that?' The answer is, unfortunately, that going fast is one thing, and going through the winning barrier is another, as we have seen. In 1980 Watson made a remark even more intriguing than his negative bet with Roger Penske. He told a journalist, 'I want to be World Champion not for the things it would give me, but because I want the Championship to satisfy something inside me. I'm like a hydrogen bomb waiting to explode. When it goes off, the fallout will be felt for miles. All it needs to trigger it is some success'.[10] I leave the reader to consider the implications of such a statement.

Winning demands a great deal of all sportsmen, but it demands even more of those who are intelligent and thoughtful, and who have been brought up in a background where sports achievement is something very special. When *these* athletes win, whether it be

Grand Prix races or anything else, they deserve rather more than the prize money. As Norwich soccer boss John Bond said of his star son Kevin, 'I can't think of too many young players who could have stood up to what Kevin has endured. . . . I think I would have gone under.'[11]

11

The Guinea-Pigs

Throughout this book I have avoided the term 'guinea-pig' when referring to the athlete's role in the sport experiment. Though we may see him in every extremity of desperation; though he is often brought by pressure to a state of panic, violence or vicious competitiveness, a sportsman's humanity nevertheless lends dignity to what he does, and grandeur too. It is difficult to come away from any sports performance, however outrageous or abysmal, without feeling that man is indeed a noble creature, capable of astonishing courage and cleverness, and never truly beaten while he lives. The term 'guinea-pig' would surely have demeaned him, however he may be tested before our eyes. But as we come to this final section, on sports medicine and the future, 'guinea-pig' becomes a term difficult to avoid.

It has long been recognized by medical science that under stress, whether mental or physical, the body's chemistry undergoes complex changes, triggered initially by the walnut-sized hypothalmus at the back of the head as it galvanizes the autonomic nervous system to combat threats to its equilibrium. Blood supply to non-essential organs is diverted to the large muscles and brain. Chemicals such as ACTH, cortisol, catecholamines (adrenaline and noradrenaline), thyroxine and somatotrophine are released. Neurone loops through the memory stores of the central nervous system activate centres for the further secretion of hormones, for electro-chemical changes in skin resistance, changes in plasma protein fractions, and so on. In these ways the organism defends itself from stress, or prepares for fight or flight according to its ancient system of priorities. Research in the field of body chemistry, for obvious reasons, exercises all the resources of international technology. A few years ago it was discovered in concurrent independent studies on psychotropic (mood-altering) drugs that the brain has receptors in the amygdala – a centre believed to be associated with emotional function – for selecting incoming substances called enkephalines and endorphines. Further research revealed that the brain produces substances corresponding to morphine (called beta-endorphine), to analgesics, amphetamines, hallucinogens and sedatives, and that these combine with the brain's receptors to regulate behaviour and mood under stress. Because man lives in a stressful world, he has always looked for ways in which he might alter or improve the body's chemistry to cope with threats to his survival. He has synthesized substances which the body produces naturally, and found ways of introducing others into his system to alter or enhance his state of being.

Sport, as we have seen, is a ready-made laboratory for man's enquiries into stress, as many enthusiasts have inadvertently observed. Ex-Olympic athlete Christopher Brasher, who writes for the *Observer*, recently met British Olympic team psychologist Maurice Yaffe. Brasher enthused: 'He endeared himself to me when he said that, "The sports arena is a wonderful laboratory for observation." '[1]

Arnold Beisser MD, author of *The Madness in Sports* and a practising psychiatrist who numbers among his patients many prominent American sportsmen, is himself a keen fan and advocate of sport as a social safety valve. But Beisser notes the following: 'Games are played to be observed, and the investigator has an excellent opportunity for such observation just by attending an athletic event. In many experimental settings the presence of an investigator is foreign to the actual life circumstances, thus distorting the results. In most sports, however, for only the price of admission, studies can be made in the natural environment. The observer is indistinguishable from other fans and has no perceptible influence on the results. The provisions for spectators, ranging from a single park bench alongside a neighborhood tennis court to hundreds of concentric rows of numbered seats in football stadiums, invite the psychologist to examine the life dramas that unfold there.'[2]

Beisser is not suspicious of these contrivances; nor does he anywhere suggest that this is the purpose of sport, as I have done. But other astute commentators have made similar guarded observations about the usefulness of sport for experimental purposes. Dr Richard Suinn, US Olympic team psychologist, sent me a paper he had presented at the Association for the Advancement of Behaviour Therapy in Atlanta, Georgia in 1977. This paper is full of scientific methodologies Dr Suinn has applied to sport in the course of his work. One of his findings is that, 'Unusual competition conditions may stir unique emotional responses; the Olympic Games hold such a prominent place in our values as to precipitate unusual reactions.'[3] Dr H. T. A. Whiting, who very kindly offered to let me work in connection with his Vakgroep Psychologie at the Free University in Amsterdam, is greatly respected for his work in the field of sports psychology. Dr Whiting includes in one of his books on the subject a paper by P. K. Bridges on physiological arousal, in which Bridges says, 'Sports situations would be very convenient in which to observe stress responses but it is not easy to avoid the obvious component of physical exercise involved. However in relation to such aspects as reaction times, anticipatory alerting and performance, study of the relationship of bodybuild may have a contribution to make.'[4] Dr Arnold Beisser puts it more succinctly: 'The sports stadium is a nearly ideal laboratory for psychological investigation.'[5]

It should surprise no one therefore, though it should perhaps alarm us all, that man has begun to use this excellent 'laboratory' to test his drugs. There is no substance, capable of being introduced into the body to improve its performance under stress, that has not, somewhere in the world, been placed on a saucer in a sportsman's locker with the assurance, 'if you take this, you will win'. The recent display of righteous indignation on the part of the British Amateur Athletic Board and other Western sports authorities concerning the use by Eastern bloc athletes of anabolic steroids, blood-doping, and so-called 'brake' drugs for retarding puberty, was as naïve as it was pious. Sportsmen in the West have been using drugs for a very long time, and anabolic steroids for as long as they have been available. One of the tragedies of the sportsman's situation is that he earns his keep by competition. If he finds his opponents with some advantage, he naturally feels that he must have it too, or some alternative, if he is to do his job successfully. This means that he is open to suggestions from anyone wishing to experiment with his mind or his body, and vulnerable to any authority anxious for him to win by short-term means.

An enquiry by a task force of the US Olympic Committee in 1978[6] discovered that drug-taking in sport has now reached what it called 'epidemic' proportions. Dr Tony Daly, an orthopaedic surgeon, concluded, 'Athletes are trapped. Based on peer pressure and folklore, they feel that in order to improve they have to experiment.' Experiment being the operative word, Swedish discus-thrower and Olympic bronze medallist Ruicki Bruchs appeared on British television in September 1978 amid the growing storm on anabolic steroids. He told BBC TV's 'Tonight' interviewer Donald McCormick that, in common with '101 per cent' of the competitors he met in the 1976 Montreal Olympics, he had taken drugs, notably anabolic steroids, for ten years. He described how his own mother had failed to recognize him at the airport on his return from America. He had put on 100 pounds in weight, had six knee operations (anabolic steroids erode calcium and stunt the long bones), a fractured vertebra and various internal illnesses. He had also suffered a nervous breakdown. Other casualties included a Russian whose drug regimen had caused his testicles to burst, and a Swedish girl who developed cancer after being given 'brake' drugs to retard her normal physical development. More recently, sprinter Renate Neufeld escaped to the West from East Berlin. She could hardly walk for the pain in her legs, and said she had been forced to take anabolic steroids in training for the 1980 Olympics.

Jack Scott, author of *The Athletic Revolution* and himself an ex-athlete, was one of the first to raise the alarm on drug-taking in American football and athletics (another was the extremely responsible American magazine *Sports Illustrated* in its three-part series in the summer of 1969). Scott covered the Mexico Olympic Games as a journalist. Talking frankly with the athletes there from all over the world (and particularly America's track and field stars), he discovered that they were not so much taking drugs, as holding pharmaceutical teach-ins.[7] At a hearing of a California State Legislature sub-committee on Drug Abuse and Alcoholism held in Los Angeles in October 1970 – the first official government inquiry into drugs and sport in American athletic history – Scott and several others testified to the widespread use of dope in US sport. Their testimony was largely ignored in the press.[8] Dave Meggyesy, for seven years a line-backer with the St Louis Cardinals, gave evidence on the use of drugs throughout American pro football, and in the college game also. Paul Lowe, referring to his career with the San Diego Chargers, reported, 'We had to take them [anabolic steroids] at lunch time. He [the trainer] would put them on a little saucer and prescribed for us to take them and if not there might be a fine.'[9] William Campbell, Chairman of the Sub-committee, issued a statement on the hearing which included the optimistic conclusion that, 'Working together with constructive suggestions we can prevent sports from becoming the testing battleground for chemical research. The medical laboratory, not the playing field, is the proper proving ground for testing drugs, and medical treatment of the ill, not the healthy athlete, is the proper role for the fruits of such research.'[10]

Anabolic steroids are of particular concern because their side-effects can be permanently destructive. Atrophied testes, liver damage, cancer of the prostate and uterine cancer are among the possibilities. Yet Gianabol[11] and Dianabol are widely used, and their names have sadly even appeared on T-shirts and in a song (dedicated to East German female swimmers with deep voices). Christopher Brasher believes, 'There is no doubt the use of steroids is widespread and that between the Tokyo Olympics of 1964 and the Montreal Games of 1976 almost every gold medal in the heavy field events and most of the medals in weightlifting were won with the aid of steroids.'[12] He cites the example of 1956 American Olympic discus champion, Harold Connolly, who has said, 'For eight years prior to 1972 I would have to refer to myself as a hooked athlete. Like all my [fellow-]competitors I was using anabolic steroids as an integral part of my training in the hammer throw.'

The supreme irony of all this, in spite of Brasher's assertions about the drug 'winning medals', is that the connection between anabolic steroids and improved athletic performance is a tenuous one. Anabolic steroids are synthesized male hormones. Normally they are used in medicine to treat mineral imbalances because they retain fluid in the blood vessels, and cause excess fluids to be collected in areas outside the blood vessels, thus increasing body weight and mass. There is no medical evidence that they thereby increase strength,[13] although research is under way 'in some places' (according to an expert at the Drug Control Centre in London) into their myotropic effects.

Urine tests can generally detect steroid deposits only if they have been taken in the last twenty-four hours. Professor Ray Brooks of London's St Thomas's Hospital, who is now working with the research team at Chelsea College's new Drug Control unit, has developed a screening method accurate for up to fourteen days. Unfortunately drug-taking regimens are usually interrupted to allow for this, and resumed immediately afterwards, ready for the next competition. There is a blood test, using radioactive iodine, that can isolate steroid traces from drugs used six or seven months previously, though this is prohibitively costly. The Chelsea College Drug Control centre opened in November 1978, and received an annual grant of £25,000 for three years, with an additional £5000 a year to aid Professor Brooks's research. This rose to £181,000 for 1984–5 and continues to increase with the expansion of the drug testing programmes. It is hoped that here, with the world's most advanced technology, new testing methods may be found, though more funds are always needed and the Centre's Dr David Cowan told me that these may eventually come from the major chemical companies. Unfortunately, sport's drug problem does not stand still. As fast as tests and screening methods are perfected, new substances are found to circumvent them. The natural hormones testosterone and oestrogen are a particular menace in this respect, for it is difficult to devise testing procedures for, or to legislate against, natural hormones in an athlete's body, and particularly difficult in the case of female athletes on contraceptive pills (which contain oestrogen and progesterone). At the Commonwealth Games in Canada, it was decided to abandon a steroid test on female athletes who took the Pill. Another natural hormone, Somatotrophine, is causing concern after two British power-lifters were found to have taken ten times the therapeutic dose (illegally) as part of their weight-training regimens. The substance, known as Dead Man's Drug, is obtained from the glands of human corpses, and is used in the treatment of stunted growth. One of the power-lifters went into a psychotic rage and ran amok with an axe. Another development to disquiet testing authorities is 'blood-doping', the method by which an athlete is given a transfusion of his own blood just prior to an event to increase the volume of oxygen-bearing haemoglobin in his system. The blood, or a concentration of it, is usually 'banked' in cold storage ready for infusion. Detection is difficult.

Anabolic steroids are merely, for all their ominousness, the tip of the iceberg. Generally speaking, the crueller the sport, the greater the likelihood of competitors resorting to drugs to 'help' their minds and bodies withstand the pressure. Sport has every intention of testing competitors, and competitors have every intention of passing the test. This reciprocation should be obvious to even the most high-minded sports enthusiast. Whatever sanctions may be placed on drug-taking, and whatever the hue and cry against it, the more pressure is applied to an athlete, and the more gruelling his sport becomes, the more he will misguidedly turn to chemicals for support. This is the spiral from which he must be rescued, if he is to be rescued at all.

An obvious example is the Tour de France. The 149-mile stage to L'Alpe d'Huez is known, because of its torture, as The Road of the Cross. Before they reach the St Étienne to L'Alpe d'Huez stage the riders have been furiously pedalling their bikes for a mere fifteen days at an average of more than five hours and 112 miles each day. The routes are laid out according to commercial and tourist priorities, with the result that the riders are put to some trouble to get from their finish points to the start points on the following day. These hours are added to their schedule and subtracted from their sleep. Six hours a night is hardly adequate for a racer's needs, yet this is all some of them get, and less if they suffer from exhaustion insomnia. Some of the stages finish in steep climbs when the rider is already in oxygen debt and lactic acid poisoning. Up to L'Alpe d'Huez there is a 1 in 12 gradient for nine miles. The climb is 6450 feet. This is asking a lot of a fit and rested human body, but of an exhausted man after a day's hard riding on ribboned roads in the glare of publicity, it asks the near impossible. The physical pain cloud known to all sportsmen bears down on the Tour leader in his yellow jersey and threatens him with extinction. Even the most brave and conservative riders are likely to feel their bodies need help. Englishman Paul Sherwen, competing in his first Tour in 1978, said he was having daily injections of C and B vitamins. According to Michel Pollentier, disgraced in 1978 for his attempts to cheat the dope test, most of the riders take something stronger. Pollentier was disqualified, as others had been before him, for using a '*topette*' – a rubber bulb hidden in his clothes – to try to provide a dope-free urine sample. The man who took over his lead jersey, Joop Zeotemelk, had been fined and suspended the previous year as the race neared Paris – for failing the dope test.

In 1976 two Peugeot–Esso riders used the same technique as Pollentier. One of them, Rachel Dard, gave a story to the French journal *L'Équipe* saying this was nothing new, and that many of the riders used analgesics (pain-killers) containing strychnine, cardio-vascular aids and hormone regimens. He indicated that

those who did not take drugs were in the small minority, and that
doctors, race-organizers and *soigneurs* were accomplices in the
scandal. Christopher Brasher recalls the case of the Danish cyclist
Knut Jensen, during a similarly painful bike race in the Rome
Olympics of 1960, who took (or was given) a preparation called
Ronicol to dilate the blood vessels.[14] (Ronicol is a cardiac
stimulant normally given to angina-sufferers and for peripheral
vascular disorders.) In Rome the temperature was nearing 100
degrees. Jensen cycled to his death. Brasher also recounts the case
of Yorkshireman Tommy Simpson, who seven years later was on
the slopes of Mount Ventoux when the effects of a drink given him
by a spectator, and drugs he had taken under the supervision of a
Paris hospital, combined with the heat and pain to force him to
stop. Soon afterwards Simpson was dead. Some years previously
he had told Christopher Brasher, 'I am riding up there with the
stars, then I see their hand go to their mouth and suddenly they are
going away from me. I don't want to take dope.' said Tommy
Simpson, 'I have too much respect for my body – but if I don't win a
big event really soon, I shall have to start taking it.'

Long after Simpson's death, Tour de France riders continue to
resort to drugs. The penalties, such as they are, seem scarcely pro-
hibitive. After Pollentier's suspension his team *soigneur* said that
he had previously given his racers 'Allupin' (presumably meaning
Alupent, a stimulant), used in Switzerland and Italy without detection. Pollentier believed it helped breathing in the high mountains.
One of the worst drug problems in sport has undoubtedly been that
of cycling. The Milk Race, one of the three biggest amateur cycling
events in Europe, costs about £2400 in dope checks at the Chelsea
College Drug Control Centre. For a long time before the recent
Sports Council intervention, the tests were being subsidized by
Professor Arnold Beckett's department of pharmacy there. Professor Beckett is the IOC Medical Commission member with
special responsibility for dope control. Another member of the
Commission, Dr Albert Dirix of Belgium, estimates that drugs in
sport have been responsible for at least thirty deaths. Clearly some
sport experiments, such as the Tour de France, have led subjects to
tamper with the chemical variables.

Physically arduous sports like the Tour push competitors hard in
the direction of a medicine chest, but these are not the only experiments inviting chemical 'adaptation'. The more internationally
competitive and prestigious a sport becomes, the more attention is

focused on each individual taking part, and the more he fears to do badly and 'let the side down'. Sometimes the sportsman under these circumstances is 'representing' powerful groups whose criticism he dreads. Sometimes he represents a nation. This kind of responsibility, or 'honour' as it is often called, is not easily sloughed off by a normally sensible athlete. Add to this the suggestion that other competitors, other teams and clubs may be taking drugs to help their performance, and you have the shadow which looms so large over the Olympic podium, and greets the British soccer player and the American football player when they open their eyes in the morning. It is this kind of stress – the stress of shame rather than the stress of pain – that seems to be responsible for the current epidemic of drugs in sport. Athletes who are selected for their courage are nevertheless afraid to fail, and they are afraid of that because we have taught them to be.

'Ordinarily, most football players are warm, loving decent human beings. They aren't drug addicts. They have to convert themselves to attain a state of hair-trigger readiness. . . . . In large doses they [amphetamines] change a condition of nervous alert into a rage players feel they must have in a game that requires violent aggression at a precise point in time. The older the player, the more likely his dependence. He gets desperate. He won't go in against someone who's grunting and drooling with big, dilated pupils, unless he's in the same condition.'

This is a pharmacological psychiatrist, Dr Arnold Mandell, talking about his experience of treating American football players.[15] Dr Mandell observes that there is a drug problem in the NFL equivalent to the occupational hazard of silicosis in mining. He tried to alert the National Football League in 1973. They said there was no problem, and refused to introduce urine tests. Dr Mandell believes that a large proportion of the serious injuries, late tackles, fights, and 'unconscionable assaults' in the game are due to amphetamines, because the players are 'half-crazy' from drugs and psychologically induced aggression. They are deprived of pain – a natural inhibitor – by analgesics, and they do not know what they are doing to each other, because of the heavy doses of stimulants causing 'a pre-psychotic rage'. Some of the more affluent professionals are now, according to Dr Mandell, resorting to cocaine, and those who take amphetamines (he mentions '60 per cent' as a possibility) cannot be persuaded to give them up, even though they are 'certainly psychologically, and possibly physically addictive', and although the 'post-use depression is severe'. Dr Mandell had one player who lost 20 lb. in a weekend, coughing blood before games. 'I asked him how he could play in such a condition. He reached in his pocket and pulled out a handful of "black beauties" – street speed. The next day he played super.'

One doubts that the players' drug-habit will ever be curbed, not because the NFL authorities do not care, or because large numbers of people in and around football are not concerned about the problem, but because of the high level of public interest in the game, financed as it is largely by television. Once spectators have seen what they have *seen* in the way of extreme human behaviour, I doubt that they will settle for less. And I suspect that this is the real reason why urine tests have not been introduced. The experiment is more important than the players. This is the cruel truth at the back of so many of sport's problems, if we take the trouble to examine them objectively. As if to bear out Dr Mandell's allegations, the New England Patriots, losers in Super Bowl XX to Chicago, were involved in a massive post-match drugs scandal, with coach Raymond Berry referring to about twelve players with a drug problem. (Baseball has been similarly hit, with casualties to cocaine addiction.)

When an individual club or nation stamps on *its* competitors and announces that it is going to curb their drug-taking, they immediately feel they have been compromised. How can they be expected to compete with other athletes who have not been so rigorously checked? Few athletes *can* compete successfully when their confidence has been undermined in this way, even if the drugs in question made no earthly difference to their performance. They have lost the 'placebo' effect, the halo that surrounds a performer who believes he has a secret advantage. Such was the case with many of the British athletes in Prague in 1978. Since March 1977 (according to the Drug Control Centre's Dr Cowan) the British Amateur Athletic Board have begun carrying out checks of their own, in addition to those already in operation in the countries of competition. They did this with the very best of intentions, because in spite of avowed tests, they saw that some Eastern bloc countries, notably East Germany, appeared to be circumventing the checks and fielding half a side at competitions when they knew checks would be made (such as Crystal Palace). The British athletes went along to Prague and did their best, which in Steve Ovett's case happened to be better than anybody else's. But some of them felt cheated. To their eyes, their fellow-competitors loomed like incredible hulks, pumped full of steroids and stimulants. Here were they, pure as the driven snow, lambs sent by mistake to the knacker's yard. That this situation was partly fictional – the Russians, for example, carry out their own dope tests and had disqualified five athletes in eighteen such tests during 1978[16] – did not make the British athletes' situation any easier to bear. Many returned from some of their poorest performances, bitter and despondent. Daley Thompson, no doubt exhausted after his Edmonton triumph, misjudged his approach run in the pole vault and fumbled the hurdles to miss a rightful gold. In the 5000 metres final, for which Brendan Foster did not qualify, Nick Rose disappointed himself and everybody else by finishing 7th in a race of modest times. In the high hurdles semi-finals both Mark Holtom and Berwyn Price were humiliated. Price, a Commonwealth gold medallist, crashed the last hurdle and finished 5th in his heat and Holtom brought up the rear. These disasters could not really be explained by opponents taking steroids. Donna Hartley, 6th in the European Championships women's 400 metre final, commented, 'If it goes on like this I see no point in going to the Moscow Olympics at all. Why go there to get mashed up?'[17] Shot-putter Geoff Capes, who planned to increase his weight slightly to 24 stone by the Moscow Olympics, had a three-year-old sponsorship of £20 worth of meat from Dewhurst the butchers every week, and regulated his body chemistry with up to eight pints of milk and eight eggs a day – enough to give him hypercholesterolaemia one would think. Geoff was nevertheless disheartened by it all. He was involved in a scuffle prior to the shot final in Prague for sporting only one number on his vest instead of two, which officials believed he had done to start a furore. Capes said sadly, 'There is no point in the British athlete competing against a Communist bloc athlete in the field events. He will be beaten by steroids.'[18]

The Chelsea Drug Control centre has issued a warning to all athletes wishing to avoid substances on the prohibited list: play safe and regard all non-normal food substances as drugs. The names of illegal preparations fill a medical book more than an inch thick. Even if a drug is not actually listed it may be included in the banned 'pharmacological categories' by its action. The list includes all types of stimulants, including central nervous system stimulants and sympathomimetic amines, a wide range of pain-killers with stimulant action, and of course, steroids, which in addition to their anabolic (muscle building) activity also have an androgenic activity (increasing aggression and competitiveness) because they are male hormones. As Dr Cowan explained to me, this may be why athletes take them, rather than for their effect on body mass.

The testing procedures are highly complex and the equipment astronomically expensive. Detection laboratories like the Chelsea unit may be equipped for a wide range of procedures. Mass spectrometry, which gives the unequivocal identification of all substances, is prohibitively costly to consult on all samples, so 'screening procedures' are used, such as gas-liquid and thin-layer chromatography, radio-immunoassay, and so on, which monitor the presence of anabolics or stimulants. The Chelsea lab houses such sophisticated equipment as the EMIT computer system used by American narcotics squads. This is called a 'drug-abuse urine calibrator' and makes use of enzyme immunoassy. it was introduced in the States in 1972.

Sometimes, as in Prague in 1978, three tests may be used simultaneously. In Prague these were mass spectrometry, plus two screening procedures (not 100 per cent accurate) – gas chromatography and radio immunoassay. The latter was being tried out as an experiment by the Czechs. It gave a negative reading on Russian pentathlete Nadia Tkacenko, while her other two readings were positive. The Russians exploited this 'discrepancy' to the full in their efforts to save her from disqualification. They did not succeed. Since then, we have seen Finn Martti Vainio stripped of his Olympic 10,000 metres silver medal in the 1984 Los Angeles Games and 'banned for life', along with four other athletes, only to have the life ban lifted eighteen months later by the International Amateur Athletic Federation. Such is 'life' in the fight against drugs in sport.

Until 1972, when testing procedures were formally introduced at the Olympics, the list of drugs banned by the International Olympic Committee (IOC) included caffeine.[19] Coffee and coke-drinking by athletes has since become more acceptable or more difficult to legislate against, though of course caffeine is a CNS (central nervous system) stimulant. Confusion also arises over other substances. Analgesics, for example, may raise ethical problems. Some of them not only mask pain but improve performance by their actions. There appears to be some disagreement over codeine, which at the time of writing is banned by the IOC (who dismissed a Czech team doctor for administering it in 1976) but permitted by the International Amateur Athletic Federation, the committee governing track and field.[20] The latest IOC position is anomalous. Although analgesics such as codeine are officially banned, a lenient view was taken at the last Olympics of mild pain-killers. It has also been decided to reinstitute a ban on high concentrations of caffeine.

In boxing there is considerable disagreement over analgesics. British boxing views with disfavour, for example, novocaine, which US doctors like Ferdie Pacheco have regularly injected into fighters to kill pain both before and after bouts. Pacheco's patients have included Muhammad Ali, and Dr Pacheco believes that analgesics are both humane and necessary in treatment of an injured boxer's cuts and arthritic fists.[21] British boxing authorities permit only adrenaline to be used in such cases.

A similar disagreement over 'Bute' – phenylbutazone – in the treatment of international show-jumpers and three-day event horses came to a head in the 1970s in a debate of the International Equestrian Federation, whose president is Prince Philip. It was at the time decided to delay banning the painkiller (which masks bangs, bruises and arthritis) until 1981, partly because 'Bute' enabled many British horses to compete which would otherwise have been unable to do so. The drug is banned by the German Federation, who permit the widely used practice of a 'de-nerving' operation, also subject to the 1981 ban. The latest position is that 'Bute' *is* still permitted in stipulated doses. It is also used extensively in the United States. Controversy persists. (The drug has been banned for human use following a number of fatalities.)

One substance on the prohibited list both of the IOC and FIFA with which we are all now familiar is fencamfamin. Willie Johnston, the Scotland World Cup winger, was put on the first plane home from Argentina after it was discovered he had taken two tablets containing fencamfamin prior to the disastrous Scotland–Peru match. Reactivan, the proprietary product with the controversial component, is obtainable on prescription in Britain and on the Continent without one. The tablets, yellow in colour, are known to British soccer players as 'uppers'. Fencamfamin itself is a stimulant which dilates the blood vessels and improves breathing capacity. Professor Beckett of the Drug Control Centre wonders, 'Why is it that a doctor for an English League team (Dr Roger Rimmer of West Bromwich Albion) can prescribe a drug which is banned by FIFA?'[22] Dr David Cowan, also of the Centre, asked a similar question: 'Why aren't the Football Association carrying out some tests? We've offered them facilities; the Sports Council has offered subsidized rates for these people. But far from proving their house is in order, they're actually saying, No, our people don't take drugs – yet they've got no evidence to back it up.' Since then, the FA's own investigations have found soccer in perfect health.

After revelations on drug taking, alleged to have been given by England and QPR forward Stan Bowles to the *Daily Star* in November 1978, the FA had announced that they were making enquiries. Gordon Taylor, Chairman of the Professional Foot- ballers' Association, said that players would be willing to submit to dope tests if the list of prohibited substances were amended. 'Virtually all the population takes drugs of some sort. A lot of those on the banned list wouldn't harm a baby,' said Taylor.[23]

England team doctor Peter Burrows was a member of the FA drug committee set up after the Willie Johnston scandal. Burrows advocated random checks 'to explode the myth of widespread drug abuse in soccer'.[24] Stan Bowles's alleged disclosures, which he subsequently withdrew, perplexed the authorities. League secretary Alan Hardaker protested, 'He has painted a completely inaccurate picture of the average player'[25] and thought Bowles should never be allowed to play football again 'until he substan- tiated his statements'.

Award-winning sports writer Jeff Powell paints a similar picture, however. 'One well-known coach has confided to me: "When I changed clubs I couldn't believe the situation I walked into. Pep pills were all over the place. You felt you could hear players rattling. I was shocked. Then it dawned on me I must have come from one of the few clubs not taking the tablets." One of the Scotland players in the World Cup commented, "Pills were lying around on the dressing-room table like sweets." '[26]

It was originally thought that Willie Johnston took (or was given) the Reactivan tablets for his hay-fever. This was rather ridiculous, although according to an ex-Arsenal doctor[27] it is 'quite common' for fencamfamin to be taken by soccer players to *counter* the depressant effects of anti-histamines and cold cures. Most of us assumed that Johnston had taken the pills to make him more aggressive – his position as winger is normally an aggressive one. I asked him on the telephone if this was right. Willie said no, it was not. 'You get very tense and nervous just before a game. They weren't to make me more aggressive; they were just the opposite.

You need something to calm you down. That's what they were for. Some of the players on an occasion like that are in the toilets till five minutes before the kick-off. Some of them are sick. The crowd get you up – you don't need stimulants. You're as excited as you're ever going to be in your life. People don't take into consideration the tension and nervousness. They just look at it objectively. After all, we're paid to do a job. They don't have to take our feelings into account.'

Willie Johnston should surely be taken at his word, which is that he did not need yellow tablets to make him more excited. In front of close on a billion television viewers and a few thousand salivating Scotsmen, on a day he had dreamed of all his life, he was feeling rather excited already. Johnston is not a doctor or a member of a narcotics squad, and I doubt that his knowledge of drugs would extend to the pharmaceutics of vaso-dilation and pupillary changes. Players who know that 'uppers' help performance do not necessarily know how this comes about. Many drugs are taken by sportsmen in ignorance, as much for their placebo effect as anything else. Willie Johnston took his yellow pills because he was nervous, afraid he would not be able to do his best. This would go some way to explaining his eventual poor performance, and it is borne out by MacLeod's statement after the game that the Scotland–Peru disaster was due to 'nerves, tension'.[28] The people who *are* in a position to know exactly what fencamfamin does to a sportsman's body-chemistry are the doctors who prescribe it. In March '79, the FA issued a statement to the effect that its own six-month investigation had 'found no evidence at all' of drugs in soccer, and declined to introduce regular random tests. Confidential checks might be made, to 'test their conviction of the cleanness of the sport'.

The problem is not new to Britain's national sport. In 1962 the England centre forward Gerry Hitchens, who was playing for the Italian club Internazionale of Milan, was asked to provide a sample for a dope test which proved positive. One of the reasons why stimulants have been given to players – and this is true of other sports apart from soccer – is to *counter* the effects of sedatives and sleeping pills. According to one national newspaper, 'The most widely used sleeping tablet in football is Mogadon, a fairly powerful sedative which many clubs insist their players take, whether or not they have trouble getting to sleep. Most of soccer's household names eventually acquire some degree of dependence on Mogadon.'[30]

Here is a dilemma which appears to lie at the very heart of sport. Should tranquillizers and sleeping pills be banned? They are used in many sports because competitors feel that they cannot produce their normal performance, or do what is expected of them, if they are anxious – especially if this anxiety is bad enough to upset their stomachs and make them weak and debilitated. Would we prefer to see these players afraid? Or are we genuinely interested in their sporting skills?

The question of tranquillizers has been rather a sticking point for the IOC. They decided, for example, to bypass the beta-blocker Inderal (which researchers claim has a CNS activity) in their testing programme for the 1980 Olympics, a decision which aroused considerable criticism from those wishing the drug to be included. It would have added a further $150,000 to the $1.4 million budget already allocated for testing procedures at the 1980 Winter Olympics in Lake Placid, New York.[31] Since then beta-blockers including Inderal have been banned by the IOC. This total prohibition comes after a fiasco at the 1984 Olympics when the drugs were permitted 'if the athlete could show a medical certificate'. Many took advantage of the proviso and said beta-blockers were just what the doctor ordered. A comparable case is that of the British driving test, and the recent storm of controversy surrounding the tranquillizer Oxprenolol. Following suggestions by Dr Ian Meurig James, a clinical pharmacologist and physician at London's Royal Free Hospital, that drivers might be helped over the problem of 'test-jitters' by Oxprenolol, at least one motoring authority spokesman retorted that the driving test was as much of nerve as driving ability.[32] Is sport as much a test of nerve as sporting ability? One strongly suspects that it is, because sport is so often referred to as 'character-building'.

The seriousness of sport's drug problem was highlighted in 1985 by a Sports Council symposium on the subject, at which the Council took off its gloves to the ninety-odd governing bodies in its pay and declared its intention to cut off grant aid and use of its facilities to anyone refusing to institute drug checks (urine tests for both sexes). Since then many testing programmes have got underway. Unfortunately for the Sports Council's laudable initiative there is a problem over the definition of 'random' drug checks. Ideally these would include tests both in and out of competitions (to catch athletes on long-term interrupted drug regimens) but some sports bodies prefer to confine 'random testing' to competitions so as to give their sports a 'clean bill of health'. Unfortunately too, the

Sports Council's influence is for the most part confined to amateur sports. Professional bodies must be left to put their own houses in order. Following front-page drug scandals, several have done exactly that. After the affair in which Kirk Stevens was accused of being 'high as a kite' by a fellow-player, snooker began testing along IOC guidelines, and cricket instituted random checks after allegations concerning Ian Botham and other England team-members in 1982–3. In tennis the Men's Professional Council agreed to begin drug tests at Wimbledon 1986, though John McEnroe strongly objected and said he would not co-operate. He is passionately opposed to such an invasion of the athlete's privacy.

Since sport stands on the frontier of man's knowledge of himself, it is at least clinically plausible that he should seek to advance his understanding of medicine there, where human beings called sportsmen volunteer to withstand stress under observation. Dr David Cowan, Assistant Director of the Drug Control Centre, emphasized to me that testing laboratories like the Chelsea unit are opposed in principle to using sportsmen as guinea-pigs, and seek only to prevent them from taking drugs. Yet even Dr Cowan had to admit that the sportsman offers science a golden opportunity by his very circumstances: 'There are some aspects of the research making use of sportsmen that I think are very good, desirable for the sportsmen, desirable for the society. You know how many people suffer from back injuries: that's a really big problem to modern society. Well, there are sports injury clinics, for example, that actually look into these problems. And I suppose scientifically, sportsmen are a good controlled population, which is all that the scientists desire; and it is very difficult to get a subject and suitable controls so that results can be obtained which are going to be significant in some way rather than just blurred by the normal variation in human response.'

Of course in the West, research is supervised by ethical committees. 'If we take for example what we're intimately involved with, which is giving drugs to people: we can't just say, Right, well, come along you, we'll give you some drugs. We'd have to get that cleared by the appropriate committee, who would say, Why are you doing this work? What suffering could be caused to the subject? Is it a safe drug that you are testing; has it been approved by the government? So there are controls.'

Before 1965, when the Department of Pharmacy at Chelsea

College began to specialize in sport's drug control problem, it had been engaged in research on 'the fundamental aspects of drug metabolism and distribution and kinetics in man'.[33] *Any* pharmaceutical laboratory may conduct research of either a preventative or explorative kind. There is also a vicious-circle argument, to which some researchers subscribe, that the only way to prevent sportsmen from misusing drugs is to demonstrate, by means of tests, that they do not work. This would involve using either volunteers or sportsmen themselves in the research. And even testing procedures must themselves be refined by research with human subjects.

'Fundamental information about drug absorption, distribution and elimination, and particularly the time-course of these processes, is required, if the analytical scheme is to be realistic. Unfortunately, for many drugs such information is inadequate. Therefore, ideally, the validity of the assay procedure for each drug considered should be tested by analysis of samples from volunteers to whom the drugs have been administered in normal doses.'[34] So said Professor Beckett in 1967.

What this may mean, if the drug detection centres intend to turn to chemical companies to help finance their research, I leave the reader to consider. As Dr Cowan observes there are few opportunities in Western society for examining 'a good controlled population'. Sportsmen are a rare commodity in this respect. Human beings generally choose to weather stress in private if they can, or in congenial circumstances, rather than under potentially hostile public scrutiny. Sport is therefore unique in its usefulness to those wishing to explore physical or chemical potential, for whatever purpose. And if there is a clinically plausible connection between sport and drugs, there is an equally plausible connection between sport and psychology, as we shall see.

12

The Experimenters

The East Europeans are nothing if not practical. While the West holds spectator sport to be a physical contest, displaying technical skill and muscular proficiency, the East Europeans, being somewhat harder, more pragmatic peoples, long ago abandoned this façade, and admitted that sporting events were not held for this purpose at all. The Communists cut a swath through Western hypocrisy about sport. They saw that the Western nations held sport experiments called 'spectator sports,' which were designed to subject the players to mental and physical stress. They also saw that Western values prevented the West from admitting exactly what was being done to these individuals. It was pretended that the events were 'for fun', even though the spectator sports were obviously organized with great care to be observed by large numbers of people, and even though they involved extremes of emotion and competitiveness. The West refused to admit the inherent seriousness of sport. The events were to entertain; to celebrate strength, skill with bats and balls, or jumping high and going fast.

The Communists, by discipline practical and iconoclastic, found the discrepancy amusing and ridiculous: typical of imperialist chicanery, in fact. Why, they wondered, should the Western sportsman be trained purely as a *physical* combatant, when the physical side of his sport played a comparatively small part in winning and losing? Surely these sporting events involved such a high degree of stress that they could reduce the strongest of human bodies to incapacity. Surely, they thought, the mind governs the body. And if it did not, it could be trained to do so.

The Communists put two and two together, and came up with some training systems of their own. These were practical systems, designed scientifically to prepare their sportsmen to stand up to the sport experiment, and to deal with its mental and physical stresses better than their Western opponents. Of course, physical training was included in the programme, and anabolic steroids and other chemicals might enhance physical capacity. But the greatest possible emphasis was placed on training the athlete's *mind*, to handle the pressure which could destroy his whole performance, and deprive him of all his physical skill. The Communists knew that if their athletes were practised in handling pressure, they would, in spite of all Western enthusiasm, callisthenics and technical proficiency, come home with the Olympic hardware. US Olympic sports psychologist Richard Suinn:

'Olympic and world-class athletes of several European nations rely routinely on sports psychology. It is no surprise that Russia has so dominated the Winter Olympic Games; their athletes make a career out of competition. Yet the Soviets also recognize that the mind helps determine athletic success. East Germany, a relatively recent entry into the Olympic arena, has introduced rigorous psychological training for its athletes.'[1]

In a sense, the Eastern bloc have been the spoilers of sport. They have openly admitted the name of the game. Spectator sport is not 'fun' for the athletes concerned. It is cruel, and it is in deadly earnest. It promotes the study of human behaviour by putting men on circuits and fields, like white mice in mazes, to see how they react when a reward is offered, or an obstacle placed in their way. It sets one group against another. It puts men in rings and arenas like bulls, to see how long they last before they fall down, or lose their teeth, or break their bones. It tests them. If they are successful, it tests them again and again until they are beaten. Some sportsmen are never broken or demoralized. These must be probed to see what makes them 'tick'.

The Communist athletes are cruelly trained to withstand cruelty. The East Europeans pull no punches with their sports performers. They let them know, from a very early age, exactly what they are in for when they compete at high levels, and internationally. They tell them frankly: this isn't a game; you are on the line, and you are representing the Communist people and Communist efficiency. They subject them to batteries of tests: personality tests, psycho-motor tests, physiological tests. They watch over their training – recording, measuring, questioning. They put them in lab experiments to see if they can withstand pain, if they have courage, strong will, motivation. They shift them from the laboratory to the playing field and from the playing field to the high altitude chamber. If necessary, they discreetly give them drugs to prepare them for competitive careers. And then they tell them, on the day, deliver the goods. Sadly, from the point of view of Western sensibilities, most of the athletes do exactly that.

The Eastern bloc have 'sports scientists', as they call the behavioural psychologists who handle athletic training. ('Behaviourism', as its name suggests, has to do with the study of observable behaviour, response to stimuli, and objective variables. It is distinct from branches of so-called 'depth' psychology which seek to explore the roots of personality and experience. The Communists have generally shunned the latter as unscientific.[2]) Western sports psychologists, on the other hand, have divided themselves in two camps.

The first group, which we could call value-orientated, are concerned with remedial research, and with helping sportsmen overcome their personal and individual anxieties not only about competition, but about themselves. These psychologists work, usually, on a face-to-face basis with the athletes concerned, and are often not at liberty to divulge their findings. They address themselves to the problems of human beings who happen to be sportsmen, and do not need to be reminded of the principles involved in their work. They are concerned with sports performance only inasmuch as they are concerned that talent should not be wasted.

The other, much larger, group of Western sports psychologists, which could be called value-free, are more closely related to the East European behavioural sports scientists referred to above. This group comprises all those researchers interested in the sportsman as an athletic animal. Such an animal, they hold, exhibits a fairly predictable pattern of traits in personality tests. This gives them reason to suppose that a standard definition of the genus 'athlete' may be arrived at. The animal is capable of a wide variety of adaptations under competitive stress, some of these more successful than others. When it does not produce a good performance the animal may be of concern to such investigators, not because of any distress involved, but because of its 'psycho-motor inefficiency'. The sports scientists of this persuasion are attempting to remedy psycho-motor inefficiency by training programmes meticulously devised, by testing, probing and quantifying athletic animal's behaviour (in the laboratory if necessary), and t weeding out or screening individuals called 'problem athletes' who have either failed to respond to training, or who might weaken what the investigators conceive to be 'superior' athletic strains. To their great credit, these sports scientists have not allowed themselves to be intimidated by any of the mythology surrounding sport: so far as they are concerned the athletic animals in their charge are subjects in an international experiment, which they may examine with impunity in experiments of their own. Their research provides vital insights into human behaviour under stress, just as vivisection provides valuable information on animal physiology. It is left to the reader to consider the dignity of such work, and to whom it is ultimately accountable.

Sports scientific experiments have been well documented in East Germany, Russia, Bulgaria, Poland and Czechoslovakia. Since the early 1920s and even before, the institutes of physical culture in Moscow, Leningrad, Leipzig, and other cities, have had productive sports research departments, complete with laboratories. Although the literature is not freely available in the West, sports scientists here are well acquainted with some of the research.

In 1970 a remarkable book appeared in the West, celebrating the progress made by East European sports scientists in their work with athletic animals. Much of the work to which it refers has been carried out in laboratories and field tests by experimental and behavioural psychologists and physiologists. The authors make no apologies for the nature of the research or the methods used. Indeed, they warmly recommend such investigations by Western sports scientists concerned to produce successful athletes, and there is every indication that such investigations are already underway. This startling and informative book, *Psychology and the Superior Athlete*,[3] deserves to be examined in some detail, with appropriate allusions to other studies to help the reader form a clearer picture of recent international research. It may well provide him with an insight into sport he never had before. The authors, Bryant J. Cratty of the University of California in Los Angeles, and Miroslav Vanek, of Charles University, Prague, are leading authorities in the field of sports psychology. Dr Cratty is a former coach and former president of the North American Society for Psychology in Sport and Physical Activity. Miroslav Vanek is

President of the International Society of Sports Psychology, and is paid by the government of Czechoslovakia in his capacity as a sports psychologist.

In the Foreword, Dr John E. Kane, a leading British sports psychologist, points out, 'The increasing interest in the psychological aspects of athletic performance probably reflects both the search by athletes, teachers and coaches for the more elusive non-physical determinants of success, and the discovery by psychologists *that the athletics arena is a fruitful laboratory for behavioural research*' (my italics).[4]

The book opens with one of the most comprehensive reviews anywhere to be found of the literature, Russian, European and American, on athletic performance over the past fifty years. The authors suggest that one of the general benefits afforded humanity by the research has been 'to formulate principles pertinent to the understanding of behaviour under stress'.[5] It proceeds to the very significant subject of personality tests commonly administered to sportsmen; including the Knobloch Neurotic Scale (considered unsuitable by the authors), the Eysenck Personality Inventory, the Raven Picture IQ Test, Taylor's Scale of Manifest Anxiety, the Cattell 16 PF (Personality Factor) Inventory, the Guess-Who Sociometric Test, the Edwards Personal Preference Schedule, the Maudsley Psychological Inventory, the Minnesota Multiphasic Personality Inventory (MMPI), and a Self-Rating Scale invented by V. Hosek, in which the sportsman is 'required to write a brief autobiography, including the characteristics of his family upbringing, the nature of the family unit, as well as other pertinent information'.[6] Other factors evaluated in such personality tests 'include the degree of self-criticism, social ability, introversion, neurotic symptoms, maniac [sic] symptoms, depressive symptoms, paranoid symptoms, and physiological stability that the athlete may evidence'.[7] Both authors experienced some hostility from sportsmen required to fill out long questionnaires, and concluded, 'More than two sessions of about two hours in duration will usually prove oppressive to athletes.' The Self-Rating Scale is designed to elicit information on the athlete's feelings about the training camp, his coach, his leisure activities, and his sex life, and the interview is repeated frequently, sometimes every second or third day.[8]

The Personality tests for sportsmen discussed here by Cratty and Vanek are very widely used in sports scientific research. Two well-known American sports psychologists, Bruce Ogilvie and

Thomas Tutko, have devised a test they refer to as 'the instrument',[9] the Athletic Motivation Inventory (AMI), a 190-item multiple-choice questionnaire which has so far been given to more than 75,000 athletes (including high school children) throughout America. *Sports Illustrated* in 1971 reported that 'the instrument' is at least theoretically 'subject to tinkering' by the respondent. The work of Tutko and Ogilvie originally aroused considerable hostility from both athletes and coaches. Ogilvie 'almost got into a fistfight' with a heckler at one clinic, and at presentations 'they have had coaches literally turn their backs on them'. The magazine also reports another incident, in which Tutko was lured into an impromptu session with a group of black players who wanted to know what exactly he intended to do with his information.

Jack Scott, author of *The Athletic Revolution* and himself a former college athlete, gave a paper to the North American Society for Psychology in Sport and Physical Activity, in Seattle during the spring of 1970, in which he told the assembly, 'It is inexcusable and socially irresponsible to put psychological information about athletes in the hands of the typical coach, for there is an excellent chance he will use this information, not to help the athletes, but to further manipulate and exploit them.'[10] Scott has something to say, too, about Tutko and Ogilvie: 'One of the things they are doing at the present time is sending out psychological tests to coaches who request them. The coach has whatever athlete he wants to take the test, and it is then returned to Ogilvie and Tutko. For a fee of $3.00 per college athlete ($1.50 per high school athlete) they provide the coach with a psychological analysis of the athlete. According to one coach they work with, "These tests give us information so we can know the right buttons to push in order to get maximum performance from our boys".'[11]

A recent development has been the appearance of a new book by Thomas Tutko and Umberto Tosi entitled *Sports Psyching*.[12] It contains a forty-two-item questionnaire for the aspiring sportsman to try out on himself. This test, called the Sports Emotional-Reaction Profile (SERP) purports to evaluate 'desire, assertiveness, sensitivity, tension-control, confidence, personal accountability and self-discipline'. Leaving aside the question of such a test's scientific validity, the reader might care to consider the uses to which such information might be put.

A number of psychologists have questioned the use of personality-trait tests on sportsmen (and indeed on anybody else).

Rainer Martens wonders what the devil Ogilvie and Tutko are up to, and points to the mass of conflicting findings of sports personality tests as a sign that they may not prove anything at all.[13] One of the co-authors of *Psychology and the Superior Athlete*, Bryant Cratty, himself reviews the personality-factor tests and questionnaires commonly given to sportsmen in another of his books.[14] Some of these, he says, are recognized in general psychology; others are not. 'At the time of this writing . . . not only are there numerous psychological trait measures of dubious value available to the uninitiated professional, but (as in industrial psychology before World War II) there are at this writing about six "mail order" psychological testing packages available to coaches that purport to measure an athlete's motivation, drive, and similar potentially important characteristics. The majority of these easily available packages are of little worth, lacking in valid norms, and potentially confusing to the coach and athlete.'[15] Such dubious tests are condemned by the Statement of Ethics of the American Psychological Association. The American National Football League Players' Association is concerned to protect its members from personality questionnaires. In February 1971 it called for an end to all psychological testing of athletes. A representative of the Association said that he could cite several instances in which coaches had misinterpreted information from the tests and mishandled players.[16]

What should perhaps concern us most about these personality tests is that they are spreading to more countries and sports. In Australia, for example, sports scientists are beginning to apply their methods to cricket. In Dennis Lillee's instruction book *The Art of Fast Bowling* his trainer, Dr Frank Pyke, tells us, 'The more professional the sport becomes in Australia, the more emphasis we'll see on a scientific approach to coaching.'[17] He refers to American football and the psychological training of players, as well as to personality tests, which 'in the long run help coaches get to know a player and his particular needs' so as to help him become a better performer.

In Eastern Europe, personality tests and measures are used, according to Cratty and Vanek, for selection and screening of sportsmen for future teams, identifying 'problem athletes', devising 'effective means for dealing with the psychological makeup of athletes who display no special personality and/or emotional problems'[18] (why these athletes should be 'dealt with' at all we are left to ponder), and for identifying the 'typical personality structure' of athletes in different sports. At the same time, the data may be used, along with other material collected by physicians and physiologists, to standardize tests internationally so as to compare sportsmen in different sports and different countries. Cratty and Vanek conclude optimistically, 'With continued investigations of the personality of athletes, a valid theoretical framework should emerge within which the personality of the sportsman may be considered.'[19]

They recommend that 'A standard definition of an "athlete" acceptable to all should be arrived at. If a comprehensive battery of personality, sociometric, self-reporting techniques and projective measures is agreed upon by researchers from various countries, fruitful intercultural comparisons may be carried out.' Additionally, 'tests evaluating the emotional states within specific situations might be constructed', for example, 'to assess feelings when losing and after winning'.[20]

Chapter 4 of this invaluable book deals with 'Assessing the Athlete through Field Tests'. Some of the 'methodologies' will be of great interest to sportsmen in the West who are not immediately anxious to be turned into White Mice Men for the benefit of behavioural research. In Moscow, structured 'field tests' were devised, in which a group of athletes representing various sports 'might be placed on a course through the forest containing obstacles with which they were unfamiliar. Observers stationed near each of the obstacles,' say Cratty and Vanek, 'would rate the manner in which each athlete negotiated the various problems.' For example, 'it would be noted whether the athlete hesitated when confronted with a particularly difficult wall to ascend or whether he unhesitatingly vaulted it'.[21]

This section is accompanied by a drawing of three white-coated observers with clip-boards, peeking through spy-holes at an athlete leaping a ditch in front of such a wall. They are taking notes. The caption underneath reads, 'Figure 1. Experiments of courage have taken many forms. In the one shown, the athlete is being observed as he traverses one of a series of obstacles. He has had no previous knowledge of the nature of the obstacle course he has just entered, nor does he know that he is being observed. The experiments record the speed with which he traverses each obstacle, the presence of reactions denoting anxiety, as well as the general "style" he may exhibit during the running of the course.'[22]

Other vital investigations are carried out under laboratory conditions; for instance, ball-handling and ball-sense tests, in which soccer players are blindfolded and required to discriminate between different balls using only their feet. Cratty and Vanek continue enthusiastically, 'Interesting experiments were carried out with athletes in a number of sports in which balance attributes were investigated.'[23] These studies attempted to discover how movement is affected by various parts of the body. 'In some studies the athlete's hearing was blocked while he attempted to perform components of the skill involved in his sport. In other research peripheral vision was eliminated with glasses' (meaning, presumably, goggles with holes in). 'Some subjects,' continue Cratty and Vanek with obvious admiration, 'had collars placed on their necks to immobilize head movements, which play a role in the maintenance of a proper orientation to gravity.'[24] It was found that vision-blocking disrupted the balance of basketball players, movement and visual interferences affected the performance of gymnasts, rowers were upset by auditory blocks, divers and figure-skaters were radically affected by both movement and visual blocks, and so on.[25]

In 1951 in Prague a dissertation appeared on 'Courage and Fear in Physical Education'. A delicate topic for the behavioural psychologist to investigate, surely, at least by experimental methods. But the experimenter in this case turns out to be one of our co-authors, the intrepid Dr Vanek. 'An interesting series of experiments exploring the nature of courage in athletes in a number of sports were carried out in Czechoslovakia in the 1950s. Subjects were obtained from several groups of participants in activities which purportedly require courage, including motorcycle race drivers, ski-jumpers, downhill skiers, parachute jumpers and gymnasts.'[26] All of the subjects were required to dive or jump into a pool off a three-metre board, regardless of their comparative skill at water sport, to see how they reacted. Hesitation, physical gestures and facial expressions were studied for signs of fear, as were the athletes' own accounts of the anxiety they experienced. About 12 per cent of the subjects actually refused to dive head first. 'Another interesting measure was taken of the subjects' ability to make perceptual judgements under the stress imposed,' say the authors.[27] This was done by flashing numbers at the unfortunate sportsmen as they left the diving board, to see if they noticed what these were. 'This phenomenon of perceptual disturbance under stressful conditions is documented with frequency in the experimental literature.' Apart from the divers (the control group in this experiment) all of the sportsmen were evidently frightened, and Cratty and Vanek note, 'there are many provocative ideas which might be explored in future research of this nature'. That the ideas are provocative, the reader may readily agree, especially since the diving experiment included *'photographic evidence of anxiety reflected in facial and bodily postures assumed as the athlete is on the board'* (my italics).[28]

The authors conclude from these investigations, that 'Further studies should attempt to determine how courage may be trained for in general and in specific sports situations.' They suggest, 'To develop a program in schools or in athletic training camps intended to enhance courage, a variety of stressful activities should be included.'[29]

There follows a brief review of some of the abundant literature dealing with 'the athletic personality'. The most ambitious at the time of writing was an extensive study by Vanek and Hosek involving 260 sportsmen from ten different sports, with data from an additional 750. To their surprise and dismay, perhaps, the investigators discovered the athletes' scores on Eysenck and Cattell personality tests did not differ significantly from the non-athletic norm, 'indicating few differences in personality trait structures when the total group of athletes was contrasted to the norms.'[30] This may come as no surprise to the reader, who probably imagined sportsmen were individuals anyway, but the authors, referring to a British compilation of 'athletic personality' studies by John Kane and F. W. Warburton, feel bound to point out: 'the delineating of some ubiquitous "animal" called an *athlete* cannot be done with any degree of certainty'.[31] Of course, this will not deter sports scientists all over the world from continuing to administer batteries of personality tests to the ubiquitous animal in question.

One of the testing experiences awaiting many sportsmen in actual competition is physical pain, and not the kind of pain to which most of us are accustomed in our lives, but the pain of mounting physical stress. The sportsman's body is stressed in much the same way as an aircraft: in the terminology of civil engineering the forces are compressive (pressing in), tensile (pulling asunder) and torque (twist, or a combination of two different forces). Serious injuries are so commonplace that, in the most violent sports,injury and pain may be regarded with some flippancy, to conceal fear. I have more than once seen an American football player lying injured on the field, ignored by his team-mates, many of whom physically turn their backs on the offending occurrence. It is not difficult to sympathize, both with the wounded player, and with the rest of the team who would prefer not to be reminded of bodily mutilation. Nor is it difficult to imagine the feelings of the team coach, who sees a vital cog in his machinery grinding to a halt, which must be either repaired or replaced. Certainly the athlete's health is never impaired by undue pity. He is lucky if his injury is countenanced at all.

Charley Taylor, former star of the Washington Redskins, talking about his college career at Arizona State: 'In spring training my sophomore year I broke my neck – four vertebrae. "Hey, Coach," I said, "my neck don't feel good." "There's nothing wrong with your neck,you jackass," he said. So the numb went away a little, and I made a tackle and when I went to get up, my body got up, but my head just stayed there right on the ground. And the coach says, "Hey, get this jackass off the field." '[32]

The more enlightened trainers and coaches consider the stress of pain a vital part of the athlete's preparation. As Vanek and Cratty observe: 'Many athletes are unaware of how it really feels to extend themselves fully in an all-out performance: they tend to run, swim, walk or work well "within themselves". Coaches of such athletes could at infrequent times during the season during practice suddenly ask the individual to extend himself at the end of a so-called "all-out performance".'[33] What exactly does this mean in practical terms? 'If he is running an 800 metre race, at what is purportedly his best time, he may be asked, just as he nears the end of the race, to "run 50 or 75 yards farther". This method should result in an athlete gaining a feeling of overload and of the pain incurred of extending performance limits in taxing endurance tasks,' say our authors. 'At the same time this technique should also aid the athlete to adapt to the pain and emotional stress endured when experiencing this type of overload.'[34]

The nature of contact sport is such that an athlete's brain may minimize the pain he experiences anyway. Thresholds of pain have been investigated by E. Dean Ryan, an American sports researcher, by the use of a cuff strapped to the lower legs of high-school students who reportedly like contact sports. By moving a football cleat beneath it gradually into the sensitive shinbone,

Ryan was able to make comparisons between pain tolerance of these children and others who did not like contact sports. He found the more vigorous children were also more tolerant: indeed, 'this type of athlete may reduce magnitude of input whether it was painful or not'.[35]

British experimenters, too, have investigated pain and exhaustion in laboratory tests, using cyclists for example, on an ergometer – an instrument for measuring muscular effort.[36] They used a 5-millimetre 'metal projection' pressed against the cyclists' shinbones by means of an inflating cuff.

Sports psychologists everywhere recommend the insertion of stress into training and practice programmes. Pre-competition activation (or perhaps 'agitation' would be the more accurate term) has been investigated in a number of studies, some of which have to do with suddenly switching the time or conditions of the competition, and monitoring the athlete's response to these changes to see if he becomes more or less nervous.[37] Coaches in America are already using recorded crowd noises in practice sessions to acclimatize their athletes. Some coaches even invite rival fans to 'observe practices and to harass their athletes',[38] so that the sportsman will not worry about these detractors looking at him during actual competition.

The final section of Cratty and Vanek's book is devoted to the Czech Olympic team, with whom Dr Vanek worked for three years prior to the Mexican Games of 1968, amassing files of information on the 124 athletes concerned, including personality scores, autobiographies, high-altitude psychomotor scores, and other laboratory data.[39] All 124, at the time of nomination to the Czechoslovakian team, were 'tested in the batteries of tests described . . . by teams of physicians and psychologists'.[40] The psychologists had surmised, from previous investigation, 'that about 15 to 20 per cent of all superior performers are what might be termed problem athletes'[41] and that about half the team had 'minor psychological difficulties' requiring attention. 'During the six weeks the team was on the Olympic site,' say Cratty and Vanek, 'a total of over 200 formal interviews were scheduled in which the problems of about fifty-five athletes were discussed.' This was in addition to informal discussions on training sites and in the dining and living areas. 'Prior to each interview scheduled the athlete's personal file containing the results of his personality and psychomotor test data would be consulted.'[42] Leisure activites chosen by the athletes were organized, and Czech household goods were strategically provided: Pilsen beer, Czech music and Czech *objets d'art* to make the athletes feel at home in Mexico.

The athletes' feelings about all this are best judged by their reactions to the sports psychologists and scientists after competition. Some were friendly and grateful for the help and attention they had received. About 50 per cent reacted in a way that Cratty and Vanek describe as neutral or 'bland' – 'almost like some kind of defence mechanism, with the athlete not quite knowing whether to thank or to ignore the psychologist'.[43] Others showed 'cool hostility' as if to say, 'my success is my own', and implying by such behaviour that the sports scientists were parasites. The book offers five case studies (out of the possible 124) for the reader's attention. One was of a girl figure-skater who, it seems, told the sports scientists to get lost. The authors note that this was a very self-sufficient athlete. The Czechs took home seven gold medals.

This memorable book, which I hope provides the reader with some insight into the advances being made by sports scientists internationally, concludes with a statement by Professor Ferruccio Antonelli, in his (then) capacity as President of the International Society of Sports Psychology. Professor Antonelli commends the 'noble message of human brotherhood' of a book co-authored by an American and a Czech, but warns against untrained coaches setting up as psychologists after reading it. He draws attention to the need for sportsmen to be treated as individuals, and after summarizing some of the author's recommendations, he says, 'But they conclude, and they are very right, that the best psychological guide for a team is the so-called "democratic" method, which means, in a practical way, the coaches and psychologists must respect the individual human dignity of the athletes (who are neither animals nor babies), their freedom, and their conscious and unconscious motivations.' Professor Antonelli will perhaps have the reader's full support when he says, 'the best sentence that I found in this book is the following one: "It is imperative that the sport psychologist be content to assume a service role, and to be discreet in his professional dealing, rather than to be placed in a position in which he appears to be sharing in the glory of success." '[44]

Let us hope, for the sake of that ubiquitous 'animal' called an athlete, that Professor Antonelli is not a voice crying in the wilderness.

13

The Growth of the Shrink

Since the end of the First World War and even before, sportsmen have attracted the attention of large numbers of psychologists, parapsychologists, psychiatrists, autogenic therapists and hypnotists. Just as there is now a burgeoning industry exploring the needs of the sportsman's body, so there is a burgeoning industry – and a very prosperous one – anxious to explore the needs of the sportsman's mind. The increasing interest in sports psychology reflects 'the discovery by psychologists that the athletics arena is a fruitful laboratory for behavioural research'.[1]

We have already seen a few aspects of the work of sports psychologists: some of the behavioural research currently being carried out in the name of sports psychology around the world might prove fertile ground for a government inquiry. But not all those studying sportsmen's minds, thankfully, are collecting data on 'athletic animals' or probing them for ways to improve motor performance of given tasks. Some sports psychologists and therapists are deeply concerned, irrespective of performance, with the sportsman's well-being under stress, and with his mental health both during and after his career. Some of them hold the view that sport serves to integrate the personality and promote mental health (a view with which I differ). Equally, the original purpose of some of the widespread personality testing of athletes was undoubtedly to weed out individuals who would be particularly vulnerable to the pressure of high-level competition and save them from pointless distress, since they would be unlikely to win, and very likely to suffer discordancies of personality in the attempt. There is much that is humane and compassionate in the literature, so individual sports psychological studies are best considered on their merits.

Ever since Norman Triplett's famous experiment with cyclists in 1898[2] in which he found that competing against others produces better times than competing against the clock, sports psychology has mushroomed as a 'science' in East Germany, Russia, the USA, Canada, Britain, France, Italy, Spain, Bulgaria, Romania, Switzerland, Poland, Hungary, Yugoslavia, Czechoslovakia, Scandinavia, Holland, Austria, Australia, Brazil, Japan, and elsewhere.[3] The earliest experiments seem to have concerned motor-learning, motor behaviour and kinesthesis. Later studies diversified. The Russians, since 1936 and especially since research carried out in Leningrad in 1958, have concentrated particularly on the study of will power.

Texts on the psychology of soccer appeared as early as 1801 in Europe. By the 1920s several universities and institutes had sports psychology on the curriculum – Leipzig and Berlin, for example. The German departments at first worked in close collaboration with the Russians who had been inspired, among other things, by the work of P. F. Lesgaft, the physician, on the possible psychological benefits of physical activity. The Russians were probably the first actually to use their leading athletes as subjects for experimentation. Russian sports scientists have had laboratories in Moscow, Leningrad and Tbilisi from as early as 1917. In 1950 the Deutsche Hofschule für Körperkultur in Leipzig opened a department under the chairmanship of Dr Paul Kunath, who was strongly influenced by Moscow and Leningrad. Its facilities included a laboratory for sports scientific research. By the 1960 Melbourne Olympics, national teams had begun to be accompanied by a sports psychologist or sports scientist, either in an active capacity or as an observer.

In 1965 an International Congress of Sports Psychology was held in Rome. By then some national societies numbered among their members the leading psychologists in the country: Italy is a notable example. 1965 was also the year in which the North American Society of Psychology in Sport and Physical Activity was formed and in three years its membership had swelled to 200. In the USA work on motor-learning began in the 1930s in PE labs at the universities of Illinois, Penn State, Iowa, and elsewhere. Following the Second World War and the pioneering work of Dr

John D. Lawther at Penn State, Clarence Ragsdale at Wisconsin, Dr Coleman Griffin at Illinois, and Dr Arthur Slater-Hammel at Indiana, Franklin Henry's laboratory at the University of California at Berkeley began training research students from all over the USA who were interested, not only in motor-learning, but in other aspects of physical education science.

In November 1968 the second International Congress of Sports Psychology was held in the USA. Over 200 behavioural scientists from sixteen countries attended the four-day meeting and over 100 papers were presented.

Some of the earliest work with Olympic teams was carried out by the Czechs (see pp. 225–6 for the 1968 Mexico Olympic team tests conducted by Dr Miroslav Vanek). Ten years previously, the Brazilians stole a march on everybody in the World Cup by sending a psychologist to accompany their team to Sweden. Many of the British soccer *cognoscenti* found this most amusing. Danny Blanchflower, then captain of Northern Ireland, wrote a mickey-taking article in the *Observer*. In 1961 an article appeared which outlined the use of post-hypnotic suggestion to 'work better together' made to the Brazilian team.[4] Apparently this worked very well, perhaps because their opponents couldn't stop laughing.

Indeed, laughter was a common reaction, in the early days, to Shrinks in Sport. One early experiment (in 1938) on an American baseball club initiated by the then president of the Chicago Cubs, Philip K. Wrigley, was a disaster. Wrigley hired the head of the psychology department at the University of Illinois to find 'the profile of a champion baseball player'. The ball players fell about laughing at the questions. 'For all the psychologist could find out,' observes William Barry Furlong, 'baseball players are the stuff that telephone poles are made of.'[5] Since then, at some of the more invasive inquiries, sportsmen have been less amused; some (e.g. the American NFL Players' Association) have considered taking legal action to protect themselves. Eastern bloc athletes, of course, have no such legal redress, and many of them by now must have come to associate sport with the inside of a laboratory or high-altitude chamber. Nor should it surprise anyone that the Eastern bloc are so far advanced in what we call sports psychology. The Russian government spends millions of roubles a year on 'para-psychology' research, which they refer to as 'bio-information'. Sport is included in this programme. Behavioural psychologists in Russian sport are called 'sports scientists'. The Soviets are dedicated materialists; they do not bother particularly with phenomenological psychology, lacking provable results.[6]

We are rather chary, in the West, of discussing psychological interference in sport. We are apt to laugh (either out of incredulity or nervousness) because sport is traditionally a 'healthy outdoor' activity. Psychologists, even supposing they accompany sportsmen to their competitions, can scarcely do them any harm, can they? The players can always guffaw, along with us, if they don't approve of the intervention. One competition that amused us all in 1978 was the World Chess Championship series, held in Baguio City in the Philippines. Viktor Korchnoi, his brown eyes bulging out of his head, resigned in the 32nd game, conceding the championship to Anatoly Karpov despite a magnificent fight-back from 5–2 down. He complained bitterly of what he called 'severe psychological pressure'. His close friend, Petra Leeuwerick, had told a journalist, 'The Soviets want to kill him in a mental way,' in revenge for his political defection.[7] Earlier in the semi-final Korchnoi had met Boris Spassky (who has since married a foreigner and moved abroad) in Belgrade. After a good start he had suddenly lost four games in a row. He accused one of his opponent's aides of trying to steal his biorhythm chart, and got angry and upset at Spassky's tactic of retiring behind a curtained cubicle between moves, so that all Korchnoi could see of him were his feet. Korchnoi believed negative 'psi' waves (sometimes wrongly referred to as microwaves) were being directed at his mind while he played. Eventually he enlisted the help of parapsychologists in Switzerland, who intercepted the waves and enabled Korchnoi to recover his composure. He won the series.

Chess has had a long history of parapsychological interference like this. Grandmasters are accustomed to the parapsychologists and hypnotists accompanying Soviet champions. Anatoly Karpov's personal parapsychologist Vladimir Zukhar is well known throughout Russia, where his techniques have been developed scientifically, and at enormous expense, for military purposes. The game of chess is one of 'supernatural tension', as Korchnoi says, and as anyone knows who has played it seriously. There are no outlets for the vehemence and humiliation which gradually build up over symbolic exchanges of territory. Survival may depend on a pawn misplaced. The World Championship has always played havoc with contestants' minds. The first Champion, Wilhelm

Steinitz, who took the title in 1866, ended his life in an asylum after suffering delusions in which he played chess against God. American prodigy Paul Morphy became upset by the idea that people were trying to steal his clothes. His fellow-countryman Bobby Fischer has been living as a recluse since he won the title in 1972. His behaviour during the contest, in Reykjavik, was outrageous and, according to some, bizarre. He became obsessed with the contest conditions, the television cameras and the size of the squares on the board, and seemed unable to stop complaining. But the latest and most significant casualty was the hitherto frostily calm Anatoly Karpov, who had held the title for a decade as Russian champion supreme and Cavalier of the Order of Lenin. In 1984, Karpov was 5–0 up in a contest with young Gary Kasparov, the 22-year-old who was eventually to snatch Karpov's crown. From this point the reigning champion went to pieces. He began calling time-outs and was on the verge of a nervous breakdown when the President of the International Chess Federation, Florencio Campomanes, brought the match to a halt to safeguard Karpov's health. The tragedy was reminiscent of an earlier Championship when the man they called 'The Carp' for his cold-blooded wiliness was in psychological ascendancy.

At Baguio City in 1978 Karpov, accompanied by the redoubtable Dr Zukhar, had successfully defended the championship he had inherited after Fischer's demise. Throughout the ninety-two-day contest Korchnoi his challenger had complained of Dr Zukhar's presence in the front rows of the stalls, and had him banished to the back of the hall for a time, by the expedient of threatening to smash his head in. Two members of the Indian Ananda Marga sect, American-born Steven Dwyer and Victoria Sheppherd, were enlisted by Korchnoi's team to help him meditate. Under their influence Korchnoi seemed to recover his confidence. He came from 5–2 down to level the score as Karpov wavered. Three of Korchnoi's aides sat behind the staring Zukhar, two of them staring at the doctor and one staring benignly at Korchnoi. Viktor said that he was very pleased with their progress and that he now had Karpov 'playing like a wet dishcloth'. Then it was borne in upon the intelligence of the Filipino authorities that Korchnoi's two meditators were on bail, accused of attempted murder. They were banished from the hall, and little by little Korchnoi lost his way. Korchnoi stared at the board; Dr Zukhar,

Karpov and unknown hosts of KGB psychics stared at Korchnoi. He raved once more at his intolerable circumstances, made errors, got into time trouble, and resigned in the 32nd game.

The reader may think, yes, but chess is different. Chess is a mental game, inviting mental interference. Sport has to do with physical activity. Well, these chess players train very hard for their contests. Korchnoi swam, jogged and punched bag. Kasparov swims long-distance, cycles and plays football. Besides, according to our definition of sport, chess fulfils all the necessary conditions of the experiment: it is competition between equals to see whose visible skill stands up under pressure, and whose breaks down. The physical aspect is, by and large, greatly over-estimated. There are Dr Zukhars in boxing. One of them is called Evil Eye Finkle, and in his heyday he incapacitated heavyweights with his stare. Finkle made a living out of it, though sometimes he was assigned to help a fighter who couldn't have won with a machine-gun. There was an interesting example of such goings-on in the Norton–Ali fight, in which Norton broke Ali's jaw. 'Norton had a hypnotist,' says Ferdie Pacheco, 'which we neutralized with Evil Eye Finkle and, as a saver, Jimmy Grippo.'[8]

'Gurus' and 'shrinks' may now be found in every nook and cranny of sports performance. Their presence is increasingly apparent in international competition. The Austrians send their Olympic ski-jumpers to an Institute of Will-Power Training. Willi Dungl, who has worked with the Austrian speed ski team, loomed large behind Niki Lauda's 1975 Formula One World championship. Australian swimmers have been trained by hypnotherapy. One post-hypnotic suggestion was apparently 'you are being chased by sharks'. Even cricket, that bastion of conservatism, has its psychologists and hypnotists. Hypnotherapist Dr Arthur Jackson, a member of the Australian Sports Medicine Federation and based in Sydney, has been influential in the careers of several cricketers, notably Bob Willis and Viv Richards. Bob Willis still has the tape recording of Dr Jackson's voice in what he calls 'that fateful hypnosis session' that changed his career. He plays it 'when I want to relax and be on my own'. Jackson say, of Willis's extraordinary performance in the Ashes series of 1977 when he took 27 wickets, 'Much of Willis's success against Australia was due to his own efforts. I do not wish to grab all the glory for hypnotherapy.'[9] Golf's Seve Ballesteros visited a hypnotist in 1981 and uses tapes in his hotel room before he plays. He is a student of the mind-over-matter programme the Spanish call 'sufrologia', based on Oriental concepts, and among his self-suggestions is this one: 'Sevvy, you are standing over this putt and you will hole it. You cannot miss.' David Llewellyn prefers Zen-style meditation: he finds it 'deeply refreshing'. The Brazilian soccer team engaged a hypnotist many years ago; in 1978 so did Hereford United. He put the team in a trance the night before a match, and they woke up 'feeling like world-beaters'. Three Welsh rugby players, Terry Cobner, Geoff Wheel and Bobby Windsor, some years ago sought official permission of the Welsh Rugby Union to consult a hypnotist about their fear of flying. A number of US football teams have availed themselves of the skills of a psychologist – the San Diego Chargers for instance – though players have tended to resist such intervention. Scouting reports, now computerized, generally 'rate' players on psychological indices and the Dallas Cowboys offices off the North Central Expressway have 2500 black dossiers lining a complete wall and part of a basement on every pro football prospect for the last eighteen years which include 'ratings' for aggressiveness, competitiveness, mental alertness and information on biorhythm patterns.[10] Other team sports have been similarly influenced. Four major league baseball teams (Chicago, Detroit, Pittsburgh, and Philadelphia) are reported to have had officially sponsored programmes in TM (transcendental meditation).[11] The Chicago White Sox took part in an experiment to see if Silva Mind Control would help their performance, and so on.

There are landmarks in sports psychology literature, as in other fields. One is entitled, 'The Hypnotic Treatment of Stage-Fright in Champion Athletes', by Gosaku Naruse, of Kyushyu University, Japan. The paper was originally presented at a meeting of the Society for Clinical Experimental Hypnosis in New York in 1963. 125 Japanese athletic champions who had just returned home from the Rome Olympic Meeting in 1960 were questioned about their experience and asked if they had suffered from 'stage-fright'. Nearly all 125 admitted that they had been troubled by it, but only 20 per cent of them attempted to find some method of overcoming it and even among that percentage, very few knew of any systematic technique that might be used. The Training Committee of the Japanese Society for Physical Culture engaged Gosaku Naruse, in his capacity as a hypnotherapist, to see what could be done. They saw that in many cases, stage-fright and nervousness in the pressure of competition had prevented leading athletes from producing their normally excellent performances.

Trainees were asked by Naruse to learn a basic self-suggestion technique, Schultz's *Autogenne* or autogenic training. This method, which because of its cathartic effects requires the supervision of a trained therapist, is now widely used in sports psychology to help athletes maintain relaxed concentration. The technique was originated by the German psychiatrist, Johannes Schultz, from research into hypnosis which began in 1905, and has proved successful in such differing fields as the training of Soviet cosmonauts and the treatment of epilepsy and schizophrenia.[12] It makes use of Schultz's discovery, in his work on hypnosis, that in a state of passive concentration the brain has a self-regulating capacity, and is 'able to perform a magnificent work which cannot be matched by the therapeutic ideas of an experienced therapist'.[13] It also has, in this condition, full command of all bodily functions. The athlete who learns *Selbstentspannung* or self-relaxation is able, by a series of exercises in heaviness, warmth, and other feelings to overcome anxiety whenever he wishes, and reach a state of mental equilibrium in which his best performances may be forthcoming. The method is not simply a meditative exercise: monitoring has shown that blood-pressure, skin temperature and brainwave frequencies respond to this control. Schultz's autogenic training, and variations of it such as psychotonic training, are widely used by Eastern bloc athletes as part of their preparation for major events. Those who believe that Olympic gold medals are won by anabolic steroids greatly underestimate the extent of Soviet and East German research in this field, and run the risk of entirely misunderstanding the demands of the Sport Experiment on human beings who take part in it.

Gosaku Naruse also used other techniques on the Japanese athletes in his charge. One of them was Edmund Jacobson's progressive muscle relaxation.[14] This method requires that the athlete find a comfortable position, so as to focus attention on the various tensions in his body. He may be asked, for example, to tense the muscles in his neck, then relax them, then tense them half as much again, relax them, and so on. Jacobson, an American physician who originated his method in the 1930s, believed that there is a connection between muscular relaxation and emotional calm; by learning to produce the one, the subject could automatically enjoy the other.

Naruse found that these self-suggestion techniques were very effective for the Japanese athletes suffering from stage-fright. He also made use of direct hypnotic suggestion and post-hypnotic suggestion, and, in some cases, 'a trance of medium depth'[15] in which the athlete was asked to imagine himself taking part in his event, so as to uncover deep-seated worries and misjudgements about his performance. Naruse always bore in mind that wherever possible it was better to use methods which the athlete could administer himself, rather than ones which needed the presence and voice of a hypnotist always on hand. He was sensitive to the independence and pride of champions; they greatly prefer their training to be in their own hands, rather than somebody else's. Many therapists around the world have made this observation: champion athletes are disdainful of 'indoctrination', whichever country they come from.

Schultz's autogenic training and Jacobson's progressive muscle relaxation have been adapted in various countries. In Prague, for example, Professor M. Machak, of the Psychology Department of Charles University, has developed a variation of Schultz's technique which places emphasis on activation. While the trainee is imagining himself in a restful pace, he is asked to tense his muscles sharply and take short breaths, preparing himself for his coming performance. After this kind of training adrenalin levels remain abnormally high for about twenty-four hours, so that the athlete is 'prepared hormonally for a high level of competition for a prolonged period of time'.[16]

Dr Herbert Benson, associate professor of Medicine at Harvard Medical School and director of the hypertension section at Boston's Beth Israel Hospital, has developed a rather different method of relaxation for clinical use which would presumably be adaptable for athletes and which is discussed by Thomas Tutko in his *Sports Psyching*.[17] This is based loosely on yoga and TM and involves the use of simple cue words (comparable to mantras) which are repeated over and over in a quiet room until tranquillity is achieved. Benson's book, *The Relaxation Response*, was a bestseller in the USA in 1975.

The Western reader may find some of these techniques disquieting in that they have been taken out of the context of clinical usage and placed in the context of sport. The sports psychologist, whose avowed intention is to improve the sportsman's performance – to 'help him fulfil his potential', as it is usually phrased – may not be the best possible guardian of the sportsman's personality. There is much that is important and congenial in psychological training of any kind so long as the sportsman's interests are uppermost in the psychologist's mind. Otherwise, the implications are grave indeed. The responsibility for implanting ideas in an athlete's head while he is in a state of ultimate receptiveness is not lightly to be contemplated. This is true of training for auto-suggestive methods and particuarly of hypnosis, and those other techniques in which the athlete's role is a passive one. Happily, the common sense and will power of most athletes seem to have prevented hypnotherapy from being anything other than a useful tool in their training. So far as I can discover, it has been helpful rather than harmful, although my information concerning work behind the Iron Curtain is obviously limited.

An English hypnotherapist I consulted, who has a practice at Crystal Palace and who has been asked to help a number of British athletes, was a little ahead of his time when, twenty years ago, he began writing articles such as 'Hypnosis in Sport' in the medical journals. 'I rather blotted my copybook,' he told me, and he has since been disillusioned as to its usefulness. The work was certainly not remunerative. Hypnotherapists worked largely at their own expense because they were interested in helping athletes sent to them; sometimes the athletes were grateful and sometimes they weren't. One thing this doctor noticed that may be of comfort to those who fear the influence of hypnosis in sport: 'It's a very curious thing. When a hypnotist starts his practice he gets spectacular results. I was getting a high success rate of post-hypnotic amnesia and post-hypnotic suggestion. But over the years, although I can still get them to relax, I haven't induced a really deep trance since about 1966 or '67, and I've spoken to a number of other colleagues who have had the same experience.'

Perhaps a note of ambivalence enters the voice, or perhaps the subject's own will power is a dynamic force we have underestimated. Whatever the reason, hypnotherapy does not appear to be turning sportsmen into automatons, as some investigators have feared. 'You can't really establish,' says the English hypnotherapist, 'whether an athlete is in fact *in* post-hypnotic suggestion' – an observation also made by a London psychiatrist I spoke to. Fast bowler Bob Willis told me about his experience of hypnotherapy with Dr Arthur Jackson. 'I was talking like a ten-bob watch beforehand,' says Bob. 'It helped my confidence especially. I used to be very nervous. I could see why everybody else was in the side, but I could never see why I was. I knew Arthur anyway – he was a mate of mine – so I wasn't worried about the hypnosis. I went right out.' Bob got out of his seat and fetched me a copy of his book, *Pace Bowling*, of which he is justly proud. 'This is it,' he said, referring me to the relevant passage: 'The hypnotherapy – and here I must stress it was just one twenty-minute session – was designed to bring home to me the importance of [the German coach Ernst] Van Aaken's running programme. Arthur was an old friend of mind, and he knew that I tended to give up at crucial moments, blaming an injury or the wicket or anything convenient. After the Centenary Test in March 1977, I asked him to help me with my insomnia. I realized my tenseness wasn't helping my bowling development, and after that twenty-minute session I felt better straight away. I was more relaxed, less talkative, more self-contained and more confident. And he had instilled into my sub-conscious the importance of a controlled planned training routine.'[18] Willis was prepared, as part of his rebuilding pro-gramme from serious knee surgery in 1975, to undergo strenuous physical training. What hypnotherapy did for him was to improve his self-image and determination, and help him sleep and relax properly. Dr Jackson sends new tapes regularly.

When the West Indian players contracted to the Kerry Packer World Series began losing form in Australia in 1975, Dr Jackson was called to the team hotel by Clive Lloyd, the captain, and the tour manager. Viv Richards, a batting genius, was very tense and nervous and suffered from the same lack of confidence as Willis. Dr Jackson talked to the players. Both Viv Richards and Alvin Kallicharran were put into deep trance, and by the use of imagery were asked to re-live their past failures, and at the same time improve their technical perception of what happened. Richards's confidence and positiveness improved to such an extent that he went on to break the world record for one year's aggregate of Test runs.

No one could reasonably suggest that Viv Richards's batting is now that of an automaton, or that Bob Willis's bowling performances were not 'his own'. Seve Ballesteros has suffered no downturn in his individuality either. Hypnotherapy seems merely to have allowed freer expression of their natural ability. Indeed, one of the most beautiful pieces of music known to us, Rachmaninov's Second Piano Concerto, could hardly be described as the work of an automaton either. Yet it was written in hypnotherapy, and dedicated to the musicians' hypnotist, Dr Dahl.

One aspect of hypnosis in sport deserves close scientific

scrutiny, and this is hypnotherapy for the treatment of injury. There have been a number of inconclusive but interesting studies, one of them by the English hypnotist Dr David Ryde, who has collected the results of 250 cases over nine years of investigation – 'forty to fifty of them athletes'. In most of these cases, Dr Ryde discusses hypnosis in its usefulness during recuperation, and where there is evidence of muscle spasm and anxiety. Dr Ryde noted 'an apparent alteration in the natural history of disease',[19] and recommends further study.

Sports psychology has not been met with open arms in every country. In the United States sports psychologists fought for acceptance for many years before they achieved their present prestige. Two of them, Thomas Tutko and Bruce Ogilvie, of San Jose State College, met with some hostility from coaches who believed they knew more about their players than 'shrinks' could do. They were nevertheless called in as consultants to many teams, including the Pittsburgh Steelers, the Dallas Cowboys, Golden State Warriors, Oakland As, the University of Southern California and the University of Nebraska. 'If we had a nickel for every time we were laughed at,' sighed Tutko in 1971, 'we could retire now.'[20] Since then the testing procedures and training suggestions of Tutko and Ogilvie have achieved wide acceptance. 'And the field of sports psychology, once thought to be on a level with voodoo, has come into its own.'[21] They are, for example, co-founders of the Institute of Athletic Motivation in America, from which emanate their personality tests. We have already alluded to certain aspects of the work of these two men, about which the author and a number of athletes have expressed concern. Evaluation of emotional profiles from questionnaires such as the Athletic Motivation Inventory may elevate behavioural psychology to the level of quizzes in women's magazines (where it quite possibly deserves to be) but it does nothing to alleviate the fears of those who believe sportsmen's personalities should not be probed and dissected in this way. The AMI has been given to more than 75,000 athletes, including high-school children, college and professional players throughout the USA. This seems at best an invasion of their privacy, if not their human rights. At worst it places information of the most personal and sensitive kind in the hands of those with no interest in the sportsmen other than that of improving their performance on the field.

On the credit side, Tutko and Ogilvie have shown great compassion in some aspects of their work, and one of these is their exploration of success phobia, in which they have adopted a more sensitive approach to the athletes in their care. The understanding which they have brought to the dilemma of athletes who flinch in sight of victory is full of insight and imagination. One's only criticism is that such cases should be described in a book called *Problem Athletes and How to Handle Them*. First, as I have tried to show in the preceding chapters, fear of success seems to be part of the experience of winning, rather than the hang-up of a particular 'problem' group, and the greatest champions encounter it to some degree. It is therefore sport that has the problem, rather than the athletes. Second, the expression 'how to handle them' sticks in the craw of anyone genuinely concerned with sportsmen as human beings, rather than heads of cattle. Still, there is no arguing with the power and clarity of something like this: 'by continually failing in the decisive moment, and by failing to fulfil his potential, the athlete not only avoids responsibility to others but avoids responsibility to himself. If he momentarily accepts this responsibility and puts forth an outstanding effort, he quickly denies his potential by failing to produce in the next instant. By abandoning responsibility, he avoids all the blame and criticism which accompany it'.[22]

Another American sports psychologist of renown, Bryant J. Cratty, we have already met in connection with *Psychology and the Superior Athlete*. Dr Cratty has also written a number of other books and articles including, in 1973, *Psychology in Contemporary Sport*,[23] which gives a full and fair summary of current trends in the field without enlarging on those aspects of laboratory work with athletes celebrated in the earlier book with Vanek. *Psychology in Contemporary Sport* is lucid and helpful on such difficult topics as aggression, anxiety, and anxiety-therapy (in which he covers a number of techniques including desensitization). To his great credit Dr Cratty gives a fairly extensive summary of personality tests currently in use, warning against the unacceptability of some, and the dangers of misuse of others.

Two other leading American sports psychologists, working in rather different fields, are Dr Arnold Beisser and Dr Richard Suinn. Dr Beisser, author of *The Madness in Sports*, is director of the Center for Training in Community Psychiatry in Los Angeles and Clinical Professor at the University of California and California

State College of Medicine. Beisser's book is respected as a classic in the field. His work as a psychiatrist has brought him in contact with sportsmen who have suffered breakdowns. Dr Beisser attributes their condition, in six of the seven cases he describes, to the interruption of their sports careers and the loss of sport as an integrating mechanism in their lives. He goes so far as to suggest, in the case of a golfer he describes, that 'Golf became *the glue which held him together* and hid the underlying paranoid schizophrenia.'[24]

Dr Beisser was himself a keen sportsman before being stricken by polio and confined to a wheelchair, as he says, to think rather than take part. His obvious love of sport encourages him in the belief that it is of great therapeutic value, and he naturally views the sportsmen who come to him as suffering from mental illness because they can no longer play. Unfortunately Dr Beisser's great fondness for sport sometimes influences his judgement. He notes, for example, that younger and younger children are 'thrust' into sports careers – 'Once they can walk training begins in earnest'[25] – but he draws no conclusions from this. Let us have a look at some statistics.

There are 10,000 British Amateur Gymnastics Association clubs in Britain (nearly all with waiting lists) for aspiring gymnasts, most of them schoolchildren, and most of them girls. In many cases, their parents have been inspired by the success of Olympic girl gymnasts such as Olga Korbut and Nadia Comaneci. In Romania, tiny girls are given identity cards and trained in special schools, such as General 7 at Deva. At about 8 years of age 'those with special talent are weeded out and made to specialize'.[26] In Moscow children are proficient at gymnastics by the age of 7 and before. Russia has 2013 gymnastic and sports schools outside the government system, financed by the trades union. Within the government system there are about 2230 sports schools, training nearly half a million children. More than 200 million of China's population are still at school. All of them receive sports instruction. Selected children are coached for eighteen hours a week. In the USA, as Dr Beisser points out, 'Before children can read they wear replicas of sports uniforms' and 'A football-shaped rattle for infants is now available to get them started right'.[27] With all due respect to Dr Beisser's professional experience and enthusiasm, one cannot but suppose that many of these children may come to find sport *anything* but the 'glue which holds them together'.

Dr Beisser also describes the pitiable case of a former boxer who had himself admitted to the hospital. The admitting doctor's notes report: 'This 34-year-old unemployed former boxer seeks voluntary admission after striking his wife. He is agitated, anxious, withdrawn. Auditory hallucinations are present saying "kill, kill, kill". He is irritable, guarded, and suspicious. The affect is flat and there are loose associations. Diagnostic impression is Schizophrenic Reaction, Paranoid Type.'[28]

Dr Beisser admits 'Almost every mental hospital has among its long-term inhabitants a formerly prominent boxer.'[29] And this is because the human skull can only protect the brain up to a point: 'Inevitably the pain of the blows is dulled, pummelling of the skull becomes increasingly vague, cheers of the crowd more distant. Eventually the brain is irreversibly damaged by the blows, the seemingly limitless earnings are plundered by the payoffs, and the fighter stands alone, a hollow hulk. In the end, there is the institution, erected by those who cheered, where their discarded creation can be hidden. The damage is done, the brain cannot be restored, and the only issue is custody. Perhaps the Roman crowd which turned thumbs down on a maimed gladiator was more merciful.'[30]

The boxer who is described in Beisser's book is anxious and frightened. He had been watching a fight on television after his own career had foundered, and in the excitement of the crowd yelling, 'Kill! kill! kill!' he had turned and punched his wife viciously in the stomach. Beisser attributes his illness to the loss of his sport, and of boxing's attraction for underprivileged minority groups he says, 'There can be little argument that if the choice is between crime and boxing, the latter is preferable.'[31]

Dr Beisser declines to comment on the relative amounts of mental illness in sport and other walks of life: he feels that because sport and acting are public professions, their casualties are more conspicuous. He does, however, acknowledge that sport may bring an athlete to emotional crises he might not otherwise have encountered. Winning, for example, crystallizes such powerful feelings that it may cause serious disorder of the personality. 'The history of sports is filled with reports of bad-luck athletes who always faltered on the threshold of victory.'[32] Dr Beisser believes that winning may be traumatic because it symbolizes something else. He takes this 'something else' to be the Freudian supplanting of the father, with all the guilt that this implies. I have no idea what

Oedipus has to do with winning, but that sport has powerful symbolic overtones is undoubtedly true; and that winning may be a harrowing experience, precipitating mental illness for some individuals, is true also. Dr Beisser describes the case of a professional tennis player of international repute who, after reaching match point several times and faltering, dropped out of tennis and into a mental institution for much of his later life.[33] 'Sometimes,' says the psychiatrist, 'becoming a winner is so disastrous for an athlete that he develops a serious psychiatric disorder when success comes his way. There have been several examples of potentially great athletes who managed every time to fail at the moment of victory. A few, through either crowd support or other seemingly fortuitous events, did win a great event. Following this they underwent severe personality disorganization. At the moment when a player sees victory within his grasp he may feel the most exquisite conflict.'[34]

One wonders, if sport has the integrative function Dr Beisser claims for it, why it should cause individuals to encounter extremities of this kind, for they do not happen by accident, and they are not incidental to other events, as they are in ordinary walks of life. A man may be successful or a failure in business and suffer a breakdown, but business did not design to place him on the threshold of his crisis. Sport, on the other hand, finds its very purpose in such emotional exigencies, and provides seating and tickets for people to come and watch what happens. One hopes, since Dr Beisser's work is now so widely respected, that those who read his book will consider its implications very carefully indeed, before turning to sport as the whole world's panacea.

One of the ways in which a nation registers its approval of sports psychology is to appoint a psychologist to its Olympic teams. For a long time the USA was reluctant to sanction such an appointment. Tutko and Ogilvie requested permission to work with America's Olympic athletes at their own expense, but their offers were turned down. 'It's like fighting with a 700-ton marshmallow,' said Tutko of their meetings with officialdom.[35] Since then, the USA has relented. Dr Richard Suinn, head of Colorado State University psychology department, in 1976 became the first psychologist officially appointed to work with the US teams. His fields, as he tells me, have included wrestling, gymnastics, skiing and track and field, though his current title is Team Psychologist, US National Nordic Ski Team and US Biathlon Team. His work received

world-wide attention when the US Nordic team ac
undreamed-of success at the Winter Olympics in Innsbr
1976. Lyle Nelson's performance in the Biathlon event, no
dominated by Russia and Finland, was partly the result of r
training programmes devised by Dr Suinn.

Some of the methods now used by the US athletes are interesting. They include sitting alone, head down, eyes closed, 'building
aggression and a feeling of hatred for the next opponent',[36] and
sitting with a towel or blanket over the head and drawing, in the
mind's eye, a series of numbered concentric circles. Dr Suinn
began working with athletes 'by accident' in 1972. He was a
behavioural therapist, particularly interested in imagery rehearsal
– the technique of visualizing in great detail what is to be done,
before doing it – and in relaxation exercises; and a ski coach at
Colorado State asked him to help out with his team, who were suffering from 'competition tensions'. Dr Suinn applied his knowledge
of mental rehearsal (he now calls this Visuo-Motor Behaviour
Rehearsal, or VMBR) and relaxation exercises, using a twenty-
minute version of Jacobson's method, described earlier. He found
these techniques worked impressively well with the skiers, and progressed to the US Nordic Ski team and other sports with equal
success. He devised a series of cue-instructions ('attack the course',
'calm and steady') which could be used to interrupt negative
thoughts during performance; the number 7 he associated in the
skiers' minds with relaxation. He had '7' taped on the back of their
protective downhill helmets so that team members riding on the
chairlift behind could see the cue.

Suinn recognized that some athletes needed calming down,
while others needed psyching up. He applied his methods to suit
each individual. To increase arousal he used autogenic training,
biofeedback techniques (by which the brain is taught to monitor the
body's level of activation) and music. To soothe athletes already
over-aroused Dr Suinn used relaxation exercises, deep muscle
relaxation with or without biofeedback equipment, and AMT –
Anxiety Management Training. 'By this method the athlete is
trained to recognize early physical-muscular signs of tension build-
up, through the use of imagery. Next, the athlete is trained in deep
muscle relaxation. Finally, the program increases the athlete's
ability to use the relaxation method as an instant means
for eliminating tensions wherever and whenever they might
occur.'[37]

Some of the techniques used by Dr Suinn are widely employed in sports psychology. VMBR, for example, is closely related to Ideomotor Practice, whose usefulness has been demonstrated in a number of studies in Russia and Czechoslovakia. In some cases the athletes were required to do their mental rehearsal prior to falling asleep, for a period of six months before their events.[38] There have also been numerous studies of mental rehearsal in the West. Thirty-nine of these are reviewed by Dorothy Mohr.[39] Thomas Tutko, in *Sports Psyching*, outlines a preparation programme for athletes which takes six weeks to learn and which includes 'mental rehearsal'. The programme begins with two weeks of relaxation exercises and one week of concentration practice, and ends with three weeks of mental and finally physical rehearsal. Of mental rehearsal he says: 'The instructions you give yourself are presented in images, for whenever you learn a sports skill in words . . . you have to translate it into images for your body to carry it out. The more vivid and detailed the image, the better your body can understand what it has to do.'[40]

Behind these techniques, and others like them, is the theory that the brain is itself a bio-computer, which can be programmed in much the same way as an inorganic computer, and that the nervous system is an apparatus for coping with the environment – a servomechanism designed to maintain equilibrium. The theory of cybernetics was originated by Norbert Wiener and though it has now achieved cult popularity, it actually dates back to 1948. The term 'cybernetics' comes from the Greek word for helmsman or guide. When the nervous system expends energy, it receives back information, both from the body and from the environment, as to the effects this energy has produced. In this way, consciousness may be seen as a kind of clearing house, processing input and output, and providing the brain with a constant 'feedback' of information which can be coded and stored for later use. The theory holds that malfunctions of the system are the result of information being fed back too slowly or in insufficient detail for the system to make the proper adjustments. For example, an athlete may be over-anxious about the coming competition, in which he is expected to do well. He is told to 'relax', and he may tell himself, 'relax Charlie', but because this is a very vague instruction, his brain doesn't know exactly what is required. Now, one of the effects of his anxiety will be to lower the resistance in his galvanic skin response – the electrical activity in his skin. If electrodes are placed (quite painlessly) on the fingers to monitor this activity by means of a variable note on a little loudspeaker, the athlete can 'hear' his GSR. Because he can hear it, he can alter it. He quickly discovers that certain feelings – such as imagining himself becoming drowsy – cause the note to be lowered and skin resistance raised. So his brain learns a direct connection between the feeling of relaxation and what is required in the way of adjustment. This is called biofeedback or bioentrainment. It is now widely accepted, not only in sports medicine, but in Britain's National Health Service (for speech therapy in the rehabilitation of stroke patients and the control of high blood-pressure) as well as in the United States, following extensive research at the Menninger Foundation, the Langley Porter Neuropsychiatric Institute and other medical centres throughout the country.

Britain, though slow to advance in the direction of sports psychology for all, did eventually engage a sports psychologist in a fact-finding capacity, paid jointly by the British Olympic Association and the United Kingdom Sports Council. He is Maurice Yaffe, a clinical psychologist in the Department of Psychological Medicine at Guys Hospital in London. In a jovial article, 'Head start for the shrink business',[41] ex-Olympic athlete Christopher Brasher describes how he met up with this gentleman, over a few beers, in Edmonton. During the day Yaffe runs a clinic for people with sex problems. The rest of the time he spends in what he terms 'a wonderful laboratory for observation' – sport. Both he and Brasher agree that sport is greatly influenced by psychology. Brasher jokes, 'I hope that does not have you shrinking away.' Yaffe explained that before he can help an athlete 'reach his full potential' he has to 'get to know' him. Sports psychologists often use this expression rather than 'give him a personality test'. Dr Yaffe went on to discuss introversion and extroversion in athletes and their relation to performance and arousal, a subject tending to confound many sports psychologists, as we may judge from their conflicting findings.[42] Yaffe said, 'We can help someone achieve bodily relaxation with mental sharpness. That, of course, is what the TCM [Transcendental Meditation] people try to do but we can do it without the mumbo-jumbo.' His published work includes suggestions on the psychological training of soccer players, and mental rehearsal techniques to enable players to cope with the stress they may encounter in that 'wonderful laboratory for observation'. It is an interesting paradox that the British Government should, through the medium of its Sports Council in conjunction with the British Olympic Association, finance Maurice Yaffe's work with British Olympic athletes, especially since his techniques include 'TCM', as he calls it, 'without the mumbo-jumbo'. Transcendental Meditation was being taught with some success by all accounts, to about a dozen girls at East Sutton Park Borstal in Kent, until the Home Office intervened in November 1978 to stop the courses. A spokesman for the Home Office said they could see no direct benefits from this type of meditative exercise and recommended the prison chaplains as a suitable alternative.[43] I asked Steve Ovett's coach, Harry Wilson, if British coaches knew about the methods used by sports psychologists. He told me, 'It's left to each individual coach. There's been very little written about it in Britain and there's very little communication between coaches on the mental side of sport. You tend to do it by instinct and personal experience.' BBC TV apparently tried to involve Harry Wilson in the material for their programme 'The Inner Game', about the psychological frontiers of sport (in which the redoubtable Maurice Yaffe appeared). Mr Wilson declined to take part. Steve Ovett had told him, 'Look, you already know this stuff. You know more about it than they do.' Mr Wilson is familiar, he says, with success phobia. 'It's what I call wanting to lose,' he added, referring me to Walter S. Tevis's classic on pool-shooters, *The Hustler*.[44] Winning, for some athletes, sits heavy, like a monkey on their backs.

'Some people try to offload the responsibility of winning. When we had David Hemery as our No. 1, the number two was John Sherwood. Now, John really enjoyed it till David retired. Then he didn't enjoy it. It was different when he was *expected* to win, and he didn't stay on very long after that.'

Denis Watts, whose experience has covered the careers of Ann Packer, Lynn Davies, and Alan Pascoe, said: 'I know the East Germans have special training, but coaching is really a question of experience. You know, or you should know, what to say to an athlete. Good coaches know instinctively what to say. I've been coaching for thirty years now, and I think the most important thing is preparation. If the athlete has been properly prepared for his event and he has confidence in his ability, he will have confidence in his training programme, and he'll be OK.'

Occasionally, an athlete's confidence may be shattered by injury and long recuperation. Denis Watts once sent a young 800-metre runner to the hypnotherapist Dr David Ryde. According to Dr Ryde, the young man was a deep subject and 'went right out'.

The hypnotherapy worked to restore his confidence, and was so effective that he went on to make the 1968 Olympic team. One of Denis Watts's more difficult problems was that of Alan Pascoe's upset stomach at nearly all of Alan's events during his retirement year. One of the authorities in sports medicine I consulted about this problem was Dr William Armour, author of *Sports Injuries and Their Treatment*, adviser to the FA, and a FIFA lecturer with wide experience of the medical problems of leading British sportsmen. Dr Armour told me that the condition I have called 'sporting stomach' is very widespread, and that it has nothing to do with 'food poisoning', or 'gastric infection' as the press like to call it: 'It is the psychological tension which produces a physical response. It's no use giving superficial medication as the problem is not confined to the digestive system: it involves the brain, the nervous system and the whole body. At Wembley I have seen football players, for instance, affected by it: in my experience sportsmen reach a situation where they are suddenly confronted by a very competitive challenge. It doesn't occur when they know they don't stand a chance, or when they think they can beat their opponents easily. It happens when there is a degree of uncertainty.'

In athletics, this kind of digestive illness affects some disciplines more than others. 'A sprinter can be incapacitated altogether, whereas a distance runner would tend to get over it.' (Some sportsmen never suffer from it at all. Dr Armour believes there are athletes who are by nature 'cool as cucumbers'.) Would relaxation exercises help? Dr Armour thought not, although he conceded that athletes predisposed to accept suggestion, such as the Russians, might be likely to respond to hypnotherapy. He also reasoned that sports in which it is possible to show direct aggression seemed less affected by the problem than others, so perhaps expending energy has a regulating effect.

The kinds of problems encountered by British coaches and athletes in the area of sports psychology seem to have received less attention from the UK Sports Council than they have in other countries. This is partly because of old-fashioned scepticism (not necessarily a bad thing) and partly because of the long-held British view that sport is almost entirely a physical phenomenon. Advances that have been made in Britain seem to centre largely on physiological aspects of sports performance. At the University of Salford, for example, experiments have been carried out to determine the degree of physical and metabolic stresses, such as lactic acid poisoning, with which the sportsman's body must cope. Brendan

Foster took part in one of these experiments, testing for oxygen debt while he ran on a revolving track. He lasted for just over eight minutes. The technician told him, 'Nobody's ever lasted ten minutes on it,' and Brendan retorted, 'I could have lasted nine: I just didn't have anything to go for.' The University of Salford research was included in the BBC2 programme, 'A Generation of Sport', in which the then sports minister Denis Howell appeared, to express his optimism about current developments. Film of Brendan's revolving-track test was greeted with some derision by the athletes in the studio. Brendan himself voiced dissatisfaction with the psychological naîveté of the test, and Alan Pascoe thought the film would cause the East Germans to roar with laughter, because they knew rather more about 'the psychological aspect'.

The future, so far as I can discover, is bleak. There is undoubtedly a chemical technology race underway in sport along the same east–west axis as the space race, the nuclear arms race, the germ-warfare race, the star wars race, and more recently the Psi race, and I cannot see any simple solution, so long as sport pursues its rather ruthless enquiries into human potential. In fact, the new drug control centres being set up around the world, because they are in constant need of funds, are in great danger of turning to the industrial chemical conglomerates for support, and if this happens, one cannot but foresee an escalation of research into how and why drugs affect performance under stress, and which are the most effective. In all of which 'advances' the sportsman will stand alone, attentive and naked as the Greek discus-thrower on his plinth. If ever he deserved his laurels or his prize money, he will deserve them then. Nor need we suppose that society will rise up in moral indignation at his plight, for society has never been particularly troubled about his plight before. It pays him handsomely 'for his pains', is jealous of his outdoor life, and has a very poor record of support for sportsmen who have lost their form, lost their health or lost their minds.

Yet these are human beings who represent us: they are carefully chosen for their skill, their dedication, their physical prowess and their courage, and to 'champion' is to represent. Let us hope, as we continue to go through the turnstiles, or examine their performances on a screen, that we shall learn to understand their behaviour better than we do, and look at them, like Aristotle, with pity and fear.

For sportsmen are our champions indeed, and where they go, we shall surely follow.

References

1 The Experiments

1 Hugh McIlvanney, 'The carnivorous eye', *Observer*, 1 April 1978.
2 Ferdie Pacheco, *Fight Doctor* (Stanley Paul, 1978), p. 66.
3 Sir Stanley Rous, *Football Worlds* (Faber 1978), p.62.
4 Colin Cowdrey, *MCC* (Hodder & Stoughton 1976), p. 35.
5 Gareth Edwards, *Gareth* (Stanley Paul 1978), p. 19.
6 Dorcas Susan Butt, *Psychology of Sport* (Van Nostrand Reinhold 1976), p. 25. Attrib. to Arnold Lunn.
7 W. Timothy Gallwey, *The Inner Game of Tennis* (Cape 1975), p. 113.
8 Roger Kahn, *The Boys of Summer* (Signet New American Lib. 1973), p. 97.
9 Gerald Ford and John Underwood, 'In defence of the competitive urge', *Sports Illustrated*, 8 July 1974.
10 T. Tutko and U. Tosi, *Sports Psyching* (J. P. Tarcher, Los Angeles, 1976), pp. 204 ff.
11 Thomas A. Harris, *I'm OK, You're OK* (Pan 1973), p. 57.
12 L. Festinger, 'A theory of social comparison processes', *Human Relations*, vol. 7 (1954), pp. 117–40, discussed in R. B. Alderman, *Psychological Behaviour in Sport* (W. B. Saunders, Philadelphia, 1974), p. 252.
13 T. Veblen, *The Theory of the Leisure Class* (The Modern Library 1934), first published 1899.
14 Alex Natan, *Sport and Society* (Bowes & Bowes 1958).
15 John McMurtry, 'Some tentative reflections on football'. Paper presented at Third International Symposium on the Sociology of Sport. Ontario: University of Waterloo, 1971. Quoted in Butt, p. 99.
16 Butt, p. 98.
17 Philip Goodhart and Chris Chataway, *War without Weapons* (W. H. Allen 1968), p. 74.

18 *See for example: Robert Moore, Sports and Mental Health* (Springfield, Illinois, Charles C. Thomas 1966), p. 74; Konrad Lorenz, *On Aggression* (Harcourt, Brace & World 1966), p. 271; L. Berkowitz, *Aggression: A Social Psychological Analysis* (McGraw-Hill 1962); B. J. Cratty, *Psychology in Contemporary Sport* (Prentice-Hall 1973), pp. 145 ff; Florence Stumpf Frederickson, in *Science and Medicine of Exercise and Sport*, ed. W. R. Johnson (Harper 1960), pp. 633 ff; A. Daniels, 'The study of sport as an element of the culture', *Int. Rev. of Sports Sociology*, vol. 1 (1966), pp. 153–65.

19 Roger Kahn, *The Boys of Summer* (Signet New American Library 1973), p. 68.

20 Ronnie Mutch, *Niki Lauda and the Grand Prix Gladiators* (Sphere Books 1977), pp. 68–9.

21 Kahn, p. 98.

22 Gareth Edwards, *Gareth* (Stanley Paul 1978), p. 77.

23 Marty Riessen and R. Evans, *Match Point* (Pelham 1974), p. 45.

24 Brian Close, *I Don't Bruise Easily* (MacDonald & Janes 1977).

25 Richard Evans, *Nastase* (Aiden Ellis 1978), p. 126.

26 'Moret to return to the Rangers . . .', *International Herald Tribune*, 27 April 1978.

27 The dangers of behaviourism in general have been highlighted by several recent studies, e.g. L. Hudson 'The choice of Hercules', *Bull. Brit. Psychol. Society*, vol. 23 (1970), pp. 287–92; R. B. Joynson 'The breakdown of modern psychology', *Bull. Brit. Psychol. Society*, vol. 23 (1970), pp. 261–9; R. B. Joynson, 'The return of mind', *Bull. Brit. Psychol. Society*, vol. 25 (1972), pp. 1–10; P. Warr, 'Towards a more human psychology', *Bull. Brit. Psychol. Society*, vol. 26 (1973), pp. 1–8.

2 The Brain Game – Cricket

1 David Frith, *The Fast Men* (Corgi 1977), pp. 62 ff.

2 Dennis Amiss with M. Carey, *In Search of Runs* (Stanley Paul 1976), p. 89.

3 Pat Gibson, 'Our batsmen had no chance', *Daily Express*, 15 February 1978.

4 Frith, p. 630.

5 Trevor Bailey (ed.), *John Player Cricket Yearbook 1975* (Queen Anne Press 1975), p. 138.

6 Irving Rosenwater, *Sir Donald Bradman, a Biography* (B. T. Batsford 1978).

7 Jim Laker, *Over to Me*, quoted in Frith, p. 187.

8 Frith, p. 196.

9 Dennis Lillee with I. Brayshaw, *The Art of Fast Bowling* (Lutterworth 1978), pp. 28 ff. (Figures rounded up.)
10 Lillee, p. 82.
11 Lillee, p. 90.
12 Lillee, p. 90.
13 Fred Trueman, *Ball of Fire* (Mayflower 1977), p. 99.
14 Bob Willis with P. Murphy, *Pace Bowling* (Pelham 1978), p. 84.
15 Frith, p. 77.
16 Frith, p. 84.
17 Frith, p. 109.
18 Scyld Berry, 'Hogg's big doubt', *Observer*, 7 January 1979.
19 Quoted in Frith, p. 149.
20 Willis, personal interview.
21 Lawton Line, 'Hadlee – the cat with the snarl of a tiger', *Daily Express*, 9 June 1978.
22 Quoted in Frith, p. 149.
23 Trueman, p. 51.
24 Trueman, p. 99.
25 John Arlott, *Fred: Portrait of a Fast Bowler* (Eyre Methuen 1971), p. 108; Trevor Bailey (ed.), *John Player Cricket Yearbook 1973* (Queen Anne Press 1973), p. 270.
26 Mike Brearley and Dudley Doust, *The Return of the Ashes* (Pelham 1978), p. 11.
27 Brearley and Doust, p. 24.
28 Brearley and Doust, p. 43.
29 Alan Thompson, 'Now a batsman is a batsman', *Daily Express*, 22 December 1978.
30 Frith, p. 64.
31 Ian Wooldridge, 'Who needs a helmet?', *Daily Mail*, 20 June 1978.
32 Ken Barrington and Phil Pilley, *Playing It Straight* (Stanley Paul 1968), p. 60.
33 Alan Thompson, 'Going soft', *Daily Express*, 15 June 1978.
34 Tony Lewis, 'Heading for state of faceless men', *Sunday Telegraph*, 11 June 1978.
35 Mike Brearley, personal interview.
36 Colin Cowdrey, *MCC: The Autobiography of a Cricketer* (Hodder & Stoughton 1976; Coronet 1977), p. 73.
37 Cowdrey, p. 61.
38 John Snow, *Moments and Thoughts* (Kaye & Ward Ltd/M. De Hartington 1973).
39 Barrington, p. 22.
40 Barrington, p. 31.
41 Barrington, p. 46

42 Barrington, p. 97.
43 Barrington, p. 105.
44 Barrington, p. 101.
45 Frith, p. 162.
46 Barrington, p. 102.
47 Trueman, pp. 107–8.
48 Roger Kahn, *The Boys of Summer* (Signet New American Library 1973), p. xviii.
49 Steve Whiting, 'Play the big boy, Geoff', *Sun*, 13 December 1978.

3 *The Fast Game – Formula One*

1 Doug Nye at Ferrari press conference, 'Ferrari on Formula 1', *Autosport*, 12 January 1978.
2 Mike Kettlewell (ed.), *Autocourse 1977–1978* (Hazelton Securities), p. 26.
3 Kettlewell, p. 172.
4 Kettlewell, p. 146.
5 Kettlewell, p. 155.
6 Kettlewell, p. 155
7 *Autocar, Grand Prix, World Championship '77* (IPC Transport Press), p. 51.
8 *Autocar*, p. 47.
9 Nigel Roebuck, 'The man from Nazareth', *Autosport*, 24 November 1977.
10 Mike Doodson on Divina Galica, *Motor*, 21 January 1978.
11 Kettlewell, p. 12.
12 Kettlewell, Alan Henry interview, p. 12.
13 Niki Lauda, *For the Record* (William Kimber 1978), p. 64.
14 'Karl Kempf's first year with Tyrrell', *Motoring News*, 9 February 1978.
15 Keith Botsford, 'Lauda's resurrection', *Sunday Times*, 23 October 1977.
16 Ronnie Mutch, *Niki Lauda and the Grand Prix Gladiators* (Sphere 1977), p. 62.
17 Stirling Moss, 'Riding the ten-ten line', *Newsweek*, 29 August 1977.
18 Doug Nye, *Great Racing Drivers* (Hamlyn 1977), p. 118.
19 Dave Kindred, 'Stewart enjoys life's Grand Prix', *International Herald Tribune*, 1 March 1978.
20 Peter Bonventure with Niki Lauda, 'Coming back blazing', *Newsweek*, 29 August 1977.
21 Lauda, *For the Record*, p. 126.

22 Lauda, *For the Record*, pp. 130 ff.
23 David Benson, *Hunt v. Lauda: Grand Prix Season 1976* (Daily Express 1976), p. 65.
24 James Hunt with Eoin Young, *James Hunt, Against All Odds* (Hamlyn 1977), pp. 169–71.
25 Kettlewell, Ian Henry interview, p. 12.
26 *Competition Cassettes*, Argentine and Brazil Grands Prix 1978, Martin Cartwright Association Ltd.
27 Kettlewell, p. 109.
28 Saudia–Williams press release.
29 Hunt, p. 171.
30 Chris Witty, Tico Martini interview, *Autosport*, 9 February 1978.
31 Ralph Thoresby, 'Private view', *Motor*, 1 February 1978.
32 Mutch, p. 92.
33 Peter Bonventure with Niki Lauda, 'Coming back blazing', *Newsweek*, 29 August 1977. Ferrari interview.
34 *Sunday Times*, 23 October 1977.
35 Lauda, *For the Record*, p. 40.
36 Benson, p. 15.
37 Benson, p. 129
38 *International Herald Tribune*, 1 March 1978.
39 Lauda, *For the Record*, p. 81.
40 Niki Lauda, *Formula 1* (William Kimber 1977), p. 204.
41 John Watson's report on the Brazil Grand Prix, 'Wattie', *Motor*, 8 February 1978.
42 Gordon Murray interview, Doug Nye, *Autosport*, 26 January 1978.
43 *Autocar*, p. 5.
44 Hunt, p. 164.
45 Mike Kettlewell (ed.), *Autocourse, 1974–1975* (Haymarket Publications), p. 13.
46 *Autocar*, p. 51.
47 Kettlewell, *Autocourse, 1977–1978*, p. 189.
48 *Autocar*, p. 10.
49 Kettlewell, *Autocourse, 1977–1978*, p. 12.
50 Benson, p. 50.
51 Benson, p. 74.
52 Lauda, *For the Record*, p. 187.
53 Lauda, *Formula 1*, p. 20.
54 Lauda, *Formula 1*, p. 16.
55 Lauda, *Formula 1*, p. 218.
56 Lauda, *Formula 1*, p. 173.
57 Lauda, *Formula 1*, p. 165.
58 Benson, p. 100.
59 Benson, p. 96.

4 *The Slow Game – Golf*

1 Tom Place, 'One run ends while another carries on', *Golf International*, 1 June 1978.
2 Tom Place, 'Close encounters of a legendary kind', *Golf International*, 13 April 1978
3 Arnold Palmer with W. B. Furlong, *Go for Broke* (William Kimber 1974), p. 240.
4 Jack Nicklaus with K. Bowden, *Golf My Way* (Pan 1976), p. 236.
5 'What makes Jack run', *Golf Digest*, April 1976.
6 *Golf International*, 13 April 1978.
7 Palmer, p. 133.
8 Palmer, p. 134.
9 Nick Seitz, 'Hogan relives his unparalleled 1953 season', *Golf Digest*, March 1978.
10 Michael Hobbs, *Great Opens* (David and Charles 1976), p. 115.
11 Frank Deford, 'Still glittering after all these years', *Sports Illustrated*, 25 December 1978 and 1 January 1979.
12 Alan Booth, 'Laughing Lee looks on the serious side', *Golf International*, 7 September 1978.
13 Dudley Doust, 'The triumph over fear', *Sunday Times*, 25 June 1978.
14 Tom Place, 'Simons takes his $50,000 share', *Golf International*, 15 June 1978.
15 Peter Alliss in *Play Golf with Peter Alliss* (BBC Publication), Part 4: 'Around the Green', in *Golf International*, 16 March 1978.
16 Mark Wilson, 'That old challenge', *Daily Express*, 16 July 1978.
17 David Morley, *Golf and the Mind* (Pelham 1978), pp. 78–9.
18 Alistair Cooke, 'Self-torture disguised as a Game', *New York Times*, quoted in Morley, p. 37.
19 *Daily Express*, 12 July 1978.
20 Palmer, p. 17.
21 Liz Kahn, 'Women's golf: the new boom', *Golf International*, 16 March 1978.
22 Richard Todd, 'Howard Clark, the secrets of success', *Golf International*, 1 June 1978.

5 *Elbow, and the High-Strung Game – Tennis*

1 James Lawton, 'Borg dream', *Daily Express*, 13 June 1978.
2 David Emery, 'Jimbo keeps that sharp edge', *Daily Express*, 7 June 1978.
3 Peter Bodo, 'Tennis superstitions: the surprising fetishes of the pros', *Tennis*, April 1977.

4 Walter S. Tevis, *The Hustler* (Michael Joseph 1960), p. 80.
5 Virginia Wade with Mary Lou Mellace, *Courting Triumph* (Hodder & Stoughton 1978), p. 124.
6 Rod Laver with J. Pollard, *How to Play Tennis* (Mayflower 1970), p. 11.
7 Laver, p. 14.
8 Laver, p. 97.
9 Arthur Ashe with Frank Deford, *Portrait in Motion* (Stanley Paul 1975), p. 174.
10 Evonne Goolagong and Bud Collins with Victor Edwards, *Evonne* (Hart-Davis, MacGibbon 1975), p. 170.
11 Arthur Ashe, post-match press conference.
12 Frank Deford, 'Raised by women to conquer men', *Sports Illustrated*, 28 August 1978.
13 *Sports Illustrated*, 28 August 1978.
14 *Tennis World* Nov./Dec. 78, Sue Barker, interview, with Nigel Clarke.
15 W. Timothy Gallwey, *The Inner Game of Tennis* (Jonathan Cape 1975), p. 113.
16 Lendl talking to Malcolm Folley, 'Secrets of the Man in the Iron Mask', *Daily Mail*, 5 November 1985.
17 *World Tennis*, December 1977.
18 Arnold R. Beisser, *The Madness in Sports* (Appleton-Century-Crofts, New York 1967), pp. 175 ff.
19 Curry Kirkpatrick, 'Guillermo Vilas', *Sports Illustrated*, 29 May 1978.
20 *Sports Illustrated*, 29 May 1978.
21 Lance Tingay, 'Borg substitute for champion Vilas', *Daily Telegraph*, 30 August 1978.
22 Björn Borg Story (Pelham 1975), p. 80.

6 *Taking the Gas*

1 Leon Tec, *The Fear of Success* (Readers Digest Press 1976). B. C. Ogilvie and T. A. Tutko, *Problem Athletes and How to Handle Them* (Pelham 1966), pp. 86 ff. Miroslav Vanek and Bryant J. Cratty, *Psychology and the Superior Athlete* (Macmillan 1970), p. 95, Bryant J. Cratty, *Psychology in Contemporary Sport* (Prentice-Hall 1973), pp. 192–3. David Morley, *Golf and the Mind* (Pelham 1978), pp. 77 ff.
2 Tony Jacklin, *Jacklin* (Hodder & Stoughton 1970), p. 11.
3 Tom Place, 'For my next trick', *Golf International*, 30 March 1978.
4 Alex Lancaster, 'Mighty Nicklaus is unnerved by loss of rhythm', *Daily Telegraph*, 21 February 1978.

5 Gary Player with Floyd Thatcher, *Gary Player, World Golfer* (Pelham 1975), p. 49.
6 Tom Place, 'Gary gets his hat-trick', *Golf International*, 18 May 1978.
7 Tom Place, 'One run ends while another carries on', *Golf International*, 1 June 1978.
8 Player, p. 126.
9 Arnold Palmer with William Barry Furlong, *Go for Broke*, (William Kimber 1974), p. 100.
10 Palmer, p. 35.
11 Palmer, p. 36.
12 Gordon Richardson, 'Grateful Coles accepts a gift', *Golf International*, 29 September 1977.
13 Gordon Richardson, 'That Dawson nightmare is over', *Golf International*, 29 June 1978.
14 Niki Lauda, *Formula 1* (William Kimber 1977), p. 208.
15 Ronnie Mutch, *Niki Lauda and the Grand Prix Gladiators* (Sphere 1977), p. 101.
16 James Hunt with Eoin Young, *James Hunt: Against All Odds* (Hamlyn 1977), p. 59.
17 Roy McKelvie, editorial comment, *Tennis World*, July 1975.
18 'Pascoe very disappointed', *Scotsman*, 39 August 1978.
19 David Benson, *Hunt v Lauda: Grand Prix Season 1976* (Daily Express 1976), p. 72.
20 Hunt, p. 160.
21 *Autocar, Grand Prix 1977* (IPC Transport Press), p. 11.
22 Hunt, p. 141.
23 Leslie Nichol, 'Kenny the King', *Daily Express*, 21 July 1978.
24 Hunt, p. 157.
25 Benson, p. 125.
26 Mutch, p. 69.
27 Hunt, p. 43.
28 Clive Gammon, 'King James drives for a crown', *Sports Illustrated*, 27 September 1976.
29 Keith Botsford, 'Lauda's resurrection', *Sunday Times* (supp.), 23 October 1977.
30 See, for instance, Marvin B. Scott, *The Racing Game* (Aldine 1968), p. 26.
31 Scott Ostler, 'Afterward Sutton can only cry', *International Herald Tribune*, 19 October 1978.
32 *International Herald Tribune*, 19 October 1978.
33 Fred Trueman, *Ball of Fire* (Mayflower 1977), pp. 107–10.
34 John Arlott, *Fred: Portrait of a Fast Bowler* (Eyre Methuen 1971), p. 168.

7 *The Mediums*

1 A phrase of the social psychologist Abraham Maslow in *Towards a Psychology of Being* (Van Nostrand Reinhold 1968), and *Motivation and Personality* (Harper 1970).

2 Nandor Fodor, *Between Two Worlds* (Parker Publishing NY, 1967).

3 Arthur Ashe with Frank Deford, *Portrait in Motion* (Stanley Paul 1975), p. 180.

4 W. Timothy Gallwey, *The Inner Game of Tennis* (Jonathan Cape 1975), *Inner Tennis: Playing the Game* (Random House 1977).

5 Arnold Palmer with W. B. Furlong, *Go for Broke* (William Kimber 1974), p. 118.

6 Mike Spino, Syracuse University distance runner; from 'Running as a spiritual experience'; reproduced in Jack Scott, *The Athletic Revolution* (Free Press, 1971), pp. 222 ff.

7 M. Stevenson, *Yorkshire, A History of County Cricket* (Arthur Barker 1972), p. 165.

8 Colin Cowdrey, *MCC, The Autobiography of a Cricketer* (Hodder & Stoughton 1976), p. 33.

9 See, for example, S. Ostrander and L. Schroeder, *Psi: Psychic Discoveries Behind the Iron Curtain* (Abacus 1970).

10 Dudley Doust, 'Instinct v. Reason, Brearley's ball game', *Sunday Times*, 14 August 1977.

11 Ashe, p. 179.

12 *Autocar Grand Prix Yearbook, World Championships 1977* (IPC Transport Press 1977), p. 6.

13 Richard Evans, *Nastase* (Aidan Ellis 1978), p. 234.

14 C. Plumridge, 'Undoing what comes naturally', in William Davis, ed., *The Punch Book of Golf* (Hutchinson 1973), p. 99.

15 Tony Jacklin, *Jacklin* (Hodder & Stoughton 1970), pp. 163–4.

16 Gary Player, with Floyd Thatcher, *Gary Player, World Golfer* (Pelham 1975), pp. 136–7.

17 The Lawton Line, 'Hadlee the cat with the snarl of a tiger', *Daily Express*, 9 June 1978.

18 Dennis Lillee with I. Brayshaw, *The Art of Fast Bowling* (Lutterworth 1978), p. 29.

19 Ken Barrington with P. Pilley, *Playing It Straight* (Stanley Paul 1968), p. 97.

20 Neil Amdur, 'Figure skating championships', *International Herald Tribune*, 13 March 1978.

21 Count Toptani, *Modern Show-Jumping* (Stanley Paul 1954), p. 55.

22 See, for instance, Ostrander and Schroeder, pp. 38 ff.

23 Ostrander and Schroeder, p. 305.

24 Miroslav Vanek and Bryant J. Cratty, *Psychology and the Superior Athlete* (Macmillan 1970), pp. 137 ff.
25 Vanek and Cratty, p. 137.
26 Eugen Herrigel, *Zen in the Art of Archery* (Routledge & Kegan Paul 1953).
27 Gilbert Rogin on Ali, *Sports Illustrated*, 22 November 1965.
28 Herrigel, p. 92.
29 Herrigel, p. 54.
30 Gallwey, *Inner Game*, p. 21.
31 Michael Murphy, *Golf in the Kingdom* (Abacus 1976), p. 32.
32 Murphy, p. 24.
33 Ostrander and Schroeder, p. 40.
34 Jack Nicklaus with K. Bowden, *Golf My Way* (Pan 1976), p. 79.
35 Palmer, p. 53.
36 Palmer, p. 119.
37 Jacklin, p. 174.
38 Niki Lauda, *Formula 1* (William Kimber 1977), p. 166.
39 Jose Silva and Philip Miele, *The Silva Mind Control Method* (Souvenir Press 1978), p. 172.
40 Silva and Miele, p. 103.
41 Gallwey, p. 122.
42 Barry Tarshis, *Tennis and the Mind* (Atheneum 1977), p. 68.

8 *Split Mind*

1 Arthur Ashe with Frank Deford, *Portrait in Motion* (Stanley Paul 1975), p. 193.
2 Marty Riessen and Richard Evans, *Match Point* (Pelham 1974), p. 184.
3 Richard Evans, *Nastase* (Aidan Ellis 1978), p. 192.
4 B. C. Ogilvie and T. A. Tutko, *Problem Athletes and How to Handle Them* (Pelham 1966).
5 Derek Underwood, *Beating the Bat* (Stanley Paul 1975), p. 155.
6 Underwood, p. 40.
7 Underwood, p. 38.
8 Mike Stevenson, *Yorkshire, A History of County Cricket* (Arthur Barker 1972), pp. 80 ff.
9 Stevenson, p. 85.
10 Dennis Lillee with I. Brayshaw, *The Art of Fast Bowling* (Lutterworth 1978), p. 81.
11 Ian Chappell, *Cricket in Our Blood* (Stanley Paul 1976), pp. 80 ff.
12 David Frith, *The Fast Men* (Corgi 1977), p. 161.
13 Colin Cowdrey, *MCC, The Autobiography of a Cricketer* (Hodder & Stoughton 1976), p. 58.

14 Cowdrey, p. 61.
15 Cowdrey, p. 65.
16 Cowdrey, p. 50.
17 Brian Close, *Close to Cricket* (Stanley Paul 1968), p. 89.
18 Close, p. 102.
19 Alex Bannister, 'Boycott apology – then he is snubbed again', *Daily Mail*, 13 December 1978.
20 Dennis Amiss with M. Carey, *In Search of Runs* (Stanley Paul 1976), p. 18.
21 Ken Barrington with Phil Pilley, *Playing It Straight* (Stanley Paul 1968), p. 136.
22 Roger Kahn, *The Boys of Summer* (Signet New American Library 1973), p. 101.
23 Kahn, p. 284.
24 P. K. Bridges, 'Some factors influencing physiological response to arousal', in H. T. A. Whiting, ed., *Reading in Sports Psychology* (Kimpton 1972), p. 214.
25 Tony Jacklin, *Jacklin* (Hodder & Stoughton 1970), p. 107.
26 Liz Khan, 'The great American debate: Tony Jacklin', *Golf International*, 2 March 1978.
27 Jack Nicklaus with K. Bowden, *Golf My Way* (Pan 1976), p. 217.
28 Thomas Tutko and Umberto Tosi, *Sports Psyching* (J. P. Tarcher 1976), pp. 29–30.
29 David Morley, *Golf and the Mind* (Pelham 1978), pp. 61 ff., 89, 94, 106, 166.
30 Theo B. Hyslop, *Mental Handicaps in Golf* (Bailliere Tindall 1927), p. 70.
31 Hyslop, p. 25.
32 *Times* articles on the Moorgate Tube Disaster 1975: March 1, (*ST*) 2, 3–8, 11–16, 20, 21, 25.
33 Graham Gauld, *Jim Clark* (Hamlyn 1968), pp. 106 ff.
34 James Hunt with Eoin Young, *James Hunt: Against All Odds* (Hamlyn 1977), pp. 171–2.
35 Gosaku Naruse, 'The hypnotic treatment of stage fright in champion athletes', *International Journal of Clinical and Experimental Hypnosis*, vol. 13, 1965, no. 2, pp. 63–70.
36 John H. Salmela and B. Petiot, 'Olympic gymnastics: a task analysis', in *British Proceedings of Sports Psychology*, University of Salford, 1974.

9 *The Violent Games*

1 For example: Jack Scott, *The Athletic Revolution* (Free Press 1971), pp. 173 ff; Rainer Martens, *Social Psychology and Physical Activity*

(Harper & Row 1975), pp. 108 ff; B. J. Cratty, *Psychology in contemporary Sport* (Prentice-Hall 1973), pp. 150 ff; R. B. Alderman, *Psychological Behaviour in Sport* (W. B. Saunders 1974), pp. 225 ff; Thomas A. Harris, *I'm OK – You're OK* (Pan 1973), pp. 257 ff.

2 Martens, p. 122.

3 John Underwood, 'Brutality – the crisis in pro football', 'Punishment is a crime', and 'Speed is all the rage', *Sports Illustrated*, 14 Aug. 1978, 21 Aug. 1978 and 28 Aug. 1978.

4 'Injury may paralyse Stingley for life', *International Herald Tribune*, 14 August 1978. William Wallace, 'Stingley injury brings NFL violence into sharp focus', *International Herald Tribune*, 18 August 1978.

5 Peter Gent, *North Dallas Forty* (Morrow 1973), p. 260.

6 Gent, p. 261.

7 D. Riesman and R. Denney, 'Football in America: a study of culture diffusion', in John W. Loy and Gerald Kenyon, eds., *Sport, culture and Society* (Macmillan, New York, 1969), pp. 308 ff.

8 Sir Stanley Rous, *Football Worlds* (Faber 1978), p. 32.

9 David Irvine, *The Joy of Rugby* (William Luscombe 1978), p. 17.

10 Irvine, p. 17.

11 Irvine, p. 21.

12 Iain MacKenzie, 'When tough is violent', *Sunday Times*, 22 October 1978.

13 Irvine, p. 23.

14 Terry O'Connor and Peter Jackson, 'Wales Crack Down With a Ban Threat'. *Daily Mail*, 5 November 1985.

15 Gareth Edwards, *Gareth, an Autobiography* (Stanley Paul 1978), p. 118.

16 Edwards, p. 79.

17 Peter Jackson, 'I didn't put the boot in says Thomas', *Daily Mail*, 20 November 1978.

18 Edwards, p. 76.

19 Alan Hubbard, 'As Jacopucci dies, the weight on boxing's mind', *Observer*, 28 July 1978.

20 Edward Grayson, *Sport and the Law (Sunday Telegraph* 1978), p. 39.

21 Rob Hughes, 'The dead fighter who lurks in the mind of Alan Minter', *Sunday Times*, 5 November 1978.

22 Hugh McIlvanney, 'Little war at Wembley', *Observer*, 5 November 1978.

23 Hugh McIlvanney, 'Pride goes before', *Observer*, 12 November 1978.

24 Sydney Hulls, 'Alan slams Tonna in six', *Daily Express*, 8 November 1978.

25 Arthur H. Steinhaus, 'Boxing – legalized murder', *Look*, 3 January 1950.
26 S. Kirson Weinberg and Henry Arond, 'The occupational culture of the boxer', in John W. Loy Jr and Gerald Kenyon, eds, *Sport, Culture and Society* (Macmillan, New York, 1969), pp. 439 ff.
27 Weinberg and Arond, p. 447.
28 Dudley Doust, 'The champion who walks a rough path from the ghetto', *Sunday Times*, 24 April 1978.
29 Loy and Kenyon, p. 446.
30 *Scotsman*, 20 October 1978.
31 Ferdie Pacheco, *Fight Doctor* (Stanley Paul 1978), p. 32.
32 Pacheco, p. 141.
33 *Look*, 3 January 1950.
34 W. E. Tucker and Molly Castle, *Sportsmen and their Injuries* (Pelham 1978), pp. 35–6.
35 Brian Scott, 'Ally faces a backlash', *Daily Mail*, 6 June 1978.
36 Mike Aitken, 'Masson's nightmare', *Scotsman*, 5 June 1978.
37 Scott, pp. 143 ff.
38 Steve Curry, 'Fury', *Daily Express*, 4 December 1978.
39 Ronald Crowther, 'Big-kick Kidd so sorry now', *Daily Mail*, 27 November 1978.
40 Brian Scovell, 'It's sickening!', *Daily Mail*, 27 March 1978.
41 'Hockey 1977–78', *Sports Illustrated*, 17 October 1977.
42 Robert Fachet, 'Hockey on thin ice', *International Herald Tribune*, 1 November 1978.
43 Rous, p. 47.
44 Rous, p. 16.
45 Rous, p. 29.
46 George Orwell, *Collected Essays, Journalism and Letters of George Orwell*, vol. 4 (Secker & Warburg 1968), pp. 41–2.
47 Edward Grayson, *Sport and the Law* (Sunday Telegraph Publication 1978), p. 10.
48 Grayson, p. 33.
49 Grayson, pp. 31–2.
50 Arthur Miller, 'The trouble with our country', *San Francisco Chronicle*, 16 June 1968.

10 *The Thoroughbreds*

1 Barry Tarshis, *Tennis and the Mind* (Atheneum/SMI 1977), p. 163.
2 Grace Lichtenstein, *Behind the Scenes in Women's Pro Tennis* (Robson 1975), p. 88.
3 B. C. Ogilvie and T. A. Tutko, *Problem Athletes and How to Handle Them* (Pelham 1966), p. 91.

4 Frank Deford, 'Raised by women to conquer men,' *Sports Illustrated*, 28 August 1978.
5 Colin Cowdrey, *MCC: The Autobiography of a Cricketer* (Hodder & Stoughton 1976), p. 38.
6 Fred Trueman, *Ball of Fire* (Mayflower 1977), p. 18.
7 Richard Sink, 'Tom Weiskopf the unpredictable', *Golf International*, 23 November 1978.
8 Michael Williams, 'Watson's lapse in Open explained,' *Daily Telegraph*, 7 August 1978.
9 David C. Morley, *Golf and the Mind* (Pelham 1978), p. 32.
10 Malcolm Folley, 'Failure! I had been stripped of my pride', *Daily Express*, 22 May 1980.
11 Malcolm Folley, 'Bond and son beat rule,' *Express* 8 March 1979.

11 The Guinea-Pigs

1 C. Brasher, 'Head start for the shrink business', *Sunday Observer*, 6 August 1978.
2 Arnold R. Beisser, *The Madness in Sports* (Appleton-Century-Crofts 1967), pp. 152–3.
3 Richard Suinn, 'Psychology and sports performance: principles and applications', unpublished paper presented at the Association for the Advancement of Behavior Therapy, Atlanta, 1977, p. 7.
4 P. K. Bridges, 'Some factors influencing physiological responses to arousal', in H. T. A. Whiting, ed., *Readings in Sports Psychology* (Henry Kimpton 1972), p. 222.
5 Beisser, p. 152
6 Reported in Neil Amdur, 'Epidemic of drug use', *International Herald Tribune*, 22 November 1978.
7 Jack Scott, *The Athletic Revolution* (Free Press 1971), p. 148.
8 Scott, p. 145.
9 Scott, p. 145.
10 Scott, p. 144.
11 See Scott, p. 148.
12 C. Brasher, 'Drugs and sport', *Observer*, 11 June 1978.
13 'Steroids muscle in', *International Herald Tribune*, 20 November 1978.
14 *Observer*, 11 June 1978.
15 Jeff Powell, 'Threatened by the plague of anger' (on drugs and football, referring to *Sports Illustrated*, 28 August 1978), *Daily Mail* 4 January 1979.
16 Roy Moor, 'Bans for Russians caught by dope test', *Daily Mail*, 6 November 1978.

17 Ian Wooldridge, *Daily Mail*, 2 September 1978.
18 *Daily Mail*, 2 September 1978.
19 *International Herald Tribune*, 22 November 1978.
20 *International Herald Tribune*, 22 November 1978.
21 Ferdie Pacheco, *Fight Doctor* (Stanley Paul 1978), pp. 42 ff, 175 and 202
22 Chris Brasher interview, *Observer*, 11 June 1978.
23 'Bowles, what I said for £1000', *Daily Mail*, 28 November 1978.
24 *Daily Mail*, 28 November 1978.
25 *Daily Mail*, 28 November 1978.
26 Jeff Powell, *Daily Mail*, 4 January 1979.
27 'England's dope secret', *Daily Mail*, 6 June 1978.
28 Mike Aitken, 'Masson's nightmare', *Scotsman*, 5 June 1978.
29 A. H. Becket, G. T.Tucker and A. C. Moffat, 'Routine detection and identification in urine of stimulants and other drugs', *J. Pharm. Pharmac.*, 1967, pp. 19, 273–94.
30 *Daily Mail*, 6 June 1978.
31 *International Herald Tribune*, 22 November 1978.
32 Roy Spicer, 'Pill to beat L-test jitters', *Sunday Mirror*, 26 March 1978.
33 Geoff Nicholson, quoting official statement, 'The drug counter', *Observer*, 28 May 1978.
34 Beckett, Tucker and Moffat, p. 274.

12 *The Experimenters*

1 Richard Suinn, 'Psychology for Olympic champs', *Psychology Today*, July 1976.
2 S. Ostrander and L. Schroeder, *Psi: Psychic Discoveries Behind the Iron Curtain* (Sphere 1973).
3 Bryant J. Cratty and Miroslav Vanek, *Psychology and the Superior Athlete* (Macmillan 1970).
4 John E. Kane, Foreword to Cratty and Vanek, p. v.
5 Cratty and Vanek, p. 3.
6 Cratty and Vanek, p. 54.
7 Cratty and Vanek, p. 53.
8 Cratty and Vanek, p. 54.
9 Joe Jares, 'We have a neurotic in the backfield, doctor', *Sports Illustrated*, 18 January 1971.
10 Jack Scott, *The Athletic Revolution* (Free Press 1971), p. 134.
11 Scott, p. 132.
12 Thomas Tutko and Umberto Tosi, *Sports Psyching* (J. P. Tacher 1976).
13 Rainer Martens, *Social Psychology and Physical Activity* (Harper & Row 1975), p. 155.

14 Bryant J. Cratty, *Psychology of Contemporary Sport* (Prentice-Hall 1973), pp. 66 ff.
15 Cratty, p. 68.
16 Cratty, p. 74.
17 Dennis Lillee with I. Brayshaw, *The Art of Fast Bowling* (Lutterworth 1978), p. 35.
18 Cratty and Vanek, p. 55.
19 Cratty and Vanek, p. 56.
20 Cratty and Vanek, p. 57.
21 Cratty and Vanek, p. 59.
22 Cratty and Vanek, p. 60.
23 Cratty and Vanek, p. 63.
24 Cratty and Vanek, p. 63.
25 Cratty and Vanek, p. 63.
26 Cratty and Vanek, p. 41.
27 Cratty and Vanek, p. 71.
28 Cratty and Vanek, p. 73.
29 Cratty and Vanek, p. 74.
30 Cratty and Vanek, p. 84.
31 Cratty and Vanek, p. 82.
32 Charley Taylor, *Sport*, December 1970, p. 70, quoted in Scott, p. 203.
33 Cratty and Vanek, p. 130.
34 Cratty and Vanek, p. 130.
35 Cratty, p. 195.
36 J. D. Brooke, E. J. Hamley and P. T. Stone, 'Disturbances of attention . . .', in H. T. A. Whiting, ed., *Readings in Sports Psychology* (Henry Kimpton 1972), pp. 198 ff.
37 Cratty, p. 169.
38 Cratty, p. 199.
39 Cratty and Vanek, p. 153.
40 Cratty and Vanek p. 157.
41 Cratty and Vanek, p. 159.
42 Cratty and Vanek, p. 160.
43 Cratty and Vanek, p. 163.
44 F. Antonelli, in Cratty and Vanek.

13 *The Growth of the Shrink*

1 John E. Kane, Foreword to Bryant J. Cratty and Miroslav Vanek, *Psychology and the Superior Athlete* (Macmillan 1970), p. v.
2 Norman Triplett, 'The dynamogenic factors in pacemaking and competition', *American Journal of Psychology*, vol. 9, pp. 507–33.
3 For details of national sports psychology societies, see Cratty and Vanek, preface.

4 E. Power and M. Lerner, 'Hipnosis v depórte' (Hypnosis and sport), *Rev. Del Derechno Deportivo*, 1961, p. 2.
5 William Barry Furlong, 'Psychology of the playing fields', *Psychology Today*, July 1976.
6 S. Ostrander and L. Schroeder, *Psi: Psychic Discoveries Behind the Iron Curtain* (Sphere 1973), p. 262.
7 Gavin Young, 'Duel in a damp Shangri-la', *Observer*, 30 July 1978.
8 Ferdie Pacheco, *Fight Doctor* (Stanley Paul 1978), p. 123.
9 Peter Deeley 'Hypnosis helped Bob Willis skittle the Aussies', *Observer*, 6 November 1977.
10 Neil Amdur, 'Organization the secret to Cowboys' success', *International Herald Tribune*, 26 January 1978.
11 Thomas Tutko and Umberto Tosi, *Sports Psyching* (J. P. Tarcher 1976), p. 131.
12 J. H. Schultz and W. Luthe, *Autogenic Therapy*, vol. 1 *Autogenic Methods* (Grune & Stratton 1969), p. xiv.
13 Schultz and Luthe, p. 187.
14 E. Jacobson, *Progressive Relaxation* (University of Chicago Press 1938). *Anxiety and Tension Control* (J. B. Lippincott 1964).
15 G. Naruse, 'The hypnotic treatment of stage fright in champion athletes', *Int. Journal of Clin. & Experimental Hypnosis*, vol. 13, 1965, no. 2, p. 67.
16 Cratty and Vanek, p. 123.
17 Tutko and Tosi, p. 117.
18 Bob Willis with P. Murphy, *Pace Bowling* (Pelham 1978), p. 39–40.
19 David Ryde, 'Hypnosis in sport', *Encyclopaedia of Sports Sciences & Medicine* (Macmillan, New York, 1971).
20 Joe Jares, 'We have a neurotic in the backfield, doctor', *Sports Illustrated*, 18 January 1971.
21 Tutko and Tosi, p. 3.
22 B. C. Ogilvie and T. A. Tutko, *Problem Athletes and How to Handle Them* (Pelham 1966), p. 89.
23 Bryant J. Cratty, *Psychology in Contemporary Sport* (Prentice-Hall 1973).
24 Arnold R. Beisser, *The Madness in Sports* (Appleton-Century-Crofts 1967), p. 71.
25 Beisser, p. 10.
26 John Moynihan, 'Nothing less than gold in Karoly's classroom', *Sunday Telegraph*, 8 October 1978.
27 Beisser, p. 10.
28 Beisser, p. 100.
29 Beisser, p. 29.
30 Beisser, p. 91.
31 Beisser, p. 111.

32 Beisser, p. 155.
33 Beisser, p. 176.
34 Beisser, pp. 175–6.
35 *Sports Illustrated*, 18 January 1971.
36 Richard Suinn, 'Psychology for Olympic champs', *Psychology Today*, July 1976.
37 Richard Suinn, 'Psychology and Sports Performance: Principles and Applications', unpublished paper presented to Association for Advancement of Behavior Therapy, Atlanta, 1977, p. 12.
38 Cratty and Vanek, pp. 70 ff.
39 D. Mohr, 'Mental practice I', *Encyclopaedia of Sports Sciences and Medicine* (Macmillan, New York, 1971), pp. 52 ff.
40 Tutko and Tosi, p. 145.
41 Chris Brasher, 'Head start for the shrink business', *Observer*, 6 August 1978.
42 See, for example, Cratty, p. 92.
43 Tim Miles, 'Ban on mystics', *Daily Mail*, 1 December 1978.
44 Walter S. Tevis, *The Hustler* (Michael Joseph 1960).

Index